maps of difference

maps of difference

CANADA, WOMEN, AND TRAVEL

wendy roy

MCGILL-QUEEN'S UNIVERSITY PRESS
MONTREAL & KINGSTON | LONDON | ITHACA

Legal deposit second quarter 2005
Bibliothèque nationale du Québec

Printed in Canada on acid-free paper that is 100% ancient forest free (100% post-consumer recycled), processed chlorine free

This book has been published with the help of grants from the Canadian Federation for the Humanities and Social Sciences, through the Aid to Scholarly Publications Programme, using funds provided by the Social Sciences and Humanities Research Council of Canada, and the University of Saskatchewan, through the President's Publications Fund.

McGill-Queen's University Press acknowledges the support of the Canada Council for the Arts for our publishing program. We also acknowledge the financial support of the Government of Canada through the Book Publishing Industry Development Program (BPIDP) for our publishing activities.

LIBRARY AND ARCHIVES CANADA CATALOGUING IN PUBLICATION

Roy, Wendy, 1957–
Maps of difference : Canada, women, and travel / Wendy Roy.
Includes bibliographical references and index.
ISBN 0-7735-2866-0
1. Women travelers – Canada.   2. Travelers' writings, Canadian (English) – History and criticism.   3. Jameson, Mrs. (Anna), 1794–1860. Winter studies and summer rambles in Canada.   4. Hubbard, Leonidas, Mrs. A woman's way through unknown Labrador.   5. Laurence, Margaret, 1926–1987. Prophet's camel bell.   6. Women and literature – Canada.   I. Title.
CT3203.R69 2005   910.4'082   C2004-906883-0

Set in 10.25/13 Sabon LT and CE with Frutiger display
Book design & typesetting by zijn digital

for garth | who shares this adventure

contents

illustrations

acknowledgments

The list of people who have helped me with this study is a lengthy one. I would like to thank, in particular, Nathalie Cooke for her encouragement and good advice during the research and writing of the initial stages of this study, and Sherrill Grace for her thoughtful comments on the completed manuscript. Warm thanks are also due to Brian Trehearne, whose advice during research for the chapter on Margaret Laurence's writings and whose later comments on the chapter on Mina Hubbard were invaluable.

I owe large debts of gratitude to Sherrill, Anne Hart, and Roberta Buchanan for generously meeting with me and sharing their research on Mina Hubbard, and for pointing out omissions and possible reinterpretations in my research, in particular on Hubbard's mapping and photographs. Many thanks also to the staff members at the Centre for Newfoundland Studies and its archives, who helped immeasurably with primary research into the Hubbard and Elson diaries during my visits in 2000 and 2003. I am extremely grateful to the Ellis and Laurence families for giving me permission to use their family members' photographs; to C.J. Martin for generously providing me with copies of his Somali photographs and permission to reproduce them; and to the Toronto Public Library for permission to reproduce sketches by Anna Jameson. Thanks are also due to the Royal Ontario Museum and the City of Victoria Archives for permission to reprint selected illustrations. In addition, I would like to express my gratitude to Marianne Stenbaek, whose astute questions helped to send my work on Laurence in new directions; Irene Gammel, Suzanne Morton, and Maggie Kilgour, whose comments on an earlier version of this project made me rethink notions of mapping and being "first"; David Brooks and Caroline Pennington, who answered questions related to Laurence's and Alys Reece's African works; Marguerite Mackenzie for supplying me with a translation of an account of Mina Hubbard's meeting with an Innu group; Jeff Muehlbauer and Clare Cook for consultations related to Cree and Inuktitut syllabics; Aurèle Parisien, Elizabeth Hulse, and Joan McGilvray for helpful editorial advice; and Neil Sawatsky for his expert scans of many of the illustrations.

This book has been published with the help of a grant from the Canadian Federation for the Humanities and Social Sciences, through the Aid to Scholarly Publications Programme, using funds provided by the Social Sciences and Humanities Research Council of Canada, and a grant from the University of Saskatchewan, through the President's Publications Fund. I acknowledge and thank SSHRCC, McGill University, the Fonds québécois de la recherche sur la société et la culture, and the University of British Columbia for generous financial and institutional support for research toward this project that I conducted during my doctoral and post-doctoral studies.

Parts of my research have appeared in *Canadian Literature* as "'Here is the picture as well as I can paint it': Anna Jameson's Illustrations for *Winter Studies and Summer Rambles in Canada*" (no. 177, 2003) and "Anti-imperialism and Feminism in Margaret Laurence's African Writings" (no. 169, 2001), and in *Studies in Canadian Literature* as "Visualizing Labrador: Maps, Photographs, and Geographical Naming in Mina Hubbard's *A Woman's Way through Unknown Labrador*" (vol. 29, no. 1, 2004). I have tried all available avenues to locate copyright holders for illustrations reproduced in the book; information about any omissions should be forwarded to me in order that future editions can be corrected.

Lorna Hutchison, Linda Morra, and Irene Roy all provided much personal support and friendly and motherly advice during various stages of my work. And finally, my thanks and love to Garth Cantrill, whose gift of the first edition of *A Woman's Way*, with its pullout map, began my investigations into mapping, and whose willingness to "pull in double harness" made this book possible.

maps of difference

introduction | MAPS OF DIFFERENCE

Map, n. *1*. A representation of the earth's surface or a part of it, its physical and political features, etc., or of the heavens, delineated on a flat surface of paper, etc., according to a definite scale or projection.

Map, v. *2*. Map out. b. fig. To record minutely; to plan out (a course of conduct, one's time, etc.).

The *Oxford English Dictionary* defines "mapping" as both a literal and a figurative endeavour. Mappers represent the physical details of the earth's surface to scale on a piece of paper or other flat surface. They also plan out where they will go and what they will see, and record their experiences in detail. As it appears in the title of this book, "mapping" links the works of three Canadian travel writers to a literal meaning of the verb "to map" but also refers to mapping in its metaphoric sense, as a minute record of cultural, gender, race, and class difference.

My interest in the relationship between mapping and travel writing began a number of years ago with a gift my husband, Garth Cantrill, gave me when I graduated from the University of Saskatchewan. It was a first edition of Mina Hubbard's *A Woman's Way through Unknown Labrador*, a book I had earlier read in reprint. The first edition had a maroon-coloured cloth cover, on which was embossed in gold a silhouette of a woman sitting in the middle of a canoe, framed by caribou antlers and bookended by male paddlers in the front and back of the canoe (fig. 1.1). I was intrigued by that gold silhouette, by the wonderfully evocative photographs of people and landscapes scattered throughout the book, and by the original eighteen-by-twenty-inch two-colour map folded and tucked into an envelope in the back cover. These visual representations of Hubbard's 1905 journey formed my first impression of the people and places evoked in her narrative, and as I reread that

I.1 Cover, *A Woman's Way through Unknown Labrador* (London: Murray, 1908)

narrative, I returned repeatedly to those photographs and that map as a way of testing my second, third, and fourth impressions.

I identified in those visual media the same issues of gender and imperialism that were played out in Hubbard's narrative, in sometimes contradictory and sometimes complementary ways. Her map and photographs thus became central to my analysis of her text and in turn encouraged me to look more closely at the visual material associated with the other travel narratives I was studying – the sketches that Anna Jameson made on her 1837 journey on Lake Huron and the photographs and map that appear in Margaret Laurence's account of her life in Somaliland during the early 1950s. Mapping was something with which these women all engaged in a literal sense, but the term "mapping" also became a way for me to describe their figurative activities as they researched and wrote their travel books. Thus I read Jameson, Hubbard, and Laurence as women who made their own maps, but whose activities were at the same time mapped by their societies. Their published and unpublished writings, especially Jameson's *Winter Studies and Summer Rambles in Canada* (1838), Hubbard's *A Woman's Way through Unknown Labrador* (1908), and Laurence's *The Prophet's Camel Bell* (1963), provide a plan of the physical, political, and relational features of the areas through which they travelled, and of their own social, cultural, and political positions.

The word "mapping" has been used figuratively in previous literary analyses, including to great effect in two discussions of Canadian women's literature. In *Mapping Our Selves: Canadian Women's Autobiography in English* (1993), Helen Buss uses the word to describe methods for representing female identity in life writing, while in *Paths of Desire: Images of Exploration and Mapping in Canadian Women's Writing* (1997), Marlene Goldman explores the figurative uses of mapping in fiction. Rather than employing mapping as a metaphor for self-representation or examining metaphors of mapping, I consider the way that women travellers position themselves both through literal acts of mapping and through representations of interactions with others. I argue that while their positions within their societies do not necessarily ensure insight into relations of gender, class, culture, and imperialism, they do help to highlight and, indeed, to map out such relations.

The activities of travel writers and map-makers often overlap, as do critical discussions of the two endeavours. Both cartographers and travel writers investigate areas of the world that are little known to their contemporaries and provide reports to those contemporaries that use words but may also include pictures and diagrams. Historical studies of maps, like early studies of travel writing, interpreted the works as increasingly objective representations of political, geographic, and relational space.[1] Mappers and travellers were discussed in terms of their adventurousness and heroism and lauded for their achievements. But judgments about the objectivity, altruism, and achievement of both explorers and cartographers have in recent years come under critical scrutiny. According to Graham Huggan, maps are "neither copies nor semblances of reality but modes of discourse which reflect and articulate the ideologies of their makers" (11).[2]

Alison Blunt and Jane Wills demonstrate that geographers have only recently begun to write "in critical and contextual ways" about their discipline's "complicity" with imperialism, rather than simply "celebrating exploration, 'discovery', and heroic explorers and geographers" (193). In his influential 1988 essay on the politics of mapping, for example, J.B. Harley calls maps "weapons of imperialism" and notes that because lands were "claimed on paper before they were effectively occupied, maps anticipated empire" (282). If geographers have only recently noted map-making's entanglement in ideologies of imperialism, they have also only recently observed its gendered politics. In those investigations, public space has been identified historically as the domain of the masculine, and private space as the domain of the feminine or domestic (Blunt and Rose 2). Because women's movement into public space (such as that involved in unchaperoned travel or exploration) was traditionally discouraged, and women who entered public spheres were at risk of such consequences as sexual violence (Rose 160), women seldom travelled to "unmapped" areas of the world or were involved in mapping. Thus their few contributions to geographical knowledge were initially recognized as akin to (although even more unusual than) those of male geographers – in other words, as heroic activities by individuals participating in "firsts." As a complication of the recovery and celebration of women explorers and map-makers, feminist geographers have more recently begun to raise questions about "white women's historical complicity with and resistance to hegemonic and, specifically, imperialist mapping strategies" (Blunt and Rose 19). They have begun to show the ways in which women's mapping ventures are like and unlike their male counterparts' in terms of their relationship to imperialism.

In a similar way, feminist researchers of travel narratives have explored the gendered nature of travel, travel writing, and criticism of such writing. In her 1992 book *Imperial Eyes: Travel Writing and*

Transculturation, Mary Louise Pratt identifies the typical traveller and writer of the eighteenth and nineteenth centuries as "European, male, secular, and lettered" (30). Karen Lawrence, in *Penelope Voyages: Women and Travel in the British Literary Tradition* (1994), more explicitly questions the way that studies of travel narratives "encode the traveler as a male who crosses boundaries and penetrates spaces," while "the female is mapped as a place on the itinerary of the male journey" (2).[3] She and many other critics, however, point out that despite the fact that women travellers and writers were rare before the nineteenth century, and despite their traditional metaphoric positioning within literature as "home" rather than "away," women could and did travel, and could and did write about those experiences of travel. They in fact produced travel narratives as soon as they could travel, read, and write. In *The Witness and the Other World: Exotic European Travel Writing, 400–1600*, Mary B. Campbell identifies a woman traveller, the late-fourth-century pilgrim Egeria, as the first *travel writer* because she was the first to write about both "journey" and "self" (15). Even women who were not literate could be travel writers of a sort: Margery Kempe dictated *The Book of Margery Kempe* (which relates, in part, her travels as a pilgrim) to two different men from about 1435 to 1440 (Barratt 177).

Autobiographical theorist Sidonie Smith points out that women "have always been in motion and for a variety of complex reasons" (xiii). In Canada some of the earliest travel narratives by European women were written by wives such as Elizabeth Simcoe and Frances Simpson who accompanied or assisted their husbands on journeys of governance, trade, and exploration (Fowler, *Embroidered Tent*, 17–51; Warkentin 384–96). Recognizing the contradiction posed by the fact of their travels, as opposed to their own symbolic function, which limited them to domestic or private space, such women often stressed in their private writings that their journeys were embarked upon at the direction of male relatives. Women who ventured further into the public sphere by publishing their travel narratives often claimed that their texts were published at the suggestion of others (Smith 18; Foster 19–20). Indeed, the three narratives that I discuss all had relational impetuses, revealed to greater or lesser extents in the narratives themselves, since Jameson initially travelled to Canada at the request of her husband, Hubbard's journey in Labrador was conceived of as a completion of an earlier failed expedition that resulted in her husband's death, and Laurence accompanied her engineer husband to British Somaliland.

In traditional analyses of travel writing, those relational motivations have often been employed to bar women's literature from discussion. In his introduction to the first section of *The Norton Book of Travel* (1987), Paul Fussell effectively excludes women such as Jameson, Hubbard, and Laurence who accompany or are motivated by their husbands by arguing, "To constitute real travel, movement from one place to another should manifest some impulse of non-utilitarian pleasure" (21). This notion has continued to be espoused; Casey Blanton suggests in *Travel Writing: The Self and the World*, written ten years later, that the only "genuine" travel narratives are those researched and written by people who travel "for the sake of travel itself," independent of outside influences or relationships (5). Dennis Porter, meanwhile, acknowledges in *Haunted Journeys: Desire and Transgression in European Travel Writing* (1991) that he discusses male authors because he focuses on father-son relationships, but at the same time he notes that he includes only writers who "pose or cause to be posed questions of central significance for European society in their time" (16). Porter thus implies that questions of "central significance" both were not posed by women travellers and writers and do not include questions of gender.

The gendered definitions of travel put forward by writers such as Fussell, Blanton, and even Porter encompass what James Clifford ironically calls "[g]ood travel," in the sense that it is characterized as "heroic, educational, scientific, adventurous, ennobling" (105). (Clifford's words find an echo in Blunt and Wills's comments about what might be called "good mapping," which also celebrates "exploration, 'discovery', and heroic explorers and geographers" [193]). Many women in fact travel for none of these "good" motives. Surely, however, their narratives are no less valid as subjects of study than those by men who travel for supposedly altruistic or objective interests – interests that can be reread and reinterpreted as commercial or imperialistic instead of "heroic, educational, scientific, adventurous, ennobling."

The omission of women authors from studies of travel writing, and of non-heroic motives for men's travel, is now being rectified.[4] The two most comprehensive of these combined studies, and the ones to which I return repeatedly, are Sara Mills's *Discourses of Difference: An Analysis of Women's Travel Writing and Colonialism* (1991) and Pratt's *Imperial Eyes*. Mills theorizes discourses of gender and imperialism using a Foucauldian framework and then analyzes such discourses in works by three writers of the nineteenth and early twentieth centuries. Pratt asks questions about how travel writing (mostly by male writers but including a few women) "*produced* 'the rest of the world'" for Western readers, and how such writing practices legitimated "economic expansion and empire" (5). Both studies are useful because of their comments on what I read as one of the fundamental problems of women's travel writing: conflictual representations of issues of gender and imperialism.

My choice of books by Jameson, Hubbard, and Laurence is based on the presence of such conflicts in these women's writings. Historically, women travel writers in Canada have occupied a unique position as reporters on and critics of colonialism. While they are implicated in the British colonial enterprise as a result of their position within the dominant culture, their gender places them on the periphery of colonizing society. Whether they are Canadians (such as Hubbard and Laurence) or British visitors with a vested interest in the colony (such as Jameson), they have a unique first-hand perspective on the colonial process. They adopt and help to implement the imperial goals of their parent society, but because of their geographical position and their gender, they are distanced from the imperial centre and are often held in disdain by it. While authors in these positions necessarily write within the literary and political parameters of their parent society, their peripheral status allows them to be critical of at least some of that parent culture's imperialist and patriarchal manifestations.[5]

Since the effects of both patriarchy and British imperialism continued to be felt in various ways throughout the nineteenth and twentieth centuries (and indeed, up to and including the present), I avoid reinscribing artificial temporal and geographic divisions. I investigate a range of texts widely separated in time and place, and at the same time I locate these narratives in their own historical and geographic moments. Jameson travelled in pre-Confederation Canada when it was popular for English writers to journey to North America and write about their experiences. Hubbard's book came just after the turn of the twentieth century, when Canadians were drawn to narratives of northern and western adventure and when relatively new technologies such as railways and portable cameras were making it easier to travel and to represent travel. Laurence journeyed in the mid-twentieth century, when Canadian writers were venturing off the continent and using their books to discuss not only the political situations they encountered but also the personal transformations sparked by those situations. Although I begin with Jameson and end with Laurence, my study does not trace a historical progression in these women's narratives. I do, however, note differences among the three texts in their analyses of the issues under discussion.[6]

The writings of Jameson and Hubbard do not evince the mid-twentieth-century self-consciousness that Laurence's travel book demonstrates in relation to her own position within imperialism. Yet Jameson and Hubbard were also conscious of issues of race and gender – Jameson most clearly in her philosophical discussion of the status of Anishinaabe (Ojibwa) women and the morality of warfare, Hubbard in her careful naming of both her companions and herself and her acute awareness of her own contradictory position as woman to be cared for and as leader of an expedition. Jameson's detailed discussion of the preconceived notions with which travellers begin their journeys helps to pave the way for the assertion that all travellers and writers are shaped by their societies. Jameson, Hubbard, and Laurence undoubtedly began their travels with preconceptions, which often amounted to what I call an imperialist discursive inheritance. Yet, at the same time, their texts indicate that they were altered by their experiences in their various "contact zone[s]" (M.L. Pratt 6), especially through individual relationships and through the attention they paid, in their ethnographic investigations, to the specifics of the cultures of their travelling companions and the peoples they encountered on their travels.

The texts themselves work in varying ways as reconciliations of feminist, colonial, and anti-colonial approaches. Jameson makes philosophical connections between mid-nineteenth-century feminist and anti-racist theoretical approaches; Hubbard provides insights into an early twentieth-century woman traveller's relationship to First Nations men, who have both more and less power than she; and Laurence serves as a witness to and astute reporter on women's oppression by specific colonial and patriarchal forces during the mid-twentieth century. Jameson's ambivalence about notions of progress, evident in her questioning of distinctions between "savagery" and "civilization," alerts readers to the parallel problem inherent in making value judgments that posit a temporal progression from her text to Hubbard's to Laurence's regarding sensitivity to issues of gender and culture.

The methods these three writers employ are of course determined by their own historical and social periods. Jameson, Hubbard, and Laurence map culture and gender in many disparate ways, including through attention to different indigenous languages and literatures, to specific colonial situations, and to the particular people, landscapes, and geographies they encounter on their journeys. At the same time, negotiation of issues of gender and imperialism is equally evident in each of these narratives, most notably in each author's depiction of artistic and cultural forms in the visited society, representation of her own and others' sexuality, description of the "native" men of her party (and especially of their hunting of wild animals), portrayal of arming herself or considering arming herself to prepare to fight off supposedly hostile attackers, and construction or critique of herself or others as "first" or as alone on the journey.

This positioning is evident not just in the women's writings about their journeys but in the other tasks they engaged in. Jameson sketched what she saw and recorded oral Anishinaabe literature. Hubbard photographed and mapped. Laurence took notes for future stories and transcribed and translated Somali oral poetry and stories. My study examines the whole of the authors' work related to their journeys, including texts, sketches, maps, photographs, and translations. It includes alternative accounts, sometimes from the authors themselves in the form of articles, fictional writings, letters, or journals and sometimes from people who travelled with or met them or who provide accounts of comparable travel experiences. These alternative perspectives help to question the notion of travel narratives as uncomplicated, objective accounts. They help to show, as Sara Mills argues, that such narratives cannot and should not be read as "straightforward transcriptions of the lives of the women travellers" (36) or, as Canadian travel theorist I.S. MacLaren demonstrates, "straightforwardly as eyewitnesses' reports" (41).

Cultural geographer Derek Gregory points out that, historically, only certain groups of people have been identified as travellers, while others are the "natives" who are visited (13–14). People who travel out of necessity, such as Innu who follow caribou herds or Somali camel-herders who move from place to place in search of water or grazing land, are not considered travellers. Neither are people who travel as a result of compulsion, such as Africans transported to the Americas as slaves. My investigation focuses on three women who, because of their gender and their relational motives for travel, fall on the margins of the traditional privileged group named as travellers. As a result of that marginal position, their narratives make reference to others who might in fact be classified as locals or "natives" but who can provide alternative perspectives on the experience of travel. Jameson was accompanied on a segment of her journey by a part-Anishinaabe woman, Jane Schoolcraft, who wrote a letter regarding those travels and who relayed Anishinaabe stories to Jameson. Hubbard journeyed with four First Nations or Métis men, including her chief guide and collaborator, George Elson, who kept a journal on the trip; she also encountered Innu women who left behind oral descriptions of the meeting. The accounts of Schoolcraft, Elson, and the Innu women thus serve as counter-narratives that both reinforce and contradict Jameson's and Hubbard's narratives.

As these parallel accounts show, travel writers do not write in isolation. Because their narratives may be challenged by contemporary narratives and influenced by texts written by precursors, my study places Jameson, Hubbard, and Laurence in the context of their literary predecessors and colleagues. Most travel writers acknowledge previous travel books about the areas they plan to visit. Indeed, Simon Gikandi rightly argues that "the narrative of travel derives its authority from its pre-texts as much as from original observations" (97).[7] Thus while Jameson writes of the influence of Alexander Henry the Elder (1809) on her itinerary and opinions, Hubbard sets out to counter the narrative of her husband's earlier failed journey written by his travelling companion, Dillon Wallace (1905), and Laurence consciously rewrites the early and influential narrative of Somalia of Sir Richard Francis Burton (1856). My study makes reference to these earlier works but also places the writers in the context of their contemporaries – people, especially other women, who travelled through similar areas at the same time or wrote about contemporaneous experiences in other countries. Those accounts, including books by Catharine Parr Traill (1836), Agnes Deans Cameron (1909), and P.K. Page (1987), are particularly useful in serving as comparison texts for an analysis of the writers' attitudes toward "native" peoples and toward women's roles.

In the same way that travel literature has often been studied as providing objective records of real events, the sketches, photographs, and maps that accompany that literature have been interpreted as straightforward illustrations of places, people, and landscapes. All the illustrations in Dorothy Middleton's *Victorian Lady Travellers* (1965), Mary Russell's *The Blessings of a Good Thick Skirt* (1986), and Dea Birkett's *Spinsters Abroad* (1989) are included in order to show readers only the women travellers and writers, although these women are often pictured in the locations in which they travelled. Similarly, in her 1994 study of Mary Kingsley's travels in Africa, Alison Blunt includes Kingsley's photographs of Fan men and women to illustrate the book's portrayal of those people, but never comments on the photographs themselves or on the relationships of gender and imperialism they might illustrate. But photographs, sketches, and maps cannot be presented only as value-free illustrations of textual accounts, since they are inflected by – and demonstrate – their authors' subject positions, time periods, and geographical locations. In this book, therefore, I examine in detail the sketches, photographs, and maps that were either published with the travel narratives or produced at the same time. I find in these visual materials revealing and often contradictory representations of self and other, in terms of gender and of imperialism.

This book is structured as a detailed examination of writings and illustrative material by the three authors, compared to the work of their predecessors and contemporaries. In chapter 1, I turn to the earliest of the three writers, Anna Jameson, and in particular to the third section of her 1838 book, *Winter Studies and Summer Rambles in Canada*. I analyze the way in which Jameson positions herself, through letters as well as book, as both refined and adventurous. In making her "rambles," she consciously follows in the footsteps of Alexander Henry, from whose sometimes imperialistic *Travels and Adventures* she quotes. While she is at first content to allow what she reads in Henry and others to shape her approach to First Nations people, personal interactions and relationships eventually alter both her attitude toward indigenous people in general and her discussions of women, and allow her to make broader philosophical connections between the two. Jameson differs from contemporaneous British visitors to North America such as Harriet Martineau and Frederick Marryat and immigrant Canadian writers such as Catharine Parr Traill because of her emphasis on investigating relationships between the settlers and their government, on one hand, and the area's indigenous inhabitants, on the other. Her contribution to ethnography is examined through her transcription of Anishinaabe oral tales. Finally, I argue that her drawings strikingly demonstrate the ways in which imperialist and anti-imperialist discourses can coincide in ethnographic work and, at the same time, position her as alone and thus "first" both to travel and to represent those travels through words and sketches.

In chapter 2, I consider Mina Hubbard's *A Woman's Way through Unknown Labrador* (1908), as well as her travel diary and her magazine articles. Hubbard's direct literary predecessors include both her husband, whose mantle as travel writer she adopted after his death, and his travelling companion, Dillon Wallace, whose *The Lure of the Labrador Wild* (1905) she set out to counter. I examine the way that Hubbard positions herself within private versus public space, through relational naming and through the inclusion of masculine narratives at the beginning and end of her book. Her discussions of race are compared to those of contemporaneous travel writers, including Wallace, Sara Jeannette Duncan, and Agnes Deans Cameron. I then compare her book to her diary, to the diary of her part-Cree travelling companion, George Elson, and to two brief Innu oral narratives, in order to demonstrate the existence of alternative accounts of the journey and show the ways in which her published narrative is constructed to downplay sexuality and put forward her claims to be "first." Finally, I examine photographs of the Innu people she met for evidence of her notions of primacy and her attitudes toward gender and race, and demonstrate that the mapping in which she was engaged was part of the British imperial project.

In chapter 3, I turn to Margaret Laurence's *The Prophet's Camel Bell* (1963) and to thematic and structural continuities in her fiction, translations, and literary criticism. Laurence's travel narrative, I argue, reveals an enduring engagement with the legacy of colonialism as well as an interest in the effects on women's lives of pre-existing patriarchal structures. Unlike other travel writers of the same era, such as Alys Reece and P.K. Page, Laurence self-consciously identifies herself as a "colonial" and thus as someone who is interested in an anti-imperialist stance, while at the same time acknowledging her position as a peripheral member of the colonizing group. She attempts to negotiate those contradictory positions by recognizing the value of Somali culture through her translation and transcription of Somali oral literature. She also makes a conscious attempt at a counter-imperialist narrative and, at the same time, hints at her own imperialist discursive inheritance by rewriting narratives of her predecessors, including Richard Burton and O. Mannoni, from her own political perspective. Finally, I compare Laurence's treatment of gender and sexuality, especially compulsory maternity, child prostitution, and female genital mutilation, in her travel book and in her novel *This Side Jordan*. Because of the self-consciousness of her position on these subjects, I suggest, she is able to begin a reconciliation of contradictions between feminist and postcolonial theoretical positions.

As I noted at the beginning of this introduction, my initial interest in the visual component of travel narratives was sparked by Mina Hubbard's map and photographs. Like other map-makers, she inscribes herself and her family members (including her dead husband and her nieces) on the landscape of Labrador by naming geographical features such as lakes in their honour. Hubbard appropriates a usually masculine, patriarchal activity and ensures that women's names are remembered through their attachment to the landscape. At the same time, she overwrites existing Innu names for the territory through which she travelled and, in the process, claims that territory for Britain and Canada. My linkage of that renaming to the later flooding of much of that land by the Churchill Falls hydroelectric project, creating the Smallwood Reservoir, is crucial to an understanding of the implications of travel mapping. If a place can be renamed without consulting the people who live there, it can also be flooded without consulting them, and the new geographical features that result can again be given new names, this time in honour of male politicians.

Geographical renaming of this sort is evident all around us, if only we look for it. My interest in toponymy began long before I first saw Mina Hubbard's map because of my personal connection with the renaming of another part of Canada at the same time as Hubbard was naming parts of Labrador and Quebec. In the first decade of the twentieth century, an official for the Canadian Northern Railway decided to take a literary theme in naming the new station stops along a rail line in the southeastern corner of Saskatchewan. The railway stations, which became towns and villages, were named after poets and novelists. Since this was the early twentieth century, many of them were British men: Cowper, Wordsworth, and Browning among them. One station, though, was named in 1909 after Canadian Confederation poet Archibald Lampman to commemorate the tenth anniversary of his death.[8] My great-grandparents had homesteaded in the area six years earlier, and eventually I was born in Lampman hospital and attended Lampman school. I lived within sight of the grain elevators of Lampman, in a rural municipality that bore the name of another nearby hamlet, Browning, which had been named after Robert, not Elizabeth Barrett. My home for the first seventeen years of my life was in the centre of what came to be jokingly known as the "poet's corner" of Saskatchewan.

It took me many years to realize that this rather romantic naming of places had in fact elided most of the area's historical, geographical, and topographical reality. The farmhouse in which I was raised was on the edge of a large area of unbroken, rather rocky pasture land, spotted with bluffs of poplar trees. My brothers and sisters and I could, and often did, walk through our pasture to a neighbour's adjoining pasture, where we climbed onto a limestone buffalo rubbing rock and where we walked around the remains of at least one stone circle indicating where a Plains Cree lodge had been constructed. I never thought much about the cultural history of that familiar landscape, even though I now remember having spent a lot of my free time during childhood walking to and from what we called "the big rock." Only as an adult did I notice the way in which the powerful narrative of the naming of places had, in less than a hundred years, so overwritten the land as to almost completely elide its earlier names and inhabitants. The hilly area where Plains Cree people had set up their homes was now called the Doyle farm. The rock, worn smooth by the rubbing of hundreds and thousands of bison and therefore possibly a sacred place to First Nations peoples who passed through the area, became "the big rock" and our playground.

Today some of the descendants of those Plains Cree live on a reserve eighty kilometres away. Around the time my great-grandparents arrived, their ancestors were forced to share that reserve with groups of Assiniboine and Saulteaux peoples – different cultural groups, but all known simply as "Indians" to government officials – when two nearby reserves were expropriated for settlement and then, shamefully, sold for a profit. The big rock is still in the pasture, unlike another much larger and more famous Saskatchewan erratic or "big rock," which was destroyed during construction of a hydroelectric project on the South Saskatchewan River. In *River in a Dry Land*, Trevor Herriot movingly describes the destruction of that granite rock when it was dynamited in 1966 in an attempt to "preserve" it. Its resting place, the valley of the Aiktow River, which connected the South Saskatchewan and Qu'Appelle river systems, was flooded by the Gardiner Dam, which created Lake Diefenbaker – when again, names of politicians were overwritten on the landscape. The new map of that area of Saskatchewan, like the new map of Labrador after the Churchill Falls project, is an example of the more destructive manifestations of the politics of place names. But even maps such as the one of the corner of Saskatchewan that holds my childhood "big rock" and Mina Hubbard's 1908 map of Labrador demonstrate the way in which the naming of places, with the most romantic and benevolent of intentions, can indicate or even contribute to occlusions in terms of gender, race, culture, and colonialism. In this book I examine narratives by three women writers who undoubtedly contributed to such mapping, but who at the same time helped to critique it.

I cannot, I dare not, attempt to describe to you the strange sensation one
has, thus thrown for a time beyond the bounds of civilised humanity, or
indeed any humanity. | Anna Jameson, *Winter Studies and Summer
Rambles in Canada* 3: 163

When two groups of people previously separated by geography and
history meet, they enter what Mary Louise Pratt calls a "contact zone,"
in which they influence one another, albeit within "radically asymmetrical relations of power" (6–7). Anna Brownell Jameson's *Winter Studies and Summer Rambles in Canada* (1838) provides a map of just such
mutually influential, but at the same time asymmetrical, contact in pre-
Confederation Canada. Her representations of Anishinaabe people she
encountered are in part anecdotal and in part those of an ethnographer
whose purpose is to categorize the world. As someone interested in what
she calls "the condition of women in savage life," Jameson's goals also
include a consideration of gender difference (*Anna Jameson* 154).[1] The
sometimes contradictory results of her investigations are evident not only
in her travel narrative but also in the oral literature she transcribed and
the unpublished pencil sketches she produced to illustrate her journey.
All three map both an imperialist discursive inheritance and revisions
to that inheritance as a result of the mutual influence of contact.

Anna Jameson was already an established writer of biography and
travel narratives when she visited Canada between December 1836 and
September 1837.[2] Her publications included a fictionalized account of
her travels in Italy (*Diary of an Ennuyée*, 1826), three volumes of biography (*Memoirs of the Loves of the Poets*, 1829; *Memoirs of Celebrated
Female Sovereigns*, 1831; and *Memoirs of the Beauties of the Court
of Charles II*, 1831), a volume of literary criticism (*Characteristics of*

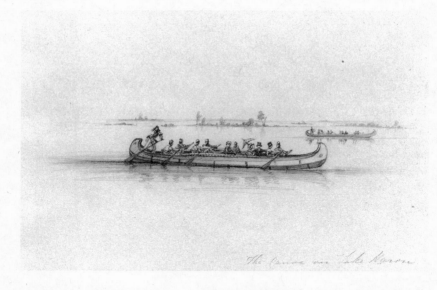

1.1 *The Canoe on Lake Huron*, pencil sketch by Anna Jameson. Courtesy of the Toronto Public Library (TRL), 966–6L–35

Women, 1832), and a three-volume work based on her travels in Europe (*Visits and Sketches at Home and Abroad*, 1834). However, the initial purpose of her Canadian journey was not to write a book; instead, she hoped to be reconciled with – or, if that was not possible, to arrange a financial settlement with – her estranged husband, Robert Jameson, who was being considered for promotion from attorney general to vice-chancellor of the newly established Court of Chancery of Upper Canada in Toronto (Jameson, *Letters* 83n).[3] By June 1837 her purpose in Canada was transformed from duty toward her marriage into a desire "to see, with my own eyes, the condition of women in savage life" (*Anna Jameson* 154; see also *Letters* 93). Shortly after Robert was awarded his new post, Anna embarked on a two-and-a-half-month journey into the interior of North America. She returned to Toronto in mid-August, at which time she wrote to her mother that "thinking it a shame to keep these wonders only to make my own hair stand on end, I am just going to make a book and print it forthwith" (*Anna Jameson* 157). In September she left again for New York, where she transformed her notes into a book as she waited for five months for a signed separation agreement, before returning permanently to England.

As an anonymous 1839 reviewer for the *British and Foreign Review* noted (148), Jameson's book bears some resemblance to Mary Wollstonecraft's *Letters Written during a Short Residence in Sweden, Norway, and Denmark* (1796). Both are travel books. Both originate from journeys embarked on at the request of a male partner – Wollstonecraft's at the request of her lover, Gilbert Imlay, to recover a ship and its contents, which had been stolen from him, and Jameson's at the request of her husband, to provide evidence of marital stability. Both are written episodically and chronologically – Wollstonecraft's in the form of undated letters and Jameson's as dated journal entries.[4] Neither author identifies her male partner or her reason for travelling, although Wollstonecraft writes of unhappiness at her loneliness, and Jameson notes that her "proper place" is "among the wives of the officials" of the Upper Canadian government (1: 152) and then acknowledges that she is known in Upper Canada as the "chancellor's lady" (2: 160).[5] Like Wollstonecraft, Jameson repeatedly addresses *Winter Studies and Summer Rambles* to a particular, unnamed, absent but loved "you." Unlike Wollstonecraft's addressee (Imlay), Jameson's hypothetical reader is not a lover but a woman modelled on her friend Ottilie von Goethe of Germany. In her preface, Jameson notes only that her book is addressed "to a friend" and "to my own sex" (1: v, vii), but in the body of the text she frequently includes comments aimed at an individual woman, such as "I always fancy *you* of the party" (3: 18). Her direction to that friendly reader to "[p]ray have a map before you when you read all this!" (3: 20; see also 2: 312, 3: 328) echoes the request she made to her real friend, Goethe in a letter from Canada, to "look at the map if you can" (*Letters* 72).[6]

Jameson's first volume, *Winter Studies*, consists mostly of considerations of education and politics in Upper Canada and lengthy descriptions of her literary studies (although she also tells of a short winter trip to Niagara Falls). She embarks on her studies, she writes early in the volume, because the cold and loneliness have caused her to lose heart, and "I *must* rouse myself to occupation; and if I cannot find it without, I must create it from within" (1: 30). The occupation that she eventually settles on as "a file for the serpent" (1: 173, quoting Byron) is translation of German texts, including Johann Eckermann's *Conversations with Goethe*. Jameson's two-volume *Summer Rambles*, in contrast, describes two much more physically active months spent travelling again to Niagara Falls and the western regions of Upper Canada, through Detroit to the American island of Mackinac in Lake

Huron, from thence to Sault Ste Marie and Manitoulin Island, and finally back to Toronto via Penetanguishene.[7] She intersperses accounts of her early travels in volume 2 with reflections on settlement, education, religion, and temperance. Volume 3 focuses almost solely on her meetings with First Nations groups, her attempts to understand and analyze their cultures and their relationships with European settlers and British and American governments, and her developing personal relationships with Anishinaabe individuals.[8] She describes, in particular, an approximately six-day stay on Mackinac Island with American Indian agent Henry Rowe Schoolcraft and his wife, Jane; a subsequent four-day stay near Sault Ste Marie with Jane's sister, missionary Charlotte McMurray, and her husband, William; and travels by boat with members of the two families.[9]

Although Jameson claims in the preface to *Winter Studies and Summer Rambles* that she is politically neutral (1: viii), she writes neither neutrally nor objectively: not about the government of Upper Canada, which she considered mismanaged (1: viii); not about Toronto, which she characterized as "most strangely mean and melancholy" (1: 2) and "like a fourth or fifth rate provincial town, with the pretensions of a capital city" (1: 98); and not about the role of women, which features prominently in both her one-volume *Winter Studies* and her two-volume *Summer Rambles*. The political tensions she describes were the precursors to the Upper Canada rebellion of December 1837, which began a few months after she left the Canadas for the United States.[10] Jameson focuses more attention on two different but related political situations: the tensions inherent in the relationship between the European colonists and the First Nations groups they were displacing, and the situation of First Nations women, in particular Anishinaabe women.[11]

Her book and her letters to friends and family (in volumes edited by Erskine and Needler and in several archives) show changes in her position on these subjects through contact with First Nations individuals. Unlike many of the narratives she points to as pre-texts or which were contemporary to hers, such as those by Alexander Henry the Elder, Henry Schoolcraft, Catharine Parr Traill, Harriet Martineau, and Frederick Marryat, Jameson's book employs a language tempered by sympathy and by a desire to be liked and accepted by the individual Anishinaabe people she met and with whom she stayed, including sisters Jane Schoolcraft and Charlotte McMurray and their mother, O,shah,gush,ko,da,na,qua (Oshaguscodawaqua), or Susan Johnston, an Anishinaabe woman who had married an Irish-born trader. Jameson's changing and sometimes contradictory responses to First Nations people are graphically illustrated in the pencil sketches she made on her journey. These were not published with her book, and until now, they have remained for the most part unpublished and relatively unstudied, although five etchings and three sketches were published in a 1958 pamphlet, *Early Canadian Sketches*.[12] In fact, many of Jameson's drawings strikingly complement, illustrate, and at times contradict her discussions of First Nations people and her careful construction of the femininity, controlled sexuality, and, at the same time, adventurousness of a pre-Victorian British woman traveller such as herself.

BREAKING FREE, BEING FIRST, REMAINING REFINED

It has become a commonplace to note that women travellers, especially those of the nineteenth century, viewed travel as an opportunity to escape from the restraints of traditional female life (Foster 8; Smith 20). Although Jameson's journey to Mackinac and Sault Ste Marie did give her a chance to leave, at least temporarily, an unworkable marriage and a city she disliked (Thomas 116), her escape from Toronto also involved a more active striving toward primacy, a striving evident in her repeated comments that she was the first of her kind to make such a journey.

Jameson's desire to be first is apparent in a letter to her mother of 17 August 1837, in which she writes that she is "the first Englishwoman – the first European female who ever accomplished this journey" and that adventures such as hers "never yet were rehearsed in prose or verse" (*Anna Jameson* 157). In the preface to her book, Jameson makes similar, although slightly more subdued, claims about being the first to experience such adventures and to write about them; she notes that she was "thrown into scenes and regions hitherto undescribed by any traveller" and "into relations with the Indian tribes, such as few European women of refined and civilised habits have ever risked, and none have recorded" (1: vi). This passage is remarkable for the way that it both establishes Jameson as the first to risk and record (thus valorizing both the doing and the recording of the deed) and also emphasizes that during her journey she remained "refined" and "civilised." As someone "refined," she is different from most British women in Canada, who are settlers from the lower classes. As someone "civilised," she is distinguished from the aboriginal women she encounters. Her refinement and civilization thus allow her to claim to be first even though other women – certainly, First Nations women and possibly other European women – have gone before her.

As Jameson later acknowledged, she was not in fact the first traveller to describe Mackinac and Sault Ste Marie: Henry had included such descriptions in *Travels and Adventures in Canada and the Indian Territories between the Years 1760 and 1776* (1809). She was not even the first woman: Martineau had included a brief description of the island in *Society in America* (1837). Jameson's belief in the need for travellers to at least claim primacy is evident when she wonders who was "the first white man" to see Niagara Falls (2: 76). Even though the falls may have been looked at for thousands of years by indigenous peoples, she implies, they were not really seen until a European man viewed them. Her own most emphatic and specific statement of primacy comes after she shoots the rapids at Sault Ste Marie in a canoe. She writes that during the seven-minute ride, she "reclined on a mat at the bottom, Indian fashion" and "had not even a momentary sensation of fear, but rather of giddy, breathless, delicious excitement" (3: 198–9). The word "reclined" emphasizes her refinement, while references to "Indian fashion," her sense of excitement, and her lack of fear emphasize her adventurous nature. She writes with pride after the event, "I was the first European female who had ever performed it" (3: 199–200).

Solitary experience and the risk of physical danger are part of Jameson's equation of primacy. Toward the beginning of the *Summer Rambles* section of her narrative, in an entry dated 8 June 1837, Jameson writes: "To undertake such a journey *alone* is rash perhaps – yet alone it must be achieved, I find, or not at all; I shall have neither companion nor man-servant, nor *femme de chambre*, nor even a 'little foot-page' to give notice of my fate, should I be swamped in a bog, or eaten up by a bear, or scalped, or disposed of in some strange way" (2: 8). In this passage, she calls attention to the potential danger inherent in solitary travel, a physical danger stemming from sources such as raw nature and the creatures (some of them human) who inhabit it. The language she uses to describe her journey emphasizes solitude even where it is entirely figurative: she writes, "I was alone – alone – and on my way to that ultimate somewhere of which I knew nothing" (2: 36–7), characterizes herself as "a wayfaring lonely woman, spiritless, half-dead with fatigue, among entire strangers" (2: 122), and calls herself a "poor, lonely, shivering woman" (3: 337). In fact, Jameson was never truly alone on her journey: other people, and sometimes large groups of people, conveyed her from one place to another and provided accommodation. But she was often without the companionship of friends or acquaintances of her own economic, cultural, and social status, and she was sometimes without female companionship.

Perhaps her most telling reference to isolation is her description of journeying from Mackinac to Sault Ste Marie. Jameson writes that as she travelled in a bateau (a small boat) with Jane Schoolcraft, Schoolcraft's two children, and five oarsmen, she was "thrown for a time beyond the bounds of civilised humanity." For "[t]wo days and nights the solitude was unbroken," and "we its [the boat's] inmates, two women, differing in clime, nation, complexion, strangers to each other but a few days ago, might have fancied ourselves alone in a new-born world" (3: 163). Jameson's belated inclusion of Schoolcraft in her solitude through the first-person plural pronoun demonstrates similarities in gender that might allow Schoolcraft to make a parallel claim to primacy based on her gender. The remainder of the sentence, however, emphasizes contrasts in race that might prohibit such a claim. Schoolcraft's children are completely excluded from Jameson's representation of her solitude, presumably on the basis of their age, while the oarsmen are also disqualified, likely on the basis of gender, race, and class.

Including another woman in her isolation and danger is one tactic Jameson employs in her continual rhetorical negotiations between boldness and adventurousness, on the one hand, and refinement and femininity, on the other. A second strategy is hinted at in a pamphlet written by Henry Scadding, whom Jameson met in Sorel, Lower Canada, on her return journey from Toronto to New York: "The hands of Mrs. Jameson were remarkably beautiful. How their extreme whiteness and delicacy were preserved during the unavoidable inconveniences and exposures of the recent extensive canoe trip was a mystery, but I think in relation to some allusion to this escape I overheard a strong hint given to one of her young lady friends, that never under any circumstances must the hands be ungloved for one moment in the out-of-door air, or sun light, a precept enforced by a reiterated emphatic *never*" (12). In order to be considered refined, Scadding intimates, women such as Jameson must zealously protect themselves from the coarsening rays of the sun. Such protection also preserves that distinctive marker of race, white skin. Jameson does not emphasize her use of gloves in *Winter Studies and Summer Rambles* (like Mina Hubbard almost seventy years later, who is sorely troubled by the loss of one of her gloves but mentions that loss only in her diary [29 June 1905]), but she does write about

1.2 *Indian Canoes on Lake Huron*, etching by Anna Jameson. Courtesy of the Royal Ontario Museum, Toronto, 961.220.5

her parasol and illustrates herself with both parasol and bonnet, in a sketch in which such markers of gender set her apart from the men also pictured (fig. 1.1 and 1.2). In a subsequent letter to Charlotte McMurray, Jameson writes that despite the care she took of her complexion, "it was however many days before my poor swelled & sunburnt face recovered its usual paleness" (Letter).[13]

Jameson's focus on her own refined femininity is particularly evident when she describes her final wilderness journey, as the only woman travelling with twenty-one men in two canoes from Manitoulin to Penetanguishene. Her narrative employs several rhetorical techniques to emphasize both the extraordinariness of her venture and her adherence to standards of refinement and civilization. First, she downplays the sexual threat (as opposed to general physical danger) inherent in travel with a large group of men by pointing out that she is accompanied by the newly appointed superintendent of Indian affairs for Upper Canada, Samuel Peters Jarvis ("Jarvis" 431). Jameson had earlier spoken of Jarvis at length, quoting long passages of his speech to the First Nations gathered at Manitoulin. Now she represents him as a trustworthy companion and protector, noting that "Providence" was taking care of her and that "nothing could exceed the politeness of Mr. Jarvis and his people" (3: 314). As Judith Johnston points out in her study of Jameson's writings, Jameson then provides herself with an imaginary woman companion by addressing her familiar implied reader

(114); she writes, "[T]hat you may accompany us in our canoe voyage, I must describe in the first place our arrangements." Next, she introduces the two other passengers in a way that emphasizes their respective ages – "the governor's son, a lively boy of fourteen or fifteen" (probably the son of Lieutenant-Governor Sir Francis Bond Head) and "old Solomon the interpreter" – and thus their harmlessness (3: 314–15). The only one of the seven men paddling the canoe whom Jameson names is "our Indian steersman, Martin." And only after she has mentioned these individuals does she write that the party consists of "twenty-one men, and myself, the only woman" (3: 316).

Jameson describes Martin in detail, as wearing "a cotton shirt, arms bared to the shoulder, loose trowsers, a scarlet sash round his waist, richly embroidered with beads, and his long black hair waving" (3: 315). She also writes that he has "the lithe agility of a snake" and is "very graceful and picturesque" (3: 316). Johnston suggests that Jameson's description is a sexualized portrayal that daringly evokes a heterosexual interest (114), but while the comparison to a snake may suggest the temptation of male sexuality, the word "graceful" contributes to an overall impression of femininity. The focus on flowing hair and finery of clothing further feminizes and thus renders harmless the one indigenous man with whom Jameson is in close proximity. Since, for white women, "the male indigene's sexuality is an emblem of fear rather than temptation" (Goldie 79), women travel writers of the nineteenth century seldom referred to sexual matters. Jameson evokes the spectre of sexual desire, but by feminizing the potential object of that desire, she renders her interest innocuous and the man's sexuality non-threatening.[14]

Jameson's description of the steersman is not the first time she has qualified her own comments about the personal attractiveness of indigenous men. After seeing the men dance on Mackinac and noting their lack of clothing, she writes that "the figures of most of the men were superb; more agile and elegant, however, than muscular" (3: 148). She describes one particularly attractive young man as "a model for a sculptor" and comments, "The perfection of his form, the graceful abandonment of his attitude, reminded me of a young Mercury" (3: 148). Her reference to sculpture, to Mercury, and by implication to artistic renditions of this messenger of the gods, aestheticizes any imagined desire. Earlier she writes of a man in scarlet leggings who expressed an interest in her by strutting about and who, when he saw her watching, "came up and shook hands with me, repeating 'Bojou! bojou!'" (3: 45). By referring to the man's "dandyism" and thus emphasizing his interest in finery, Jameson again downplays a potentially sexualized subject.[15]

In Jameson's description of the canoe trip, her itemization of some of the articles she carried with her – and her failure to mention others – further emphasizes her refinement and de-emphasizes sexual danger. Scadding reports that on Jameson's travels, "a small stiletto or poignard was secretly carried for self-defence if there should be any need" (12). Jameson never mentions the knife; instead, her description of her luggage implies that she was never really "beyond the bounds of civilised humanity" since she carried its trappings with her. She writes that she had "a pillow at my back" and "reclined in the bottom of the canoe, as in a litter, very much at my ease." With her were "necessary luxuries," as well as "cloak, umbrella, and parasol; my note-books and sketch-books, and a little compact basket always by my side, containing eau de Cologne" (3: 315). References to reclining in a litter are not accidental; Johnston notes that Jameson's use of the word "litter" "constructs the vision of the memsahib carried on the backs of the colonised" (114). Jameson was, like memsahibs everywhere in the British Empire, transported by servants, protected from unpleasant odours by eau de cologne, and shielded from the sun by a parasol. Her narrative emphasizes that the men treated her with the respect and care due her sex and class; when they provided breakfast for her, they added a bouquet of flowers to the rock she used as a table, and they pitched her tent "at a *respectful* distance from the rest" (3: 320–1, 326).

A final rhetorical strategy is Jameson's repeated contrast of herself to the men (whom she is careful to call gentlemen) in terms of their interest in hunting and fishing. They had the masculine propensity toward killing animals, she writes, while emphasizing her feminine distaste for the activity: "My only discomposure arose from the destructive propensities of the gentlemen, all keen and eager sportsmen; the utmost I could gain from their mercy was, that the fish should gasp to death out of my sight, and the pigeons and the wild ducks be put out of pain instantly" (3: 322). This passage initially indicates to readers that the pursuit of game is pure sport, but Jameson eventually admits that the animals were being hunted to provide food. She writes that "when the bass-fish and pigeons were produced, broiled and fried, they looked so *appétissants*, smelt so savoury, and I was *so* hungry, that I soon forgot all my sentimental pity for the victims" (3: 322). By describing her interest in the welfare of the animals as sentimental, Jameson stresses her femininity. Similarly, in subsequent sections she refers to the killing of a water snake as a "gratuitous piece of cruelty" (3: 329); calls the pursuit of a mink repayment of the beauty of nature "with pain and with destruction" (3: 331); describes a mother duck and ducklings as "a sight to touch the heart with a tender pleasure," for which she "pleaded hard, very hard, for mercy" (3: 331); and calls the spectacle of "poor gulls" being called by the voyageurs so that they could be killed and eaten "touching" (3: 332). Her characterization of herself in these passages as tender-hearted and the men as cruel and destructive further emphasizes the gap between them.

On the title page of her book, Jameson and her publishers have already provided confirmation of her respectability and have mitigated the dangers of her journey. Calling the two final volumes of her book *Summer Rambles* makes them appear no more arduous than an afternoon walk in the English countryside. As with most of her books, *Winter Studies and Summer Rambles* was published under her married name, "Mrs. Jameson." Sandra Gilbert and Susan Gubar argue that Victorian women writers who used only their married surnames on their publications "established their allegiance to marital respectability by acquiescing in the couverture of 'Mrs.'" (241). Although Jameson had been married in name only for a number of years, continuing to represent herself as "Mrs." allowed her the freedom to travel alone and unchaperoned, to make the kind of adventurous journey about which she wrote, and indeed, to publish the writing that resulted from such a journey. Marian Fowler suggests that Jameson's journey serves as a metaphoric moving outside "society's artificial fences which keep women dependent, delicate, and sexually innocent" (*Embroidered Tent* 159), but in fact Jameson carefully and self-consciously maintained an ambivalent position, acting independently and at the same time working from inside at least some of those social fences.

THEORIZING TRAVEL

Despite her representation of herself as bringing civilization with her, Jameson's summer rambles were in reality often arduous. She travelled from Niagara Falls to Detroit over roads that were either mired in bog or consisted of a rough "corduroy" of logs, in bakers' and farmers' carts that blistered her hands as she held on to avoid being tossed out (2: 223, 119). Although she travelled from Detroit to Mackinac by steamship, her return loop was by bateau and canoe. On those journeys, although she writes of having "a luxuriant dinner" (3: 247), she also suffered hardships that included fighting off swarms of mosquitoes. She calls the theologian who suggested that sinners would be "stung by mosquitoes all made of brass, and as large as black beetles" "an ignoramus and a bungler" because "[m]osquitoes, as they exist in this upper world, are as pretty and perfect a plague as the most ingenious amateur sinner-tormentor ever devised" (3: 167–8). Her description of these hardships thus is so poetic that their sting is softened.[16]

By providing unusual descriptions of her travels such as the one above, Jameson resists pigeonholing as a typical traveller. Karen Lawrence writes in *Penelope Voyages* that travel writers, like modernists, must always struggle to "make it new" (24). Jameson engages with this struggle in part through her focus on primacy, but also through the impressionistic nature of her descriptions. She serves notice to readers that she will not try to weed out inconsistencies and contradictions: "as I travel on, I am disgusted, or I am enchanted; I despair or I exult by turns; and these inconsistent and apparently contradictory emotions and impressions I set down as they arise, leaving you to reconcile them as well as you can" (2: 236–7). This eccentric approach is put into effect when, preparing for her first winter trip to Niagara Falls, Jameson initially presents herself as a sightseer. She is going to "see Niagara in all its wintry magnificence," she writes, contrasting her visit to the conventional trip of a European traveller on the Grand Tour: "O! in this moment I do not envy you the blue Mediterranean, nor the summer skies and orange-groves of your southern island!" (1: 63). In Jameson's description of her first sight of the falls, however, she contradicts the expectation she has set up, in which a sightseer will express the Romantic traveller's awe at viewing the falls.[17] Instead, she writes that she is so profoundly disappointed that she is no longer herself, no longer a traveller, no longer even human: "What has come over my soul and senses? – I am no longer Anna – I am metamorphosed – I am translated – I am an ass's head, a clod, a wooden spoon, a fat weed growing on Lethe's bank, a stock, a stone, a petrifaction,– for have I not seen Niagara, the wonder of wonders; and felt – no words can tell *what* disappointment" (1: 83). Jameson's inclusion of the words "translated" and "ass's head" implies that her transformation is as radical as that of Bottom in Shakespeare's *A Midsummer Night's Dream* (3.1.116, 119). In a letter to her family, she writes less poetically and less encompassingly that "the *first* glance disappointed me ... but, when I had been looking at them for a couple of hours and from different points of view, my mind began to open to

1.3 *Forest Road to Niagara, January 25*, pencil sketch by Anna Jameson.
Courtesy of the Toronto Public Library (TRL), 966–6L–3

their immensity and sublimity" (*Anna Jameson* 147; see also *Letters* 78). In the book, in contrast, she reverses the language of landscape aesthetics to describe the falls as though they are part of a painting, but one containing "neither light, nor shade, nor colour" (1: 86).

Jameson's subsequent, more close-up descriptions of the falls in *Winter Studies and Summer Rambles* are more enthusiastic; she writes that as she stood on Table Rock overlooking the falls and watched icicles hang from the cliffs and huge blocks of ice pour over the edge, she was fascinated by the "wild and wonderful magnificence" of the scene (1: 89). In contrast to Jameson's professed disappointment, Martineau, who visited Niagara Falls several times during her travels through North America a few years earlier, writes in her *Retrospect of Western Travel* that the emotion she felt during her first sight of the falls "was never renewed or equalled" (1: 153). In *Society in America* she makes viewing the falls "new" by using it as an opportunity to comment on contrasts between civilization and savagery and on the superiority of her own society. Niagara Falls is for her one of the "primitive glories of nature" that has been "dispensed to savages" who, although they

1.4 *Table Rock, June 26, being wet through*, pencil sketch by Anna Jameson. Courtesy of the Toronto Public Library (TRL), 966–6L–10

may love it, cannot bring to it "the mind of man, as enriched and stimulated by cultivated society" (1: 212). Marryat, whose travels were almost concurrent with Jameson's, muses that the first "savage" who saw the falls must have been compelled by its "thunder and awful majesty" to see it as "the dwelling of the Great Spirit," but "could not imagine that the Great Spirit dwelt also in the leaf which he bruised in his hand" (1: 160). Although all three of these responses focus on contrasts, in Jameson's narrative the contrast is not between civilization and savagery, as it is in Martineau's and Marryat's, but between expectation and reality.[18]

Jameson also makes distinctions between travel and tourism. While she never uses the word "tourist," her definitions of various types of travellers align in many ways with those of Paul Fussell, who posits that the traveller seeks "that which has been discovered by the mind working in history," while the tourist seeks "that which has been discovered by entrepreneurship and prepared for him by the arts of mass publicity" (*Abroad* 39). Jameson predicts that the beauty of the island of Mackinac will make it "a sort of watering-place for the Michigan and Wisconsin fashionables," and she writes, "I am only glad it has not yet taken place, and that I have beheld this lovely island in all its wild beauty" (3: 40–1) – in other words, before it becomes a destination for mass travel. In fact, the island was already popular with nineteenth-century tourists. Henry Schoolcraft, the American Indian agent and Jameson's host on Mackinac, peppers his *Personal Memoirs* with references to visitors such as Martineau, who called Mackinac "enchanting" and a "paradise" and decried the fact that the captain of her ship intended to spend only three hours there (*Society in America* 2: 12, 13), and Marryat, who described Mackinac as "a fairy isle floating on the water" (1: 181). Jameson was aware of those visits; she writes, "I am told that last year there were several strangers staying here, in spite of the want of all endurable accommodation" (3: 41). She herself calls Mackinac a "fairy island" (3: 151) and "a *bijou* of an island! – a little bit of fairy ground, just such a thing as some of our amateur travellers would like to pocket and run away with (if they could)" (3: 68). Thus, although she romanticizes and reduces the island through her rhetoric, she also distinguishes herself from the "amateur travellers" who would turn it into a toy.

In addition to distinguishing between travel and tourism, Jameson theorizes travel writing by pointing out the influence of prior texts on travellers. Contemporary travel theorists suggest that the authority

1.5 *Wigwams on the beach at Mackinaw – July 21*, pencil sketch by Anna Jameson. Courtesy of the Toronto Public Library (TRL), 966–6L–24

of travel narratives is as much a function of their "pre-texts" as their "original observations" (Gikandi 97). Jameson distinguishes among the types of authority provided by precursors when she notes, "In former times, when people travelled into strange countries, they travelled *de bonne foi*, really to see and learn what was new to them. Now, when a traveller goes to a foreign country, it is always with a set of preconceived notions concerning it, to which he fits all he sees, and refers all he hears: and this, I suppose, is the reason that the old travellers are still safe guides; while modern travellers may be pleasant reading, but are withal the most unsafe guides one can have" (1: 277). Jameson thus tacitly acknowledges that the experiences of travel and travel writing are discursively constructed, since both she and her readers have preconceived notions about her subject matter gained from reading previously published books. She insists that she will not repeat "well-known Indian customs" or "anecdotes to be found in all the popular books of travel" because her readers will be familiar with "the general characteristics of Indian life and manners" after having read "the works of [James Fenimore] Cooper, Washington Irving, Charles Hoffman, and others" (3: 85).

Jameson earlier indicates that the narrative which had the most influence on the direction of her own travels was Henry's *Travels and*

1.6 *Wigwam of Another Tribe of Indians*, etching by Anna Jameson. Courtesy of the Royal Ontario Museum, Toronto, 961.220.3

Adventures. Because he travelled in Canada between 1760 and 1776, into territories that had previously been unexplored by European travellers, Henry could be classified as an "old traveller" and thus a reliable source, someone who could be "quoted as first-rate authority" (3: 17). Jameson was lent *Travels and Adventures* while she was in Toronto, and she notes that it struck her so forcefully that it "had some influence in directing the course of my present tour" (3: 17). Indeed, Henry's descriptions of Mackinac and Sault Ste Marie led her to travel to that area. As she describes travelling through the same territory, Jameson quotes Henry repeatedly, citing him as an authority on history and culture. On Mackinac she recalls his "vivid description" of the murder of seventy British soldiers at Fort Michilimackinac (3: 57n), and she visits particular sites about which he writes, such as "a spot of romantic interest," a cave in which he was hidden by an Anishinaabe friend during a time of danger (3: 67; Henry 108–9).[19]

Henry's motive for travel was at wide variance from Jameson's. His purpose was almost wholly economic – to set up trade routes and thus to make money from his contact with First Nations – while Jameson's travels were impelled by a more disinterested ethnographic curiosity. She does not emphasize the economic basis for Henry's travels, but instead places his writings into the long discursive tradition of writings about travel by comparing them to the *Odyssey*, one of the oldest existing European narratives that includes a description of travel. In arguing for the necessity of using *Travels and Adventures* as her source and model, Jameson writes:

He is the Ulysses of these parts, and to cruise among the shores, rocks, and islands of Lake Huron without Henry's travels, were like coasting Calabria and Sicily without the Odyssey in your head or hand,– only here you have the island of Mackinaw instead of the island of Circe; the land of the Ottawas instead of the shores of the Lotophagi; cannibal Chippewas, instead of man-eating Læstrygons; Pontiac figures as Polypheme; and Wa,wa,tam [the Anishinaabe man who hid Henry after the massacre] plays the part of good king Alcinous. I can find no type for the women, as Henry does not tell us his adventures among the squaws, but no doubt he might have found both Calypsos and Nausicaas, and even a Penelope, among them (3: 18–19).[20]

Jameson's comparison of Henry's travels to the *Odyssey* reinforces her awareness of the discursively constructed nature of travel. Because she has read this classic tale of travel and adventure, she reinterprets Henry's narrative in terms of the models it proposes. In a similar way, her initial representation of the land and the people through which she travels reflects the "types" found in Henry's book – types of the cannibal, the good friend, and perhaps even the woman who waits at home.

THE TROPE OF ADOPTION

One type that Jameson borrows and reworks is that of the adopted First Nations sibling. She writes several times of Henry's friendship with Wa,wa,tam (Wawatam in the *Dictionary of Canadian Biography*), who rather than dreaming of the usual *manito* or guiding spirit during puberty rites, had dreamed of a white man who would become his brother (3: 57n, 3: 115n). According to Henry's own account, the adoption was entirely Wa,wa,tam's idea. He writes that the Anishinaabe man visited him often, brought "a large present, consisting of skins, sugar and dried meat," and then informed Henry that he wanted to adopt him "as his son, brother and friend" (73–4). Henry accepted the association because it was to his economic and social advantage to have strong links with the Anishinaabe community. Indeed, as a result of his relationship with Wa,wa,tam, he was warned of the impending danger at Fort Michilimackinac. When he ignored the warning and witnessed the taking of the fort, he was spirited to safety by Wa,wa,tam and his family.

Jameson's repeated references to Henry's adoption by this Anishinaabe family indicate her intense interest in the subject and her belief that to be a North American traveller and not a tourist, one must become part of what one travels through. If she is travelling in the region through which Henry journeyed, she must similarly be adopted. Such adoption would require several steps, comparable but not identical to Henry's experience: finding compatible siblings and parents, undergoing transformative experiences, and being renamed. Jameson found suitable relatives in Charlotte McMurray, Jane Schoolcraft, and their mother, Susan Johnston. Unlike Henry's, her motives for the adoption were not practical, and thus the suitability of her "family" was based on her own unique criteria of "Indian" appearance combined with delicacy and refinement. During her first brief meeting with McMurray in Toronto just before the start of her rambles, Jameson was "struck ... with a pleased surprise" that McMurray was different from "the specimens of Indian squaws and half-cast women I had met with." Although she had "distinctly Indian" features, they were "softened and refined," and she had a manner "free from embarrassment" and a graceful form (2: 33). When Jameson later met Schoolcraft, she wrote that although the woman's features were "more decidedly Indian than those of her sister," her use of language was "pure and remarkably elegant" (3: 36) and she exhibited a "genuine refinement and simplicity" – a refinement evident for Jameson, and for Jameson's readers, in "the exceeding delicacy of her health" (3: 69). As for Mrs Johnston, Jameson writes that she had "the strongest marked Indian features," but also "a countenance open, benevolent, and intelligent, and a manner perfectly easy," as well as an eloquence in her own language (3: 184–5). These women's "Indian features" provided them with a welcome exoticism. At the same time, the women possessed elements of Jameson's definition of refinement, including softened features, graceful movements, delicate health, easy manners, and eloquent speech.

The language of family relationship is especially evident in Jameson's description of her meeting with Susan Johnston, who possessed a "motherly dignity, becoming the head of her large family" and received Jameson "most affectionately." Jameson emphasizes in this passage that Johnston made the first move in the "adoption," calling her "Nindannis, daughter." At the same time, she highlights her difference from Johnston by comparing her "dark Indian face" to the face of Jameson's own "fair mother" (3: 185). Jameson may have become this woman's foster daughter, but her reference to her natural mother's fair complexion registers the European gentility of her own family situation.

Once she has found her adoptive family, Jameson must undergo a transformative experience to confirm her acceptance into it. For Henry, that transformative experience was surviving the massacre with the help of his "brother"; for Jameson, it was shooting the rapids at Sault Ste Marie in a canoe with the help of her own soon-to-be adopted "brother," Mrs Johnston's son, George. In her account of canoeing down the rapids, Jameson claims to be "first" and also paradoxically stresses both her bravery and her refinement. The experience of shooting the rapids, she writes, allowed her to become part of the Johnston family; she notes that her "Neengai" (mother) "laughed, clapped her hands, and embraced me several times. I was declared duly initiated, and adopted into the family" (3: 200). Jameson's adoption was sealed with a new name. She had earlier recorded a name bestowed by her Anishinaabe friends at Mackinac: "Being in manners and complexion unlike the European woman they have been accustomed to see," she writes, they call her "the *white or fair English chieftainess* (Ogimaquay)" (3: 134–5). At Sault Ste Marie, she notes, the Johnston family "had already called me among themselves, in reference to my complexion and my travelling propensities, O,daw,yaun,gee *the fair changing moon*, or rather, *the fair moon which changes her place*" (3: 200). Now, she says, these two names, both of which related to her Europeanness, her refinement, and her high social status, were replaced by a name that she preferred because it highlighted her adventurous nature and her connection to the North American landscape: "Wah,sàh,ge,wah,nó,- quà ... *the woman of the bright foam*" (3: 200).[21] Jameson's renaming thus represents her own transformation and metamorphosis, including her entry into a new culture and her adoption of a new identity, through cross-cultural contact and the crossing of gender boundaries.

Jane Schoolcraft provides an alternative, and in some points contradictory, version of the events surrounding Jameson's "adoption" in a letter to her husband quoted in his *Personal Memoirs*. Schoolcraft writes, belying the impression of competence and adventurousness that Jameson projects in her narrative, "I feel delighted ... at my having come with Mrs. Jameson, as I found that she did not know how to get along at all at all." Jameson's shooting of the rapids, she continues, was accomplished "in fine style and spirits. She insisted on being baptized and named in Indian, after her *sail* down the falls. We named her Was-sa-je-wun-e-qua (Woman of the Bright Stream), with which she was mightily pleased" (563). Schoolcraft's emphasis on the word "sail" indicates that the experience might not have been as dangerous or as adventurous as Jameson's account implies. In addition, the stress in Schoolcraft's version on Jameson's own insistence on being renamed, as well as the omission of any reference to adoption, indicates that it was Jameson who sought the renaming as a way of both changing her identity and proving her acceptance by her aboriginal hosts, and thus authenticating her travels. Her new name, too, is translated slightly differently by Schoolcraft: the word "stream" suggests a watery setting that is more quiet and tame than that suggested by the word "foam," with its implications of roiling and perhaps dangerous waters.

Immediately after her "adoption," Jameson writes, "Now that I have been a Chippewa born, any time these four hours, I must introduce you to some of my new relations" (3: 200-1). Her juxtaposition of the "adoption" with a reference to the change in social status that occurs toward the end of Shakespeare's The Winter's Tale (5.2.135-7) reinforces differences in social position. At the same time, it emphasizes both the audacity of making such connections and the refinement implied by detailed knowledge of the classics of English literature. The suitability of Jameson's adopted relatives is then represented in terms of a family history of gentility (in European terms), as she refers to her "illustrious grand-papa, Waub-Ojeeg, (the White-fisher)" (3: 201) and insists that the family "exercised, even from a remote period, a sort of influence over the rest of the tribe" (3: 203).

Throughout the remainder of her narrative, Jameson reminds readers of her kinship with this "illustrious" family – she calls Johnston her "dear good Chippewa mamma" (3: 245) and Johnston's brother "my uncle Wayish,ky" (3: 243) – and she emphasizes their superiority to other First Nations people she has encountered. She writes that the interior of Wayish,ky's lodge "presented every appearance of comfort, and even *elegance*, according to the Indian notions of both" (3: 186). Even after she travelled to the gathering on Manitoulin, she was surrounded by relatives who displayed a kind of natural distinction: "the chief whom I immediately distinguished from the rest, even before I knew his name, was my cousin, young Waub-Ojeeg, the son of Wayish,ky; in height he towered above them all, being about six feet three or four. His dress was equally splendid and tasteful ... His features were fine, and his countenance not only mild, but almost femininely soft. Altogether he was in dress and personal appearance the finest specimen of

1.7 *Wayish-ky's Lodge – July 31 1837*, pencil sketch by Anna Jameson. Courtesy of the Toronto Public Library (TRL), 966–6L–31

1.8 *Wayish ky's Lodge*, etching by Anna Jameson. Courtesy of the Royal Ontario Museum, Toronto, Canada 960.220.2

his race I had yet seen; I was quite proud of my adopted kinsman" (3: 274–5). His height and his "tasteful" dress attest to his gentility, while the softness of his features indicates both his harmlessness and his refinement. As I will argue in more detail later in this chapter, Jameson's use of the word "specimen" to describe even her adopted relatives indicates the powerful influence of a discursive inheritance that, while it might posit nobility, also implies its corollary, savagery, and includes a tendency to categorize aboriginal peoples in the language of natural history inquiries.

Jameson undoubtedly became fond of Mrs Johnston and her daughters during the two weeks she spent with various members of the family. Indeed, Jane Schoolcraft wrote that Jameson "cried heartily when she parted with me and my children" (qtd. in Schoolcraft, *Personal Memoirs* 563), and Jameson wrote to her after their parting, "As long as I live, the impression of your kindness, and of your character altogether, remains with me; your image will often come back to me, and I dare to hope that you will not forget me *quite*" (qtd. in Schoolcraft, *Personal Memoirs* 567). Jameson makes it obvious from the beginning of her third volume that she has come to care what First Nations people in general think of her. On Mackinac, she writes that "Mr. Johnson [*sic*; probably George Johnston] tells me, what pleases me much, that the Indians like me" (3: 134).[22] The two-way nature of contact thus is evident in Jameson's interest in the good opinion of her First Nations friends.

THE LANGUAGE OF IMPERIALISM

Just before she embarked on her summer journey, Jameson wrote that her purpose in undertaking it was to see the "great characteristic features" of Canada and "its aboriginal inhabitants" (2: 8). She had expressed her interest in those aboriginal inhabitants soon after her arrival in Canada, and in mid-January 1837 superintendent of Indian affairs Colonel James Givins "had accordingly brought some Indians to visit us" (1: 24). She identified the three men who visited her, including one whom she named White Deer, as "Chippewas from the neighbourhood of Lake Huron," in Toronto to ask for help because their people were starving (1: 25).

Leslie Monkman calls Jameson's "private voice," evident in a letter about this meeting to Goethe, "less than attractive" (93). Indeed, Jameson writes that the men had faces that were "vulgar from the high cheek bones, small foreheads [*sic*] and want of mind" (*Letters*

1.9 *Indians*, watercolour by Anna Jameson. Courtesy of the Toronto Public Library (TRL), 966–6L–37

72). She also describes "Indians" in general as "improvident," "uncultivated," and "Barbarians," and provides a stereotypical picture of marriage in First Nations communities (72, 73). Jameson's initial views of First Nations people in Upper Canada, as this letter shows, were very much based on what she had read and heard – in other words, on her discursive inheritance. In the book, she describes the dress and facial expressions of her visitors more politely and circumspectly, writing only that their countenances were "melancholy," but her descriptions are still filled with preconceived notions. She comments that while she seated them on chairs, "they would certainly have preferred the floor," and that they ate the meal set before them with "the utmost propriety," although "they had certainly never beheld in their lives the arrangement of an European table" (1: 24, 25). Jameson's description in her letter is not entirely more negative than that in *Winter Studies*, since in her letter she humanizes her visitors by supplying all the men with names, including "The Beaver" and "The Buffalo" (*Letters* 72). She also writes, in acknowledgement of the fact that her information is based on others' reports and in anticipation of a future broadening of outlook through direct experience, that "in summer when I go up the country I shall see and find out more, and judge as well as I can for myself" (*Letters* 73).

Jameson's final summing up of the visit in her book exemplifies the kind of terminology that was then commonly in use to describe First Nations people: "On the whole, the impression they left, though amusing and exciting from its mere novelty, was melancholy. The sort of desperate resignation in their swarthy countenances, their squalid, dingy habiliments, and their forlorn story, filled me with pity and, I may add, disappointment; and all my previous impressions of the independent children of the forest are for the present disturbed. These are the first specimens I have seen of that fated race, with which I hope to become better acquainted before I leave the country" (1: 26). As this passage demonstrates, members of First Nations were exhibited to her like exotic animals and provided opportunities both for amusement and excitement, and for disappointment if they did not live up to her expectations. The words Jameson uses to describe her visitors, including "swarthy," "squalid," "specimens," "independent," and "children" – words she continues to use throughout her many meetings with First Nations people during her *Summer Rambles* – were conventional nineteenth-century shorthand to indicate "otherness." Such language tends to distance and diminish others by describing them as non-human ("specimens") or as immature ("children"). While the word "specimen" evokes the categorizations of natural history and implies "possession without subjugation and violence" (M.L. Pratt 57), the characterization of indigenous peoples as children suggests "a lack of evolutionary maturity" (Goldie 28).

Jameson's wording, especially the phrase "independent children," highlights the inconsistencies of her Romantic notions of indigeneity. The positive and negative characteristics of independence and immaturity that she simultaneously attributes to First Nations people are what Goldie calls "swings of one and the same pendulum" (10). Early in her narrative, Jameson writes that she has "yet but a vague idea of the Indian character," as though there is but one character (1: 26; see also 2: 251, 3: 69). She astutely notes, however, that "the very different aspect under which it [the Indian character] has been represented by various travellers, as well as writers of fiction, adds to the difficulty of forming a correct estimate of the people, and more particularly of the true position of their women" (1: 26–7). Jameson is aware that "the Indian character" is discursively constructed, as is knowledge about gender relations, and that these constructions are passed on to her through the works she has read. Even initially, she presents an alternative to a single, unified "Indian character," writing that Givins "says that there is as much difference between the customs and language of different nations, the Chippewas and Mohawks, for instance, as there is between any two nations of Europe." At the same time, she undermines that alternative point of view, writing that Givins's intimacy with the First Nations groups makes him "hardly an impartial judge" (2: 27).

Biographer Clara Thomas suggests that Jameson's attitude toward First Nations people is an "admixture of a romantic conception of the 'Noble Savage,' a fatalistic conviction that nothing can be done to halt the progress of their destruction, and a school-mistress' admonitory revealing of the unvarnished truth" (138). The trope of the noble savage is indeed just one of the ways that Jameson represents First Nations, and her musings about them are increasingly imbued with a recognition that there are no easy solutions to problems related to them. The contrasts between "independent" and "children," "noble" and "savage," continue to be played out in her text, even after she has become much more personally acquainted with Anishinaabe people, thus indicating the power of discursive constructions. Notions of the inevitable demise of the First Nations are evident in her repeated use of the expressions "fated race," "doomed race," and "*untamable* race" (1: 26, 2: 35, 240, 274, 3: 69–70). What Thomas calls the "romantic conception of the 'Noble Savage'" is apparent in Jameson's second-hand descriptions of North American war and political leaders such as Pontiac, Tecumseh, and Joseph Brant, whom she characterizes as both noble and heroic. Nobility is also evident to her in the Anishinaabe of Mackinac with whom she made personal acquaintance; she writes that they "realised all my ideas of the wild and lordly savage" (3: 30) and that she had never met with "a set of more perfect gentlemen, in *manner*" (3: 137).

Jameson's contradictory representation of First Nations people as, at the same time, childlike is evident in her account to Goethe of the three visitors "habited in coats of *Blanket* and caps of the same, such as children make of a sheet of paper" (*Letters* 72) and in the descriptions in her book of Anishinaabe women whose laugh "has something infantine in it" (3: 59). Even of her good friend, Mrs Johnston, Jameson writes that "she laughed softly like a child" (3: 185). Along a similar vein, Catharine Parr Traill, whose *The Backwoods of Canada* (1836) was published the year before Jameson made her trip to the North

American interior, writes about the "childishness" of a hunter and his son who, when showed some illustrations of "fashionably dressed figures," not only laughed "immoderately" at them but also insisted on showing them to their dogs (288–9). Traill interprets as "childish behaviour" an action that mocks her and her culture.[23]

As Jameson's trip progresses, her analysis of the word "children" as used to describe members of First Nations becomes more thoughtful. Initially, she quotes at second hand, through reports from missionaries and Indian agents, First Nations individuals referring to themselves as "children" and to the French and English governors as "fathers" (2: 293, 319–24, 330–1; 3: 142, 237–9). Later she quotes in detail a meeting she attended at which a government representative called indigenous peoples "CHILDREN!" and the king or his representative "your Great Father" (3: 277–85). Jameson makes it clear that she is aware of the discursive effects of calling indigenous people "children." In her final volume, she analyzes the origins of the use of this expression, noting that in Ojibwe, "father" does not just denote parentage but is also "a common expression ... of respect" (3: 83). She also explicitly critiques the lack of reciprocal respect that resulted from the continued one-sided use of these words of relationship by British colonial officials, arguing that "we acknowledge the Indians our *allies*, yet treat them, as well as call them, our *children*" (2: 328n).

Jameson's book outlines nine months spent as a visitor to Canada, compared to Traill's three years as a settler before her book was published, but Jameson appears much more interested in learning about First Nations cultures than does Traill. Admittedly, the two women's reasons for being in Canada and the purposes of their books are very different. As a visitor, Jameson did not experience first-hand, as did Traill, the conflicts between settlers and Native peoples that would have provided a barrier to understanding. Jameson's visitor status, along with the critical eye that she had already directed toward the colonial government during her stay in Toronto, may have permitted a more objective analysis of those conflicts. Indeed, Monkman argues that because Jameson's stay was temporary, "she can test European concepts of progress, civilization, nationalism, race, and religion without having to confront directly the issue of material self-interest that colours the perspective of most traders and immigrants" (86). That one of the purposes of Traill's book was to promote settlement is evident not just in its tone but also in its appendices, which provide statistical information for emigrants on subjects such as land settlements and costs of travel. In the body of her text, she focuses on settlers and downplays analysis of indigenous peoples. She refers to specific Anishinaabe individuals with whom she trades, but she writes generally only, "The race is slowly passing away from the face of the earth, or mingling by degrees with the colonists, till, a few centuries hence, even the names of their tribes will scarcely remain to tell that they once existed" (220).[24]

Traill, like most writers of the time, tends to group all First Nations peoples under the all-encompassing title "Indians," "in disregard of any cultural or physical differences" (Wolf 380). Jameson, by contrast, takes the ethnographer's care to specify exact cultural relationships, writing of meeting "Ottawas, Chippewas, Pottowottomies, Winnebagos, and Menomonies" (3: 268). At the same time, although she notes that in terms of pronunciation, "*Chippewa* is properly O,jîb,wày" (3: 59), she persists throughout her book in calling the Ojibwa people she met "Chippewa," and she occasionally lumps First Nations languages together under the rubric "Indian" (see, for example, 3: 186). She also repeatedly calls Indian women "squaws," using the word as a neutral or even respectful translation of the word "women," even though she knew that in Ojibwe "woman" was not "squaw" but *equay* (3: 82).[25] Thus she writes admiringly of "a squaw of unmixed Indian blood," describes her friend Charlotte McMurray to Goethe as "an Indian Squaw by birth," and introduces Johnston to readers of her book as a "woman of pure Indian blood ... whose habits and manners were those of a genuine Indian squaw" (1: 71; *Letters* 90; 3: 183–4). Traill also calls women "squaws," but unlike Jameson, who valued the individual "genuine Indian squaw," Traill uses the word as a way of avoiding individuation. She never provides a first or last name for a neighbouring woman with whom she repeatedly interacted, calling her instead "the squaw," "Peter's squaw," "Mrs. Peter," "squaw Peter," "the hunter's wife," "the swarthy matron," and the "old squaw" (although the woman's youngest child was three; 164, 213–15, 286–8). In contrast, Jameson carefully names the Anishinaabe acquaintances that she has also introduced as "squaws," telling readers that their names are Mrs McMurray, Mrs Schoolcraft, and Mrs Johnston. In naming her new acquaintances by using their marital status and their surnames (but not their first names), she provides them, as she does herself, with the respectability of the title "Mrs." She also stresses the exotic nature of their difference and indicates her skill as an ethnographer by providing their Ojibwe names, each of which carries the feminine ending *qua*: McMurray is "O,ge,bu,no,qua," or "the wild rose"; Schoolcraft is "Obah,bahm,wa,wa,ge,zhe,go,quà, [which] signifies literally the 'sound which the stars make rushing through the sky'"; and Johnston is "Oshah,gush,ko,da,na,qua," or "'the green prairie,' (woman)" (3: 215, 227, 242).[26]

Like other travellers of her era, Jameson uses certain adjectives as shorthand methods of evoking the exotic "other" even when she is well into her *Summer Rambles*. One such word, "dusky," which Goldie argues is "immediately suggestive everywhere of the indigene" (10), appears repeatedly in her book, along with other adjectives that signal difference, including "red" and "savage." Images of savagery are connected to the trope of First Nations people as untamable or wild and, following the logic that this wildness makes them not quite human, as "creatures," whether "splendid creatures" (1: 297), "wild creatures" (3: 289), or "wretched creature[s]" (3: 287).

Like other nineteenth-century travellers to North America, Jameson is fascinated with cannibalism, tomahawking, and scalping. Her descriptions of these practices, as with most such descriptions in Western narratives, are never first-hand (Hulme, "Introduction" 16–19) but are often sensationalist or reflective of long-standing misconceptions about the practices. At Manitoulin she writes that although she could see scalps on warriors' belts "generally without emotion or pain ... there was one thing I never *could* see without a start, and a thrill of horror, – *the scalp of long fair hair*" (3: 294). Jameson's use of italics and of the expression "thrill of horror" and her reference to fair hair together sensationalize this descriptive passage. In earlier passages comparing "cannibals" in Canada to the "man-eating Læstrygons" of the *Odyssey*, Jameson has already positioned her references to that practice within a long historical and literary tradition.[27] When she writes later about reported cannibals, however, she revises these tropes by acknowledging that cannibalism in North America was not an oft-practised social custom but instead an anomalous occurrence caused by "famine" (3: 206, 287). After she meets one group from the Red River, whom the indigenous Odawas called "cannibals," she argues that the name probably could not be taken literally but was instead given because of an animalistic appearance: "their attitude when squatted on the ground was precisely that of the larger apes I have seen in a menagerie" (3: 276). As her identification of their geographic origins implies, though, the name "cannibal" was likely given to members of the group, not because of what she identified as their subhuman appearance, but instead as a marker of their otherness.

The tolerance that Jameson's personal contact with First Nations people produced is evident when her book is compared to the two other narratives written by travellers from England, Martineau and Marryat, who visited much the same territory she did at approximately the same time. Both of those contemporaneous travellers use the generic term "Indians" to refer to the Mackinac people whom Jameson identifies as "Ottawas, Chippewas, and Pottowattomies" (2: 295). Like Jameson, Martineau uses words such as "red," "dusky," "savage," and "squaw," but she also calls members of First Nations "demon-like" (see *Society in America* 2: 14–26). Jameson only once uses similar terminology, describing her first sight of a dance of warriors as "like a masque of fiends breaking into paradise" (3: 145).

While Marryat writes of seeing "the Indians ... lying stripped in the porches before the whisky stores" (1: 182), Jameson portrays alcohol as a general problem in North American society and relates an anecdote that criticizes unscrupulous traders for encouraging alcohol abuse among First Nations populations (2: 253–66). And while Jameson names, and thus recognizes as human, not only her Anishinaabe friends and acquaintances but also some of the men who ferried her on her three wilderness lake trips (3: 246, 315), Marryat is scathingly disparaging of the Métis paddlers who took him by canoe to Sault Ste Marie, calling them "Canadian half-breeds – a mixture between the Indian and the white, which spoils both" (1: 184), "our Canadian brutes" (1: 185), "lazy gluttonous scoundrels" who behaved well only when hit with a broomstick (1: 200–1), and "our lazzaroni of half-breeds" (1: 195). Marryat's geographical displacement of "lazzaroni" – "Neapolitan street lounger and beggar" (*OED*) – represents the kind of disparaging stereotyping of cultural difference that is absent from Jameson's narrative.

JAMESON'S ETHNOGRAPHIC RECORD

One of Jameson's goals was to pass on first-hand information about indigenous cultures and practices. Her book therefore became an ethnographic project, and the third volume includes details about the history, religion, family relationships, marriage customs, languages, and stories of the groups she visited. Initially, she quotes a number of secondary sources on these subjects. As her journey progressed and as she relied less on hearsay, the information she relayed became more detailed and more immediate. Once at Mackinac, her primary source was personal observation, along with conversations with Jane and Henry Schoolcraft.[28] As a result of the novelty and immediacy of the information these sources provided, her three weeks in and around Mackinac, Sault Ste Marie, and Manitoulin, along with her return voyage through Penetanguishene, take up one full volume of a three-volume book that covers nine months spent in Canada.

Jameson insists that she does not want to repeat commonly known information about "Indian customs" (3: 85). Indeed, she hopes that her alternative focus on language, storytelling, and mythology will set her narrative apart from other similar investigations. Thus she gives translations and phonetic transcriptions of names and spends several pages discussing Ojibwe syntax and grammar, noting terms of salutation, imprecation, and endearment (3: 272–3, 80–4). She also transcribes some words phonetically, "as nearly as I can imitate the sound," and includes accurate pronunciations of words such as "wigwam" and "moccasin" (3: 83, 58). In comparison, Traill's most detailed comment is that "the Indian tongue [is] a language that is peculiarly sweet and soft in its cadences, and seems to be composed with many vowels" (215). She quotes a few words of an indigenous language but does not indicate which one (170), although she does say that the people were "Chippewas" (63, 211). When she writes of "a curious specimen of Indian orthography," it is a grammatically awkward and misspelled note in English (208). In contrast, Jameson writes with more respect and interest that her canoe party tried unsuccessfully to read hieroglyphics written on birchbark "of which we could make nothing – one figure, I thought, represented a fish" (3: 329).

A large part of Jameson's ethnographic project is the representation of traditional Anishinaabe oral literature. In transcribing three fairly lengthy stories for which she provides titles, two other untitled stories, a titled "allegory," and several pages of poems and songs, she acknowledges that the Anishinaabe have a recognizable culture in the form of an orature passed on from generation to generation. She thus revises an earlier backhanded criticism she has made that she does not "consider the Indians as an inferior race, merely because they have no literature, no luxuries, no steam-engines; nor yet, because they regard our superiority in the arts with a sort of lofty indifference" (2: 273). In her introduction to the stories, Jameson disputes Alexander Henry's description of "the dulness of the long winters, when he was residing in the wigwam of his brother Wa,wa,tam," among a people who lacked "all intellectual amusement" (3: 86).[29] Anishinaabe people have their own unique form of storytelling, she argues, and she then paradoxically tries to fit their stories into known European forms. She writes that although some are "traditional tales" or "histories," others are "allegories" or "parables" intended either to teach a "moral lesson" or to "excite wonder or amazement" (3: 86–7). Perhaps because of her religious and literary background, the stories that Jameson chooses to transcribe are for the most part those with moral lessons. The characters described often endure hardships at the hands of family members who abandon or test them. The allegory she presents, on the other hand, is a personification of winter and spring and thus an example of one of their "extravagant inventions" (3: 87).

Jameson compares several of the Anishinaabe stories to sources of European literature. Of the story "Mishosha; or, the Magician and His Daughters," she writes, "In this wild tale the metamorphosis of the old man into a maple tree is related with a spirit and accuracy worthy of Ovid himself" (3: 113). She compares what she calls a "Chippewa canzonetta" to an Italian song because of the "no-meaning and perpetual repetition of certain words and phrases" (3: 224). And during her extended discussions of Anishinaabe religion, Jameson refers to what she calls its "mythology," contrasting it to that of the Greeks and pointing out similarities between Anishinaabe "mythologic existences" and those in both Hindu religious mythology and Romance narratives (3: 129, 131).[30]

While she compares these tales to European and Asian stories and mythologies, Jameson also stresses that she is "first" in presenting them. Her claim is based on the fact that several of these stories are previously unpublished and that all originate from what she considers an authoritative source: Waub-Ojeeg, "the greatest poet and story-teller ... of his tribe" (3: 87). Their merit also stems from the fact that they are recognizably First Nations, as is indicated by Jameson's emphasis on their "wildness" and "childishness" (3: 88). Both the stories' originality and their authenticity are questionable, however. Jameson acknowledges in footnotes that "The Origin of the Robin" had already been published "by an American traveller, to whom Mrs. Schoolcraft imparted it" (3: 118n), and that her untitled tale of the funeral fire was previously published in Schoolcraft's *Travels in the Central Portions of the Mississippi Valley* in 1825 (3: 125n). In fact, all but two of the stories had already been published. Her abbreviated tale of Gitchee Gauzinee, for which she gives as her source a conversation with Henry Schoolcraft (3: 124n), had appeared in his *Travels*, and the stories both of the funeral fire and of Gitchee Gauzinee had been pirated from Schoolcraft by James A. Jones and published in his *Tales of an Indian Camp* in 1829 (M. Williams xx). The "American traveller" whom Jameson mentions was Chandler R. Gilman; in his 1836 book *Life on the Lakes*, he had published not only "The Origin of the Robin" but also another lengthy tale that Jameson includes, "The Forsaken Brother." Only "Mishosha; or, the Magician and His Daughters" and "The Allegory of Winter and Summer" indeed first appeared in Jameson's book. Within a year, those two stories and the other four were republished by Schoolcraft himself in his *Algic Researches* (1839).[31]

In a 1956 edition of *Algic Researches*, renamed *Schoolcraft's Indian Legends*, editor Mentor L. Williams speculates that similarities between Gilman's and Jameson's versions of their two common stories must be due to the fact that both Gilman and Jameson read versions of the stories in Schoolcraft's notebook (96). According to Jameson, however, they both heard the tales, not from him, but from his wife, Jane (3: 118n). Gilman himself writes that Henry Schoolcraft allowed him to "copy" the stories (1: 159; 2: 215) and that "The Origin of the Robin" "was taken down by Mrs S. verbatim, from the lips of an old Chippewa woman" (1: 159). Similarly, Jameson claims that she wrote "The Allegory of Winter and Summer" from Susan Johnston's "recitation," which was "translated by her daughter" (3: 218). All of the stories thus are heavily mediated, coming to Jameson and Gilman from Waub-Ojeeg or other Anishinaabe individuals via Waub-Ojeeg's daughter (Susan) and thence his granddaughter (Jane) and her husband. Williams speculates that the language of the stories and the occasional pious moralizing stem from Jane Schoolcraft's deeply felt Christianity (xxii). The influence of Jameson on the tales published in her *Summer Rambles* cannot be underestimated, however, since she is ultimately responsible not only for the choice of stories but also for the language of their transcription.

Each version of an oral tale that is translated and then transcribed into written language is unique; even the several versions of the same stories that Henry Schoolcraft published show significant disparities. Thus the similarities between some of Jameson's 1838 versions of the stories and Schoolcraft's 1839 versions are remarkable. Often the only differences consist in abbreviation on Jameson's part. She omits the names of the characters, which Schoolcraft includes in both stories and titles, and she omits all or part of songs sung by the characters in School-craft's transcriptions. On the other hand, Jameson's "The Allegory of Winter and Summer" is so dissimilar to Schoolcraft's "Peboan and Seegwun, an Allegory of the Seasons" that they appear to have a different source. Less obvious but still significant differences exist between Jameson's untitled tale of a warrior left for dead by his companions and Schoolcraft's two versions of the same story, "The Grave Light, or, Adventures of a Warrior's Soul" and "The Funeral Fire." Jameson's tale of Gitchee Gauzinee, meanwhile, is so much more abbreviated than Schoolcraft's as to make their comparison moot.

A joint source *is* evident in Jameson's, Gilman's, and Schoolcraft's renderings of the three titled tales, especially the story of the robin, which until the final paragraphs have almost identical wording. Each version tells the story of a boy whose father forces him to endure a fast of unusual length in order to demonstrate superiority and who, as a result of his ordeal, does not find a guardian spirit but instead is transformed into one. Jameson introduces the story by giving her interpretation of its moral, to "admonish parental ambition, and inculcate filial obedience" (3: 113), a moral that Gilman describes as "the danger of ambition" (1: 169). In telling the story, both Jameson and Gilman omit the boy's name but otherwise word the opening paragraphs almost identically to Schoolcraft, except for an occasional inversion of words. Thus while Jameson and Gilman write, "His father visited him every morning regularly to encourage him to perseverance" (Jameson WSSR 3: 116; Gilman 1: 166), Schoolcraft writes, "His father visited him regularly every morning, to encourage him to perseverance" (*Algic Researches* 106). Toward the end of the story, Jameson and Gilman begin to summarize what Schoolcraft transcribes in detail, quoting the boy as saying that "the spirit is a just one, though not propitious to me. He has shown me pity, and now I must go" (WSSR 3: 117; Gilman 1: 168). Schoolcraft, in contrast, writes the more logical and understandable "my guardian spirit is a just one; though not propitious to me in the manner I desired, he has shown me pity in another way; he has given me another shape; and now I must go" (107). Schoolcraft uses his final paragraph to quote the boy telling his father not to be unhappy, for the robin will stay near man and bring him joy, and then concludes with a seven-stanza song of the robin. In contrast, Jameson and Gilman paraphrase and summarize the boy's final statement, writing it in the third person rather than the first and omitting the song. As the similarities in wording indicate, Jameson, Gilman, and Schoolcraft were probably using the same source. If Jameson and Gilman are accurate, that source was Jane Schoolcraft's translation. Differences in wording exemplify the inaccuracy of transcription, especially toward the end of a relatively long story.

In another story, Jameson's "Mishosha; or, the Magician and his Daughters" and Schoolcraft's "Mishosha, or the Magician of the Lakes," Jameson's language is consistently more explicit than Schoolcraft's. While Schoolcraft writes that one of the characters "found cause to suspect his wife," Jameson says that he suspected the "fidelity of his wife," and when Schoolcraft refers to "her crime" (*Algic Researches* 163), Jameson calls it "her infidelity" (3: 96, 97). Similarly, when Schoolcraft writes that she "intended to have dispatched him," Jameson says that she had "formed a plan to murder him," and when Schoolcraft says that she "fled to her paramour" (163), Jameson writes that she "returned to her lover" (3: 98). Describing the rescue by eagles of the couples' son from an evil magician, Jameson writes that the birds flew over the magician "lying half asleep in the bottom of his canoe, and treated him with peculiar indignity" (3: 107); Schoolcraft uses almost identical wording but omits reference to the "indignity" (*Algic Researches* 166). The pious moralizing that Williams identifies in some of the stories is not evident in Jameson's straightforward version of this tale, thus indicating her desire to represent Anishinaabe culture accurately even though its stories might fall outside the range of subjects considered appropriate in mid-nineteenth-century women's narratives.

The most religious aspect of Jameson's versions of the stories is their archaic, almost biblical language. The language of "The Forsaken Brother" and of her untitled tale of the abandoned warrior (which Schoolcraft calls "The Grave Light") is much more anachronistic than that of Schoolcraft's later renderings of the tales, especially when she is quoting her characters' speech. While she writes in the tale of the warrior, "Thou spirit, ... why dost thou oppose me?" (3: 128), Schoolcraft says, "Demon, ... why do you bar my approach?" (*Algic Researches* 233–4). Similarly, while in "The Forsaken Brother" she writes, "I leave ye – I leave ye! thou who hast been my partner in life, thou wilt not stay long behind me" (3: 89), Schoolcraft's version reads, "I leave you in a world of care ... For you, my partner in life, I have less sorrow in parting, because I am persuaded you will not remain long behind me" (*Algic Researches* 92).[32] The formality of Jameson's language signals difference in a way that Schoolcraft's more standard English translation cannot. Jameson cannot write in Ojibwe (the original language of the stories), both because she does not know the language and because her purpose is to communicate with English-speaking readers. She can, however, give a sense of translation through use of a formal English more archaic than everyday speech.[33] As I will argue in chapter 3, the use of formality to give a sense of translation and to signal difference also motivates the stilted language of Margaret Laurence's representation of Ghanaian speech in *This Side Jordan*.

REPRESENTING TREATIES AND LAND SETTLEMENTS

Jameson visited Canada during a time of turmoil for its aboriginal inhabitants. From 1828 to 1836 the lieutenant-governor of Upper Canada, Sir John Colborne, had operated under the principle that "the best way of financing the civilizing of Amerindians would be through leasing and sale of their lands" (Dickason 234). During that period, Indian farming villages were established under the auspices of several missionary groups, including at Manitowaning on Manitoulin Island, which Jameson visited. When Francis Bond Head became lieutenant-governor in 1836, the policy changed. Head argued in his "Memorandum on the Aborigines of North America," dated 20 November 1836, that "an attempt to make farmers of the red man has been, generally speaking, a complete failure" and that "congregating them for the purpose of civilization has implanted many more vices than it has eradicated" (4). For these reasons, he wrote, "the greatest kindness we can perform towards these intelligent, simple-minded people, is to remove and fortify them as much as possible from all communication with the whites" (4). Thus at the time of Jameson's visit, Head was negotiating – or rather, compelling – the cession of large tracts of land from various First Nations. In his "Memorandum," he recorded that the Ojibwa and the Odawa "formally made over to me 23,000 islands" in Lake Huron; that the "Saugeen Indians also voluntarily surrendered to me a million and a half acres of the very richest land in Upper Canada"; that the Hurons of Amherstburg turned over two-thirds of "a hunting ground of rich land of six miles square ... on condition that one of the said two-thirds should be sold, and the proceeds thereof invested for their benefit"; and that he had convinced the "Moravian Indians ... for an annuity of 150£, to surrender to me about six miles square of black rich land, situated on the banks of the Thames river" (4–5). He advised the "Indians" whose land had been ceded to move to Manitoulin and the surrounding islands, justifying this advice by arguing that "it may appear that the arrangement was not advantageous to the Indians, because it was of such benefit to us; but it must always be kept in mind, that however useful rich land may be to *us*, yet its only value to an Indian consists in the game it contains" (5).

Another upheaval was occurring because of an American policy toward aboriginal residents of the United States. In a policy similar to Head's (and from which, in fact, Head borrowed, according to Rogers [127]), the American government was forcing the removal of First Nations peoples from the area around the Great Lakes, where settlement of European immigrants and eastern Americans was desired, and into areas west of the Mississippi River. Many members of First Nations communities who had traditionally lived on both sides of the Great Lakes chose around the time of Jameson's visit to move permanently to the Canadian side rather than to move west. They were encouraged to do so in part by the gifts distributed to them in compensation for their earlier assistance to the British in battles against the Americans. Jameson watched and described just such a gift distribution at Manitoulin Island; her account comprises eighteen pages, including eight pages in which she directly quotes the words of the superintendent of Indian affairs, Samuel Peters Jarvis. In this speech is a warning that gifts to non-resident allies would cease unless they moved permanently to British territory (3: 281); the reasons Jarvis provides for this decision echo those of Head in his "Memorandum" of the previous year.[34]

Jameson shows a remarkable willingness to grapple with the causes and effects of the problematic interactions between First Nations groups, on one side, and British traders, settlers, and administrators, on the other. She offers no easy solutions, as is clear in both her contradictory and changing responses to the issue and her direct statements about the difficulty of reconciling the needs of settlers with the rights of earlier inhabitants. Before her journey to Manitoulin, Jameson's discussions of indigenous peoples were apparently influenced by the differing points of view of former and present lieutenant-governors Colborne and Head. Thus she argues both that the only way for indigenous peoples to survive is to turn to farming and that they can never be successful as farmers: "These attempts of a noble and a fated race, to oppose, or even to delay for a time, the rolling westward of the great tide of civilisation, are like efforts to dam up the rapids of Niagara. The moral world has its laws, fixed as those of physical nature. The hunter must make way before the agriculturist, and the Indian must learn to take the bit between his teeth, and set his hand to the ploughshare, or *perish*. As yet I am inclined to think that the idea of the Indians becoming what we call a civilised people seems quite hopeless; those who entertain such benevolent anticipations should come here, and behold the effect which three centuries of contact with the whites have produced on the nature and habits of the Indian" (2: 240–1). Jameson's notions of moral law, like those of many of her contemporaries, involve a progression toward civilization. Her use of metaphors of grand forces of nature such as rolling tides and Niagara Falls emphasize and discursively pave the way for the inevitability of settlement. She then not only suggests that the First Nations man must become a farmer but also equates him with the draft animal used in farming – he must "take the bit between his teeth." Her final sentence equates civilization with benevolence, but at the same time represents the process as "hopeless" because of the negative effects of civilization on First Nations people.

Perhaps the most extraordinary part of Jameson's narrative is her examination of British and American government policies concerning indigenous peoples. At first, she appears to approve policies that deprive First Nations of their lands. In writing about the land that the Six Nations were granted in exchange for their loyalty to the British during the American War of Independence, she notes, "Great part of this land, some of the finest in the province, has lately been purchased back from them by the government, and settled by thriving English farmers." She commends this exchange because it both provides land for "thriving" farmers and uses payments for land taken from the First Nations for their "conversion and civilisation" (2: 105, 107).

Jameson fairly quickly, however, begins to question the policy of forcing indigenous peoples to give up their lands. She writes of the "tribe of Delawares," whose "twenty-five thousand acres of rich land" was sold at Head's urging to the government of Upper Canada, even though "the tribe were by no means unanimous in consenting."[35] She quotes a Moravian missionary working with the Delawares as predicting that they would soon sell the remainder of their lands, since "no doubt they would be required for the use of the white settlers, and if government urged on the purchase, they had no means of resisting."[36] Jameson is familiar with, and has some sympathy for, Head's position, arguing that if the only hope for "Indians" is to remove them from the contaminating influence of whites, it "certainly excuses the Governor, if you consider only the expediency and the benevolence, independent of the justice, of the measure" (1: 241–5).

Her comment about the justice of Head's actions indicates that she interprets as unfair the change in policies that accompanied the transition of governance from Colborne to Head. Her opinions on this question soon become more pronounced: "That the poor Indians to whom reserved lands have been granted, and who, on the faith of treaties, have made their homes and gathered themselves into villages on such lands, should, whenever it is deemed expedient, be driven out of their possessions, either by purchase, or by persuasion, or by force, or by measures which include all three, and sent to seek a livelihood in distant and strange regions – as in the case of these Delawares – is horrible, and bears cruelty and injustice on the face of it" (2: 267). Later in her narrative, Jameson emphasizes the effects of such policy changes on individuals. When she is writing her ethnographic descriptions of First Nations religions, she describes hell as "being doomed to wander up and down desolately, having no fixed abode, weary, restless, and melancholy," and she asks, "To how many is the Indian hell already realised on this earth?" (3: 121).

At times Jameson's critique contains elements of sarcasm. She quotes Head's argument that the British crown "has never exercised his paramount right" over the lands on which indigenous peoples live, "except at their request and for their *manifest advantage*," and then notes in brackets, "this is doubtful, I presume" (2: 326n). She goes on to argue that members of First Nations must be treated as adults who can make their own decisions: "no measure should be adopted, even for their supposed benefit, without their acquiescence. They are quite capable of judging for themselves in every case in which their interests are concerned" (2: 328n). Jameson recognizes that a discursive construction of immaturity can be used to justify the excesses of colonialism, because the parent-child metaphor carries implications of privileged knowledge and decision-making. She also comes to acknowledge that settlement of North America and justice for its indigenous peoples are contradictory endeavours, since "the interests of the colonists and settlers, and those of the Indians, are brought into perpetual collision, and ... the colonists can scarcely be trusted to decide in their own case" (2: 329). In *Winter Studies and Summer Rambles*, Jameson repeatedly suggests that people who think it easy to accommodate the needs of both settlers and aboriginal inhabitants should come to Canada to study the situation for themselves. When she discusses the fact that governments have reneged on land agreements, she writes that British philanthropists must become involved in any resolution of such disputes, and she compares such resolution to the abolition of slavery (2: 270).

Throughout her final volume, Jameson delineates the breaking of treaties in both Canada and the United States. On Mackinac Island, she describes a meeting in Schoolcraft's office in which one man was told that it was "useless to speak farther" on the subject of land payments (3: 47). She recounts a second, larger, gathering on Mackinac in which the First Nations assembled there were given goods instead of the money promised for the sale of their land; she calls the "mean, petty-trader style in which the American officials make (and *break*) their treaties with the Indians" "shameful" (3: 141).[37] Jameson's text is sprinkled with references to other incidents in which promises to indigenous peoples were broken: promises not to disturb an aboriginal graveyard, to build houses for those converted to Christianity, and to leave timber in unceded land standing (3: 181–2, 236, 238–9). She notes the "trifling nature" of the presents given by British representatives to the groups gathered on Manitoulin Island in exchange for their previous military co-operation, then lists those gifts (3: 269–70). She also quotes in detail Jarvis's speech, in which he told the people asssembled that, contrary to earlier promises, gifts would no longer be given to groups allied with the British crown unless they moved year-round into the Canadas and encouraged them to move to Manitoulin Island (3: 277–85). As evidence of her contradictory approach, Jameson again voices her approval of this particular plan for resettlement; she writes that it was "a means of removing them more effectually from all contact with the white settlers," and adds, "As far as I can judge, the intentions of the government are benevolent and *justifiable*" (3: 267–8). Benevolence and justice become the standards by which she judges policies related to First Nations, and prevention of contamination a commendable motive for those policies.

CONVERSION AND CIVILIZATION

As is evident from Jameson's initial reaction to the use to which money paid for land purchased from the Six Nations was put, civilization and conversion were the twin and interrelated initiatives perceived as essential in dealings with First Nations in Canada. During the nineteenth century, missionizing was often inextricably tied to ideas of civilization and progress (Smith 6, 10). Thus in the Canadian context, Traill writes,

"Certain it is that the introduction of the Christian religion is the first greatest step towards civilization and improvement" (63).

Civilization for Jameson has many trappings, including European dress and means of livelihood. She judges that the Odawa are more "civilised" than the Potawatomi, since an Odawa man is "distinguished by the decency of his dress" while a Potawatomi is recognizable by the "more savage finery of his costume" (3: 43), and she characterizes the Odawa of Arbre Croche as "more stationary and civilised," "superior in humanity and intelligence," and "more inclined to agriculture" than the Ojibwa and Potawatomi (3: 50). She also equates civilization with the beneficial inevitability of progress, which she has earlier described as a moral law.

At the same time, she represents contact as problematic for First Nations, characterizing it as "contagion" (3: 61). If the "Indians" live too close to the whites, they will be drawn to alcohol abuse (2: 250–66); they will also become "half-cast" and there will be fewer of "unmixed blood" left (2: 244, 272; 3: 62). White traders have injured Indian women, she writes, "first, by corrupting them; secondly, by checking the improvement of all their own peculiar manufactures" (3: 309). Contagion thus includes not only alcoholism and miscegenation but also the negative economic and cultural effects of the European settlers' and traders' self-interest.

Jameson questions why the "Indian" would want to exchange "his 'own unshackled life, and his innate capacities of soul,' for our artificial social habits, our morals, which are contradicted by our opinions, and our religion, which is violated both in our laws and our lives" (2: 249). Here she radically contradicts her own definition of a progressive moral world by pointing out the violation of moral codes in her supposedly more advanced society. In an essay on Jameson's representation of nationalism, Lisa Vargo points out that Jameson scrutinizes with special care "notions of the moral superiority of European imperialism" (62). Indeed, Jameson makes that scrutiny explicit when she indignantly concludes a description of the burning of large fields of corn in expeditions against Miamis and Wyandots with the words "and we complain that the Indians make no advance in civilisation!" (2: 302n).

Her most comprehensive comment about the double-sided nature of civilization and conversion comes in her report of a conversation with George Johnston in Sault Ste Marie. Susan Birkwood astutely calls their exchange "a dialogue between 'civilized' Europe and 'savage' North America" in which "the opposition between civilization and savagery is established only to be subverted" (308). Jameson began by telling Johnston that "of all their customs," the practice of killing women and children in wars "most justifies the name of *savage*!" (3: 191). She reports Johnston's explanation that the principle of aboriginal warfare was to inflict "the greatest possible insult and injury on their foe with the least possible risk to themselves" and his contention that "outrage against the chastity of women is absolutely unknown" (3: 192–3). Jameson then quotes him as pointing out that "more women and children have perished in *one* of your civilised sieges, and that in late times, than during the whole war between the Chippewas and Sioux, and *that* has lasted a century" (3: 194). Johnston's arguments silenced her, Jameson tells her reader, and led her to draw disturbing parallels between civilization and savagery and between Christianity and heathenism: "A war-party of Indians, perhaps two or three hundred, (and that is a very large number,) dance their war-dance, go out and burn a village, and bring back twenty or thirty scalps. *They* are savages and heathens. We Europeans fight a battle, leave fifty thousand dead or dying by inches on the field, and a hundred thousand to mourn them, desolate; but *we* are civilised and Christians" (3: 194). Jameson implies that her gender allows her to make this comparison: "one scalps his enemy, the other rips him open with a sabre; one smashes his brains with a tomahawk, and the other blows him to atoms with a cannon-ball: and to me, femininely speaking, there is not a needle's point difference between the one and the other" (3: 195). In this pivotal passage, Jameson first emphasizes that she speaks as a woman and then uses a metaphor of women's work to make her point. The needle – a metal object that is not a knife, sabre, tomahawk, or cannonball – can be used not just to produce needlepoint but as an anti-weapon to prove the futility and the similarity of apparently divergent masculine activities of warfare. If only the width of a needle's point separates "Indian" and European methods of warfare, there is indeed little distinction between them. The cross-cultural feminine metaphor of needlework thus supports Jameson's contention and helps her to make her case more powerfully.

THE "WOMAN QUESTION"

Jameson is not ready to discard civilization altogether, and again her hesitation is based on her gender. Nineteenth-century writers often argued that progress could be determined "by the degree to which Western women had been 'freed' from the cruel and 'dehumanizing' practices of 'backward' societies" (Smith xi). Indeed, Jameson argues that it is only with civilization that women can expect to improve their lot: "God forbid that I should think to disparage the blessings of civilisation! I am a woman, and to the progress of civilisation alone can we women look for release from many pains and penalties and liabilities which now lie heavily upon us" (3: 196). Her discussion of those "pains and penalties" recurs throughout her narrative.

Thomas points out that *Winter Studies and Summer Rambles* marks Jameson's first explicit representation of what in the nineteenth century was often referred to as the "Woman Question" (141). Jameson's book is indeed sprinkled with her views on gender relations, in numerous contexts. She argues that women actors are not necessarily immoral (1: 49). She decries the fact that a "woman, as a legal property" may be subjected to outrages against her person (1: 60). When she writes about politics in Canada, she notes, "I am not one of those who opine sagely, that women have nothing to do with politics" (1: 104). She judges that women need to "take some courage to look upon the evil" of prostitution (1: 113), and she quotes Martineau's views in *Society in America* on the necessity for women to be strong (1: 118n). She refutes Samuel Johnson's judgment that men are "*held down* in conversation by the presence of women" (1: 141–2), and she attributes marital difficulties to "inequality between the sexes" (3: 14). When Jameson learns that William IV is dead and Victoria is the new queen, she discusses the implications of the succession in terms both of gender and of the politics of imperialism. She notes that "so far her youth and sex are absolutely in her favour, or rather in *our* favour" (3: 262–3), with "*our*" referring to women and their progress toward equality. She also writes that in this "new world of woods and waters, amid these remote wilds, ... her power reaches and her sovereignty is acknowledged" (3: 262), implying that the imperial power of a female sovereign is as recognized and as influential as that of a male sovereign.

Jameson's views on the "Woman Question" are not unusual for a woman in her position: both educated and, because of the circumstances of her progressive family and failed marriage, independent. What is unusual is the way in which her discussions of women's roles and limitations converge and overlap with discussions of the situation of First Nations. Fowler contends that Jameson's "comments on Indian women 'in savage life' are merely a handy context for exposing the unhappy lot of white women in civilized life" (*Embroidered Tent* 160), but Jameson's comments also demonstrate a keen interest outside of what was then considered "civilized life." Indeed, she writes early in her first volume that she wants to travel to First Nations territory because she wishes to learn "the true position of their women" (1: 27).

Jameson's observations in the first two volumes of her book are based on what she has read and learned second-hand and what she has seen in brief and distanced exposures to First Nations individuals and groups. In a letter to Goethe shortly after she arrived in Canada, she makes broad generalizations about relations between indigenous men and women:

If you would like an Indian chief for a husband, Ottilie, you have only to come here. Bring with you a few hatchets, a couple of brass Kettles and some strings of Beads. Add a Cask of Brandy, and with such a dowry, you may choose, I can promise you, an Indian Hunter, six feet high and very prettily tattoed, one side of his face covered with red paint and the other painted with soot and oil,– will you have him? You must know how to skin a Buffalo in five minutes, and cut him up, *artistement*, and how to knock a dog on the head and put him, half dead, into a pot for a stew, and dig Jams. But all this is very easy. And if your Indian is dissatisfied, he will not kick you above six times a day and then sell you to his comrade for a gun or a Brass Kettle. And if he is satisfied with you and loves you, he will give you what is left of his dinner, and be so kind as neither to beat you or sell you. (*Letters* 73)

The sketch of indigenous life that Jameson provides for Goethe is intended as satire, but it reveals her preconceptions about women's roles and about marital relationships in aboriginal North America. Building on those preconceptions, she refers in the first two volumes of *Winter Studies and Summer Rambles* to indigenous women she sees at a distance as "busy, care-worn, and eager" (2: 80), while characterizing the men as "lounging" (1: 297, 2: 80), "lazy" (2: 80), and "indolent" (1: 298; 2: 113, 130, 244). In the third volume, Jameson makes it clear that first-hand observation after she has been on Mackinac Island for a few days has begun to change those presumptions. She writes, "I should doubt, from all I see and hear, that the Indian squaw is that absolute slave, drudge, and non-entity in the community, which she has been described" (3: 75).

Writing of individual women she has met and describing incidents she has seen or heard, Jameson begins to paint a more well-rounded picture of the position of Ojibwa and Odawa women, a position that encompasses both freedoms and oppressions. She relates an anecdote about one woman who, in an echo of Elizabeth I's decision to wed England,

1.10 Untitled pen and ink drawing of woman and child, by Anna Jameson. Courtesy of the Toronto Public Library (TRL), 966–6L–23

declined to marry, instead taking the sun as her "manito or tutelary spirit." Jameson then reports that the woman was tolerated by her people, if not imitated (3: 71–2). She identifies a few female "chiefs," but says, "Generally, the squaws around me give me the impression of exceeding feminine delicacy and modesty, and of the most submissive gentleness" (3: 78). She notes that at the gathering with government representatives on Manitoulin Island, "not one woman, outside or inside, was visible during the whole time the council lasted" (3: 276).

And she relates the story of Susan Johnston, whose father married her against her inclination to Irish fur trader John Johnston. Jameson writes that when "the pretty O,shah,gush,ko,da,na,qua" left Johnston to run home to her family, her father "gave her a good beating with a stick, and threatened to cut off both her ears." After she was returned to her husband, Jameson writes, "Johnston succeeded at length in taming this shy wild fawn" (3: 213–15). The non-judgmental description of the beating indicates that Jameson is trying to understand difference, but in the process is failing to condemn practices that oppress women. The representation of the woman she now calls "mother" as animal-like is typical of contemporaneous representations of indigenous peoples.

Jameson's investigations into the position of women culminate in a fourteen-page disquisition that makes several complex and interrelated arguments and concludes by comparing indigenous North American women to European women. She begins by pointing out that "all travellers … who have treated of the manners and modes of life of the northwest tribes, are accustomed to expatiate with great eloquence and indignation" on "the treatment and condition of their women. The women, they say, are 'drudges,' 'slaves,' 'beasts of burthen,' victims, martyrs, degraded, abject, oppressed" (3: 298–9). Jameson then launches into her complicated argument: first, she concedes, First Nations women "*are* drudges." Further, repeating her earlier judgment on women, civilization, and moral progress, she contends that "the condition of the women in any community is a test of the advance of moral and intellectual cultivation in that community" (3: 300). For indigenous peoples, she judges, the "first step from the hunting to the agricultural state is the first step in the emancipation of the female" (3: 304).

Jameson points out that because indigenous North American economies are based on hunting and gathering, women in those societies will of necessity be forced to do hard, menial work. At the same time, she writes, "however hard the lot of woman, she is in no *false* position. The two sexes are in their natural and true position relatively to the state of society, and the means of subsistence" (3: 303–4). A First Nations man cannot carry burdens in the way that his wife does, Jameson concludes, because to do so "would absolutely incapacitate him for a hunter" and thus put the family's livelihood at risk (3: 303).

She then compares First Nations women to European women and, in so doing, outlines some of the difficulties faced by women of her own culture, especially poor women. The indigenous North American woman, Jameson writes, is "sure of protection; sure of maintenance, at least while the man has it; sure of kind treatment; sure that she will never have her children taken from her but by death; sees none better off than herself, and has no conception of a superior destiny" (3: 302–3). By implication, the European woman is, in contrast, not sure of protection or maintenance and may have children taken from her (as indeed was the case under British laws of inheritance and property current at the time of Jameson's journey).[38] Jameson argues that a woman's position must be compared to the positions of other men and women in her society, and she then makes that comparison: "when we speak of the *drudgery* of the [Indian] women, we must note the equal division of labour; there is no class of women privileged to sit still while others work ... Compare her life with the refined leisure of an elegant woman in the higher classes of our society, and it is wretched and abject; but compare her life with that of a servant-maid of all work, or a factory girl,– I do say that the condition of the squaw is gracious in comparison, dignified by domestic feelings, and by equality with all around her" (3: 305). While Adele Ernstrom argues that Jameson's focus on "material conditions" may have been influenced by "utopian socialist thought" (289), Susan Birkwood characterizes Jameson's comments about the comparative equality of indigenous North American women as a "critique of the class system" in England (315). In the passage quoted above, Jameson certainly points out the inequities of that system, but her overall position in *Winter Studies and Summer Rambles* is not one of critique, since in other contexts she accepts distinctions of class and advocates that others be content within their own spheres. When she writes of the dissatisfactions of immigrant women in North America, she implies that they should be content with the manual labour and lack of intellectual stimulation that accompany their positions (2: 153–5), deficiencies that she as a woman of privilege would never tolerate, as her complaints about the lack of an appropriate social circle in Toronto attest. Jameson writes of settlement as being more successful when the settlers are of a higher class and can afford to purchase land already cleared by the lower classes; regarding Colonel Thomas Talbot's settlement, she notes that "a considerable improvement has taken place within these few years by the introduction of settlers of a higher grade, who have purchased half-cleared farms, rather than waste toil and time on the wild land" (2: 210).[39]

If Jameson's comments do not encompass an absolute critique of class relations in her own society, they certainly contain a critique of its gender relations. She points out that the obsession of European men with the chastity of their women is often only a matter of wanting to protect "property" (3: 307). While she has heard that First Nations men may offer wives or sisters to visitors, they do not use prostitutes, "those poor perverted sacrificed creatures who haunt our streets" (3: 308). Jameson concludes by asking, about the European woman, "Where she is idle and useless by privilege of sex, a divinity and an idol, a victim or a toy, is not her position quite as lamentable, as false, as injurious to herself and all social progress, as where she is the drudge, slave, and possession of the man?" (3: 312). This comment in particular won Jameson one of the few criticisms in early reviews of *Winter Studies and Summer Rambles*.[40] In an unsigned article in the *British and Foreign Review*, she was taken to task for her "constant resolution to represent any arrangement of the position and duties of her sex whatsoever, – even that where the Squaw is the Red Man's drudge in field and wigwam ..., – as more equitable and to be desired than that existing according to the present system of European civilization" (137). Clearly, while Jameson uses discussion of indigenous North American women to critique her own society, she does not suggest that their culture is better than hers. Both cultures oppress women, and the only advantage that First Nations women possess is that they do not have to contend with the additional oppression of social position.

JAMESON'S SKETCHES AND THE LANGUAGE OF LANDSCAPE AESTHETICS

Imperialist and anti-imperialist discourses and discourses of femininity coincide in Jameson's visual representations of herself, North American peoples, and their physical surroundings. Beth Fowkes Tobin argues in *Picturing Imperial Power*, "Drawings and paintings are sites where the tensions and contradictions of colonialist doctrines and practices were negotiated, more or less successfully, on an aesthetic level" (1). Negotiations of such tensions and contradictions are indeed evident in the sketches and watercolours that Jameson produced on her journey. Her sketches, like her text, were designed to provide a record of her travels, and as a result, they alternately show a distancing from First Nations subjects through an ethnographic or natural history focus and a personalized and nuanced interest through portraits and scenes that picture her First Nations hosts. Her own position within the British imperial venture and her responses to the doctrines of Romantic landscape discourse sometimes led her to construct First Nations peoples as part of the scenery or as "types" or ethnographic specimens. At other times, however, Jameson individualized First Nations acquaintances to the extent that their features were distinct and their portraits named. She also put herself in the picture, providing complex visual constructions of the pre- to early Victorian woman traveller that enrich and challenge parallel textual representations in her book.

Jameson had already illustrated some of her own books and would later publish several works of art criticism (including the well-known two-volume *Sacred and Legendary Art* [1848], which she also illustrated).[41] Her illustrations from her "rambles" in Canada and the United States are collected in two main locations: fifty-six pencil sketches, one pen sketch, and four watercolours are in an album in the Toronto Public Library's collections; and five etchings (all but one based on a specific album sketch) are held by the Royal Ontario Museum. The album was long the property of a Toronto family, but was first loaned to the Toronto library and then donated in 2000. Because of its long private ownership, only three of its sketches have previously been reproduced, along with the five etchings, in a 1958 pamphlet introduced by G.H. Needler and titled *Early Canadian Sketches.*[42] Jameson may have herself created the etchings; certainly, she wrote during her early days in Canada of preparing etchings for publication in a new edition of *Characteristics of Women* (*Anna Jameson* 140–1). Scadding notes that when Jameson visited him on her way back to England in the autumn of 1837, she "had with her numerous beautiful water-colour sketches taken during her late tour, together with many etchings by her own hand" (11).

Throughout her book, Jameson repeatedly mentions the activity of sketching. In the section in which she describes a spring visit to Niagara Falls, she notes that when she sat down to draw the falls, "in a moment the paper was wet through" (2: 73). She later mentions sketching a rude inn near Chatham and scenery on Mackinac Island, and carrying a sketchbook with her on the return canoe trip down Lake Huron (2: 225, 3:152, 315). She also describes scenes that she sketched, including Mackinac beach; the lodge of Wayish,ky near Sault Ste Marie; and her journeys, including representations of herself and her travelling companions in sleigh, bateau, and canoe. Henry Schoolcraft took particular note of her artistic endeavours: "She is, herself, an eminent landscape painter, or rather sketcher in crayon, and had her portfolio ever in hand. She did not hesitate freely to walk out to prominent points, of which the island has many, to complete her sketches ... She took a very lively interest in the Indian race, and their manners and customs, doubtless with views of benevolence for them as a peculiar race of man, but also as a fine subject of artistic observation" (*Personal Memoirs* 561–2). Schoolcraft thus identified Jameson's sketches as evidence of an interest in landscape and indigenous peoples that was artistic on one hand, and documentary or ethnographic, on the other. Jameson herself writes that she began to enjoy Toronto only in the spring, when she could sit and sketch the lake and at the same time describe it as a Romantic landscape: "Sat at the window drawing, or rather not drawing, but with a pencil in my hand. This beautiful Lake Ontario! ... – it changed its hues every moment, the shades of purple and green fleeting over it, now dark, now lustrous, now pale – like a dolphin dying." She then points out the poetic roots of her description and mocks the excesses of Romantic poetry by adding, "or, to use a more exact though less poetical comparison, dappled, and varying like the back of a mackarel" (1: 291).

As well as sketching landscapes and peoples she encountered, Jameson also occasionally included herself as a figure in her drawings, representing not what she observed but what she experienced. One illustration, of which two slightly different versions exist in the form of a sketch and an etching, is of the winter journey to St Catharines that she made with "Mr. Campbell, the clerk of the assize" (1: 36; fig. 1.11 and 1.12). The sketch, labelled *Journey to Niagara, along the Shores of Lake Ontario, January 1837*, shows a man driving a sleigh while a lone woman sits in the back, her face turned toward the viewer.[43] In contrast, a second sketch of a smaller sleigh drawn by one horse shows a back view of the female passenger and driver (fig. 1.3); no faces are visible, and the sleigh is about to disappear behind the corner of a building at the side of the sketch. At the bottom of the sketch is a dated label: *Forest Road to Niagara, January 25*. This sketch thus represents the second part of Jameson's journey, from St Catharines to Niagara with family friend John Lees Alma (*Anna Jameson* 147, *Letters* 78n). Both illustrations demonstrate the process of travel and provide a chronology – Jameson travelled through this area, at this point in time – and reinforce and complement her written version of her experience.[44] Indeed, the background scenery matches her textual descriptions of "spaces of cleared or half-cleared land, spotted over with the black charred stumps and blasted trunks of once magnificent trees, projecting from the snow drift," and of "wide openings ... bringing us in sight of Lake Ontario, and even in some places down upon the edge of it" (1: 66).

1.11 *Journey to Niagara, along the Shores of Lake Ontario, January 1837*, pencil sketch by Anna Jameson. Courtesy of the Toronto Public Library (TRL), 966–6L–4

1.12 *Travelling in a Sleigh in Canada*, etching by Anna Jameson. Courtesy of the Royal Ontario Museum, Toronto, 961.220.4

Jameson's realistic and often negative textual and visual portrayals of that landscape can be compared to Catharine Parr Traill's description of the "odious stumps that disfigure the clearings" of the Canadian land through which she travelled (Traill 111) and to the woodcuts that illustrate those descriptions. As with Jameson, Traill's publishers chose not to use illustrations by her, although she could have supplied them. In fact, Traill notes in one letter published in *The Backwoods of Canada* that she has attached a pen sketch of some of the flowers she describes (233). Instead of using this sketch, publisher Charles Knight commissioned illustrations from a London firm (Thompson 31), causing Traill to later complain about the "wretched prints many of them miserable reprints from the Penny Magazine and not one descriptive of Canadian scenery" (qtd. in Peterman xlix). Despite such discrepancies, the engravings can easily be mistaken for Traill's work because the artists are not credited in the book and the engravings appear to illustrate her words.

Although Traill's book was an edited version of letters she had sent home, it was presented by the publisher as a guide for British settlers, and thus the publisher's woodcuts portray the landscape as more tidy and idyllic than Traill's descriptions. They also diverge widely from similar scenes sketched and described by Jameson, whose goal was to provide both a record of her own travels and an artistic, documentary, and ethnographic record of the people and landscape she encountered. While one of Jameson's sketches shows her alone in the back of a sleigh being driven through a blasted landscape, facing the viewer with an almost beseeching expression on her face (fig. 1.11), Traill's illustrators present one idyllic picture of a nicely dressed couple being driven through a pretty winter landscape and another of orderly fields of cleared stumps, with a zigzag fence diagonally bisecting the scene and pointing to the sun breaking through in the background (66, 129). Similarly, the picturesque illustration in Traill's book of a log cabin set among tall pine trees, with cattle in the foreground and a woman hanging clothes at the side, can be contrasted to Jameson's bleak portrayal of a log inn in denuded land encountered on her journey (Traill 95; fig. 1.13).[45]

Although Jameson's drawings were completed by someone on the scene rather than by illustrators who had little or no first-hand knowledge of the area, they are clearly also designed to convey a specific point of view. Thus, while her visual representation of the sleigh journey shows her as the only passenger, in the textual description of the same trip, Jameson makes it clear that she and Campbell were in fact

Campbells Inn, on the Talbot road July 10. 1837.

1.13 *Campbells Inn, on the Talbot Road, July 10, 1837*, pencil sketch by Anna Jameson. Courtesy of the Toronto Public Library (TRL), 966–6L–15

accompanied by at least one other person (1: 74).[46] Her sleigh sketches illustrate her repeated and sometimes inaccurate claims that she was the first of her kind to make such a journey and that she made that journey alone. Her figurative solitude is also evident in the sketch and etching of her return trip from Manitoulin to Penetanguishene by canoe (fig. 1.1 and 1.2). Both versions of that scene show two birchbark canoes carrying eleven people each, with the four passengers Jameson identifies in her book sitting in the middle to front sections of the foreground canoe: the son of Lieutenant-Governor Francis Bond Head; the interpreter, Solomon; Jameson herself; and the superintendent of Indian affairs, Samuel Peters Jarvis. Two Métis paddlers sit in the bow, with four more in the back half of the canoe, recognizable in the sketch not only because each wields a paddle but also because each wears "a handkerchief twisted round the head." The "Indian steersman, Martin," stands in the stern. In both etching and sketch, his sleeves are rolled above his elbows, but the sketch gives a better sense of his posture and thus his "lithe agility" (3: 314–16).

Jameson is on the side closest to the viewer, her face in profile and shielded by a bonnet that, along with the parasol she mentions in the text, identifies her as the lone woman. Beside her is a man also looking at the viewer and wearing a top hat, which distinguishes him as a gentleman: Mr Jarvis. The illustration provides documentary visual evidence of Jameson's journey and, at the same time, represents in concrete terms her solitude in terms of gender and her femininity, gentility, and cultural origins.[47] Bonnets and parasols are appurtenances of the European woman, who must "never under any circumstances" allow face or hand to be exposed to "the out-of-door air, or sun light" (Scadding 12).

In her references to drawings that do not show herself on her journey, but instead show landforms, settlements, or other people, Jameson makes explicit parallels between what she sketches and what she writes by using similar language to describe the two activities. Of her arrival at Mackinac, she writes that "a scene burst at once on my enchanted gaze, such as I never had imagined, such as I wish I could place before you in words,– but I despair, unless words were of light, and lustrous hues, and breathing music. However, here is the picture as well as I can paint it" (3: 24). Jameson sketched this scene in pencil, and although her sketch is significantly less poetic than her textual introduction, it shows Mackinac to be much as she subsequently finds words to describe (fig. 1.14). In that description, Jameson uses the word "picturesque" – which William Gilpin defined in 1768 as "that peculiar kind of beauty, which is agreeable in a picture" (xii) – to refer to both land and dwellings. She also invokes a Eurocentric sense of nobility and grandeur in the landscape: "Immediately in front rose the abrupt and picturesque heights of the island, robed in richest foliage, and crowned by the lines of the little fortress, snow-white and gleaming in the morning light. At the base of these cliffs, all along the shore, immediately on the edge of the lake, which, transparent and unruffled, reflected every form as in a mirror, an encampment of Indian wigwams extended far as my eye could reach on either side. Even while I looked, the inmates were beginning to bestir themselves, and dusky figures were seen emerging into sight from their picturesque dormitories, and stood gazing on us with folded arms, or were busied about their canoes, of which some hundreds lay along the beach" (3: 24–5). As evidence of its status as a base for the colonizing forces, the island is "robed" in trees and "crowned" by the fort, like an imperial monarch, while its inmates, the Anishinaabe, are stereotypically "dusky" figures in "picturesque" dwellings.

As her use of the word "picturesque" demonstrates, Jameson's response to scenery and people in Canada is part of the Romantic tradi-

1.14 *Island of Mackinaw – Lake Huron*, pencil sketch by Anna Jameson.
Courtesy of the Toronto Public Library (TRL), 966–6L–22

tion.[48] She often employs a kind of painterly language to describe landscape, as in the above description of Mackinac. Introductory phrases such as "[o]n the East," "[o]n the opposite side," "[i]mmediately in front," and "[a]t the base" (3: 24–5), as well as a descriptive progression "from foreground to middle ground to distance," help "to place and orient the viewer" (Glickman 9). In her discussion of Jameson's descriptions of landscape, Lorraine York argues that "in *Winter Studies* one witnesses the frustrating attempt to apply artistic criteria of form and symmetry to a wild, recalcitrant landscape" (51). The result, York contends, is that Jameson's description of the expansiveness of the Canadian landscape "is not one of awesome grandeur, but one of barren desolation" (47). I would argue, in contrast, that the Canadian landscape seems to epitomize for Jameson the elements of awe and fear inherent in the Romantic sublime. An example is the passage in which she depicts a campsite menaced by fire during her trip from Sault Ste Marie to Manitoulin. She writes, "Wildly magnificent it was! beyond all expression beautiful, and awful too!" (3: 259), and notes that the scene at first "delighted" members of her party, but then inspired them with "fear" (3: 258). Indeed, Jameson's approach to landscape evokes the attitude toward danger that Susan Glickman identifies when she points to "the *prestige* of terror as an aesthetic category during the eighteenth and nineteenth centuries" (45).

This valorization of terror is a characteristic of scenic tourism, which Elizabeth Bohls suggests "inscribed disinterestedness on the landscape, constructing scenes through its process of detachment from the material specificity of land and people's practical connection to it" (103). The aestheticization of scenery by early nineteenth-century artists and travellers was criticized by at least some of their contemporaries. Henry Schoolcraft, for example, argued in 1837 that visitors to Mackinac, including Jameson, often attempted to distance themselves from what they saw by aestheticizing it. He wrote that the Englishmen and English-women who visited him "look on America very much as one does when he peeps through a magnifying glass on pictures of foreign scenes, and the picturesque ruins of old cities, and the like. They are really very fine, but it is difficult to realize that such things are." He concluded that "even Mrs. Jameson, who had the most accurate and artistic eye of all ... appeared to regard our vast woods, and wilds, and lakes, as a magnificent panorama, a painting in oil" (*Personal Memoirs* 566). In this passage, Schoolcraft astutely pointed to the depersonalizing and simultaneous containment inherent in "picturesque" approaches to landscape.

Such detachment is evident in Jameson's use of that visual term to describe the First Nations people she encountered. When applied to the individuals on Mackinac, "picturesque" comes to mean primarily the odd or curious. Jameson tells her reader that she wishes she could make a "sketch" of the people she sees in more than words: "There was not a figure among them that was not a study for a painter; and how I wished that my hand had been readier with the pencil to snatch some of those picturesque heads and attitudes! But it was all so new – I was so lost in gazing, listening, observing, and trying to comprehend, that I could not make a single sketch for you, except the above, in most poor and inadequate words" (3: 48).[49] The effect of this initial description of Ojibwa and Odawa peoples, which again metaphorically aligns writing with drawing, is to distance her from them; they are not people but objects to be delineated by her pencil and sketchbook. Her use of the languages of landscape and literature romanticizes them, reinforces their difference, and at the same time defines and contains them. Although they are "other," if they can be written about using the idiom with which Jameson is familiar, they are both knowable and controllable.

In her early Canadian drawings, Jameson also contains First Nations individuals by using compositional strategies, common to late eighteenth-century landscape painting, that position them as small figures in the foreground or middle distance to give the scene life and provide a sense of scale (Bohls 96). In one of her three sketches of Niagara Falls, for example, she places a figure of a man with feathers in his hair, leaning on a lance, in the upper central foreground (fig. 1.4).[50] In *Niagara Falls: Icon of the American Sublime*, Elizabeth McKinsey argues that First Nations individuals were included as internal viewers within landscape paintings to serve both as commentators on those landscapes and as natural components of them (28, 206–7). Jameson's representation of the man next to the waterfall undoubtedly associates him with the forces of nature and also contains him by portraying him as just one part of the landscape. At the same time, it puts Romantic landscape conventions into effect by using him to provide perspective, measurement, and commentary.

The Niagara Falls sketch was made early in Jameson's travels, before she had become well acquainted with any First Nations individuals and before she could provide the more integrated portrayal of them apparent in the third volume of her book. This integrated approach is evident in the head-and-shoulders sketch that Jameson made of two Odawa elders she met on Mackinac and Manitoulin, labelled with their names: *Mokomaun ish* and *Kee me wun* (fig. 1.15). She writes about Kim,e,wun, a name she translates as "the Rain, or rather 'it rains'" (3: 53–4), at least three times in her book (see also 3: 138, 272). In her account of her early days on Mackinac, she describes him as "one of the noblest figures I ever beheld, above six feet high, erect as a forest pine. A red and green handkerchief was twined round his head with much elegance, and knotted in front, with the two ends projecting; his black hair fell from beneath it, and his small black piercing eyes glittered from among its masses, like stars glancing through the thunder clouds. His ample blanket was thrown over his left shoulder, and brought under his right arm, so as to leave it free and exposed; and a sculptor might have envied the disposition of the whole drapery – it was so felicitous, so richly graceful" (3: 54). In this passage, Jameson interprets Kim,e,wun through the trope of the noble savage, a trope evident in her other descriptions of First Nations acquaintances. While her allusions to pine trees and stars also equate Kim,e,wun with nature, the description of his blanket characterizes him as a work of art – a

1.15 *Mokomaun ish* and *Kee me wun*, pencil sketches by Anna Jameson. Courtesy of the Toronto Public Library (TRL), 966–6L–58

sculpture – and thus to some extent objectifies and contains him. Indeed, in sculptural terms, Jameson's head-and-shoulders drawing presents a kind of "bust." The rather rough sketch was likely made during a meeting between Indian agents and First Nations groups on Mackinac, at which Jameson recognized individual characteristics of which she approved in the men she encountered while at the same time representing them as objects of artistic study; she writes of "five or six who had good heads – well developed, intellectual, and benevolent ... my friend the Rain ... conspicuous among them" (3: 138). Another possible occasion for the sketch was a gathering later at Manitoulin when she saw her "old acquaintance the Rain, looking magnificent" (3: 272).

At that second gathering, Jameson twice identifies the other figure on the portrait page. She notices one of the "remarkable chiefs of the Ottawas ... Mocomaun,ish, (the Bad-knife;)" (3: 272–3), and then writes that when Superintendent Jarvis stopped speaking to the council, "a fine Ottawa chief (I think Mokomaun,ish) arose, and spoke at some length" (3: 285). The portrait of Mokomaun,ish (labelled *Mokomaun ish*) shows a man with a serious expression; his face is turned away from the observer in three-quarter profile, and his eyes appear to gaze at the side of the page. The drawing of Kim,e,wun (labelled *Kee me wun*) portrays him facing in the same direction, in complete profile. Anne Maxwell demonstrates in *Colonial Photography and Exhibitions* that artistic representations in which the subjects are turned from the viewer and thus are not allowed to return the viewer's gaze are the most objectifying (13–14). Since Mokomaun,ish and Kim,e,wun turn away from the observer, it could be argued that these men are presented primarily as objects of the artist's and viewer's gaze. On the other hand, Tobin points out that portraits by definition "imply an empowered subject. However delicate and complex the negotiations among sitter, artist, and patron, portraits are of somebody: an individual with a name, a family, and a home" (17). While the men in Jameson's portraits do not gaze at the observer, they have at least "achieved the status of subject" in that both are represented as individuals (Tobin 17). As an exemplification of that status, their names are attached to their images, they are described in the text, and an attempt has been made in each portrait to capture distinctive features and personalities.[51]

In his essay on Jameson's sketches and watercolours, Thomas Gerry refers to five "close-up portraits of individuals" which he argues show evidence of "warm contact with the native people" (45). He does not, however, point to the head-and-shoulders portraits of Kim,e,wun and Mokomaun,ish, possibly because the page of the album on which they are pasted is incorrectly labelled to indicate that the portraits were drawn on Jameson's return trip to England through the United States.[52] The five illustrations that Gerry mentions are not what I would define as portraits – none of the people in them is named or identifiable – and do not represent any of the individuals with whom Jameson had "warm contact."[53] Instead, these five full-figure illustrations signal the intense interest of the ethnographer in what she sees on her journey. They provide examples of what Tobin calls, in another context, "a visual description of what were presented as specimens of exotic species" (145). Indeed, the sketches graphically represent Jameson's repeated textual use of the word "specimen" to refer to First Nations individuals. Included among them are a pen sketch of a woman carrying a baby in a cradle on her back (fig. 1.10), a watercolour grouping of three adults and a child (fig. 1.9), and three watercolours of men dancing (fig. 1.16, 1.17, 1.18). All exemplify descriptions in Jameson's book intended to give readers a "picture" of the peoples she encountered and of their cultural artifacts and social practices, including their dress, their modes of transporting children, and their dances.

1.16 Untitled watercolour of man dancing, by Anna Jameson.
Courtesy of the Toronto Public Library (TRL), 966–6L–27

According to Tobin, ethnographic art, "despite its focus on the human figure, does not share portraiture's goals of reproducing an individual's countenance and conveying a sense of the subject's character. Instead, ethnographic art seeks to represent the typical and to suppress the individual" (147). While these five pictures are unusual for Jameson in that they are in pen and watercolour, for the most part they represent types rather than (as her two pencil portraits have done) individuals. Thus her untitled pen sketch illustrates her description of a woman on Mackinac with a baby "in one of their curious bark cradles" (3: 30).[54] Similarly, although the watercolour tableau of the three adults and a child has a sense of deliberate artistry rather than solely of scientific illustration, it is labelled at the bottom simply *Indians*. These people are carefully posed, but the sketch is designed most of all to show dress, cultural practices, and, through the guns the men either carry or lean against, the encroachment of European technology.

In *Winter Studies and Summer Rambles*, Jameson describes in detail two separate dances put on for her benefit, one at Mackinac and the other at Manitoulin. In her watercolour sketches of three of the dancers in motion, none is recognizable as any one of the individuals she describes (3: 145–9, 292–4), and indeed, none is named, unlike her portraits of Mokomaun,ish and Kim,e,wun. The men appear instead to be "types" of dancers, composites dressed in various combinations of loincloths, moccasins and leggings, beads, paint, and feathers. Because these sketches are in colour, all the figures are portrayed with very dark skins; the paintings therefore have a documentary focus designed to emphasize cultural difference. At the same time, two of the men look directly at the observer, and each has distinctive features. Thus although these three dancers are clearly objects of ethnographic investigation, they are allowed some individuality and some engagement with the investigator and the viewer. As Tobin notes, the "powerful narratives" belonging to the subjects of ethnographic art "cannot be completely suppressed" (18).

The three watercolours, like the descriptions of the dancers in Jameson's text, exemplify her fascination with the men's state of undress: "Of their style of clothing, I say nothing," she writes, "– for, as it is wisely said, nothing can come of *nothing*" (3: 145). In his study of travel writing, Dennis Porter argues that "the shock of such encounters with naked or seminaked peoples of color seems to reside in the perception of similarity within radical difference" (12). Jameson's paintings register that shock, as do her textual accounts of the scene, which focus

1.17 Untitled watercolour of man dancing, by Anna Jameson. Courtesy of the Toronto Public Library (TRL), 966–6L–28a

1.18 Untitled watercolour of man dancing, by Anna Jameson. Courtesy of the Toronto Public Library (TRL) 966–6L–28b

both on nakedness and on purported warlike tendencies. Earlier she has described in detail one individual, whom she provides with the European descriptor dandy. She writes that "he had neither a coat nor any thing else that gentlemen are accustomed to wear; but then his face was most artistically painted ... and conspicuous above all, the eagle feather in his hair, showing he was a warrior, and had taken a scalp – *i.e.* killed his man" (3: 44). The juxtaposition of the words "dandies" and "gentlemen" with references to paint, feathers, and scalping emphasizes both the jarring juxtaposition of the familiar with the unfamiliar and the fascination of the traveller with potential violence.

Tobin maintains that feathers and jewellery "code their wearers as exotic" (139). Such finery also marks them as "uncivilized," as Jameson's connection of the eagle feather with scalping indicates. Writing half a century before Jameson, Wollstonecraft suggested, "An immoderate fondness for dress, for pleasure, and for sway, are the passions of savages; the passions that occupy those uncivilized beings who have not yet extended the dominion of the mind" (*Vindication* 319). Jameson, too, connects civilization, or the lack of it, with dress (3: 43). In addition, her dancing subjects are feminized, appearing, in common with the oarsman Martin, to have "superb" figures, "more agile and elegant, however, than muscular ..., with small and well formed hands and feet" (3: 148).

In other sketches, Jameson shows Anishinaabe people who are also not individualized in terms of features, but at least are placed in relation to their natural surroundings, to everyday activities such as fishing or canoeing, and to their dwellings and their modes of transportation. An example is *Wigwams on the beach at Mackinaw – July 21*, which shows tents, canoes, and people in a specific location on a specific date (fig. 1.5; see also the more dramatic etching of that scene, fig. 1.6). Jameson's documentary record is also sometimes explicitly tied to individuals whom she knew and described in detail. Her sketch and etching of a lodge near Sault Ste Marie illustrate both the dwelling of an Anishinaabe man of high status and that of a warmly regarded acquaintance (fig. 1.7 and 1.8). The sketch is labelled in a way that identifies it with an individual at a specific time and place: *Wayish-ky's Lodge – July 31 1837*. In her book, she writes: "The lodge is of the genuine Chippewa form, like an egg cut in half lengthways. It is formed of poles stuck in the ground, and bent over at top, strengthened with a few wattles and boards; the whole is covered over with mats, birch-bark, and skins; a large blanket formed the door or curtain, which was not ungracefully looped aside. Wayish,ky, being a great man, has also a smaller lodge

1.19 *Sault Ste. Marie, 1845*, painting by Paul Kane. Courtesy of the Royal Ontario Museum, Toronto, 912.1.9

hard by, which serves as a storehouse and kitchen" (3: 186). Jameson's description and the accompanying illustration can be compared to the painting by Paul Kane titled *Sault Ste. Marie, 1845* (fig. 1.19). Kane's painting, of the same location eight years later, has very similar composition: lodges in the foreground, river in the middle distance, and the opposite shore in the background. While the painting is, like Jameson's sketch, clearly documentary, it exemplifies a much more deliberate sense of artistry, evident not only in the use of colour but also in the formal grouping of the central figures (who appear to represent the concept of the "noble savage"), the draping of blankets in doorways and over bushes, and the use of compositional features such as the large tree in the left foreground.

When Henry Schoolcraft described Jameson's 1837 visit to Mackinac Island, he linked her sketches to landscape paintings by the seventeenth-century French painter Claude, whose works epitomized Gilpin's notions of the picturesque (Brennan 16; McKinsey 58–9). Jameson's host wrote that when she "stepped out on the piazza and saw the wild Indians dancing; she evidently looked on with the eye of a Claude Lorraine or Michael Angelo [*sic*]" (*Personal Memoirs* 562). While Schoolcraft may have compared Jameson to well-known artists only because he wanted to stress her artistic activities, his comment also points to the containment of difference, the turning of people into parts of the landscape, evident in some of her sketches and in sections of her narrative. Bohls argues that women writers of the Romantic era made use of, but at the same time radically revised, the distancing aesthetic of early Romantic discourse of landscape. She contends that their writings "point to the often inhumane consequences of denying the connection between aesthetic practices and the material, social, and political conditions of human existence" (10). Jameson's detailed and personalized descriptions and illustrations of Wayish,ky's lodge and of Mokomaun,ish and Kim,e,wun indeed make concrete the connection between aesthetic practice and practical human existence, unlike some of her other classifications of First Nations abodes and people as picturesque or as types, and unlike Kane's painting or the illustrations for Traill's book.

THE MUTUAL INFLUENCE OF CONTACT

Jameson's adherence to standards of civilization, despite her "adoption," is evident in the textual and pictorial mapping of herself and the people she met during her *Winter Studies and Summer Rambles in Canada*. As those representations demonstrate, while she may have been adventurous and may have wanted to be seen as "first," she took care to ensure that she would always be perceived as respectable and refined. Her first-hand experience altered her textual and visual interpretation of First Nations, but she continued to view "civilization" as essential both for indigenous peoples and for women of all societies. While Jameson's travel writing displays evidence of its discursive roots in other, earlier, and often more imperialist narratives of travel, it at the same time revises those narratives. She came to understand that, contrary to Alexander Henry's representations to his readers, the Anishinaabe did possess a complex language and literature – elements of her own definition of a superior race (2: 273). She also came to believe that shifting policies toward the First Nations were unjust.

Vargo points out, "From the perspective of the twentieth century, it is hard to escape the thought that Jameson herself exploited Canada's colonized subjects through what she brought away with her. But at the very least she used what she acquired to unsettle accepted wisdom" (66). The figurative maps that Jameson left of her travels in North

Indians, watercolour by Anna Jameson. Courtesy of the Toronto Public Library (TRL), 966–6L–37

Sault Ste. Marie, 1845, painting by Paul Kane. Courtesy of the Royal Ontario Museum, Toronto, 912.1.9

Untitled watercolour, by Anna Jameson. Courtesy of the Toronto
Public Library (TRL), 966–6L–27

Untitled watercolour, by Anna Jameson. Courtesy of the Toronto Public Library (TRL), 966–6L–28a

Untitled watercolour, by Anna Jameson. Courtesy of the Toronto Public Library (TRL) 966–6L–28b

America, in her book, her letters, and her sketches, indeed unsettle accepted wisdom and also provide evidence of the mutual influence of contact. If she recorded the Anishinaabe culture, she also documented her dawning awareness that such a culture existed. If she described the reality of the discharging of treaty obligations, she also recorded her altered opinions about the fulfillment of such obligations. Anna Jameson was profoundly influenced by what she saw and experienced, and that influence is evident in her pictorial and textual mapping of her North American journey.

chapter two | "WHERE THE WOMEN DIDN'T DO WHAT THEY WERE TOLD" | Mina Hubbard's Mapping of Physical Space

The men ... said they had been on lots of trips before, and where there were women too, and they said to me they never were on a trip before where the women didn't do what they were told. | George Elson, quoted in Mina Hubbard's *A Woman's Way through Unknown Labrador* 130–1

In *Winter Studies and Summer Rambles in Canada*, Anna Jameson makes a metaphoric link between Alexander Henry's travels and the mythic journey outlined in the *Odyssey*. Henry was of course a male traveller and thus an appropriate subject of comparison for Odysseus, but Jameson's text makes it clear that women too have long been travellers. Travel theorist Karen Lawrence points out that despite the experiences of travellers and writers such as Jameson, women have had to struggle to revise the "Western cultural truism that Penelope waits while Odysseus voyages" (ix). The subject of this chapter, Mina Benson Hubbard's *A Woman's Way through Unknown Labrador: An Account of the Exploration of the Nascaupee and George Rivers* (1908), provides a radical revision of that cultural truisim.[1] Hubbard's narrative is that of an early twentieth-century Penelope whose Odysseus does not return from his voyage and whose death sets the stage for her decision to voyage in his stead, to tell her own tale, and in so doing, to provide her own figurative and literal maps of human relationships and geographical locations in Labrador.

By making her 1905 journey, Mina Hubbard intentionally rivalled one of her husband's original travelling companions, American lawyer Dillon Wallace, who also set out in 1905 to complete Leonidas Hubbard's earlier failed journey. At the same time, she acted as an unintentional rival to her husband's 1903 expedition through unmapped sections of Labrador, which had ended in his death. Using the same guide, George

2.1 "On the Trail," *A Woman's Way through Unknown Labrador*. Courtesy of Betty Ellis

Elson, her expedition succeeded where Leonidas Hubbard's had failed. It was better planned and executed than both his 1903 expedition and Wallace's of 1905, and, most importantly, she lived to write an account of the journey and to present a map and photographs that documented the land through which she travelled and the Innu people she encountered.[2] In so doing, Hubbard made a claim to the physical space of the Ungava Peninsula that is still in effect today.

Mina Hubbard has been presented most often in popular histories in a manner similar to her characterization in contemporaneous reviews: as a plucky and romantic adventuress who honoured her husband's memory by becoming the first white woman to traverse continuously by canoe and subsequently to map the Naskaupi and George River systems (Cooke, 1960; Berton, 1978; Davidson and Rugge, 1988; Merrick, 1992). Judith Niemi argues, "There was not much precedent for being a lady explorer, but the role of grieving and dutiful widow could be understood by the public" (221). Indeed, most of the reviews of Hubbard's book characterized her journey as a tribute to her husband, and many of those reviewers wrote as many words about his expedition as about hers.[3] Typical is the 1909 review by J.G. Millais, who writes that "she leaves us with the impression of a charming and plucky little woman, whose devotion to her husband and his dreams is pure and true" (402–3), and the 1908 headlines "Love's Labour" (*Evening Standard*) and "Through Unknown Labrador: Explorations of a Plucky Woman" (*Western Mail*). Indeed, Leonidas Hubbard's journey had received so much coverage in the American press of the day, and Mina Hubbard was herself so determined to keep him in the public mind, that her expedition was often read as a footnote to his, a reading that has continued to be influential.[4] Only recently has her expedition been reassessed on its own, in particular in terms of its gender implications. And only in the past few years has her book been examined as a textual artifact, along with the travel diary on which it is based.[5] *A Woman's Way* undoubtedly serves as documentation of the negotiations necessary for women travellers of the early twentieth century to claim physical and discursive space. Hubbard is not just a woman, however, but a white middle-class Canadian woman travelling through a contested part of the British colonial empire.[6] Throughout her book, her journal articles, and the travel diary that serves as a rough draft for all of them, she reveals not only the compromises necessitated by restrictions of gender but also the complexities of race, class, and colonialism.

Women travel writers have often negotiated "a dominant position of race and a subordinate one of gender" (Sharpe 12). Hubbard was nominally the head of her expedition, which included four guides who were Cree, Métis, and Inuit. In terms of race and class, she would have been considered superior; they were Native and they were her servants. Her inferior position in terms of gender and wilderness knowledge, however, meant that those men – George Elson, Job Chapies, Joseph Iserhoff, and Gilbert Blake – often told her what to do. (In contrast, her husband had repeatedly made decisions about his expedition that might better have been left to Elson.) Mina Hubbard negotiated this inferior-superior position in order to be able to do the exploring, mapping, measuring, and recording that were an essential part of her project. In her written accounts of the journey, such conflict is evident when the "we" of the shared adventure changes to "I" of the explorer-narrator.

Lisa LaFramboise has ably argued that the change from "we" to "I" is in part a function of the negotiations of femininity versus control evident in the writings of many early twentieth-century woman travellers ("Just a little" 9). The authority of Hubbard's narrative is also dependent upon her spatial (and racial) separation from her travelling companions. Hubbard makes a claim to physical space by travelling, domesticating, naming, and mapping, and she deals with place in a metaphoric way in order to compensate for the fact that she is moving outside "woman's place" (Lawrence x). She does so by claiming to travel in her "husband's name" (WW 50) and by making complex claims about the nature of home. Hubbard defuses potential criticism that she has stepped outside woman's place by declaring all of Labrador to be "home." Her husband's metaphoric presence helps not only to domesticate Labrador but also to allay potential suspicions of sexual impropriety with her companions.

Hubbard was not writing in isolation; the *Evening Standard* noted in one of its two reviews of her book that it had received other accounts of "feminine exploration and adventurous journeyings" ("Love's Labour" 5). Her contemporaries included women travellers who published book-length travel narratives, such as Sara Jeannette Duncan, Georgina Binnie-Clark, and Agnes Deans Cameron. Duncan's *A Social Departure: How Orthodocia and I Went Round the World by Ourselves* (1890) is a fictionalized account of her travels with friend Lily Lewis from eastern to western Canada and from thence to Japan, Ceylon, India, Egypt, and England. The chapters on Canada form a species of railway narrative – Duncan and Lewis took the train from central Canada to Vancouver, with stops along the way – unique in that, as the title *A Social Departure* indicates, the two young middle-class women departed from social conventions by travelling unchaperoned. Duncan's is a witty and often humorous account that also touches on matters related to colonial government and to the gendered relations of travel.[7] Binnie-Clark's *A Summer on the Canadian Prairie* (1910) outlines her trip to Canada via steamship and rail and her impressions of farming on the Canadian prairies; it is particularly scathing in its condemnation of effete and incompetent middle- and upper-class British men who aspire to be farmers.[8] Cameron's *The New North: Being Some Account of a Woman's Journey through Canada to the Arctic* (1909) describes a journey she took with her niece by rail from Chicago to Edmonton, by stage coach from Edmonton to Athabasca Landing, and from thence along several connecting waterways to the Arctic Ocean.

All three of these narratives provide a sense of how Canadian and British women wrote about experiences of travel in Canadian territories during the late 1800s and early 1900s. Cameron's book is also about the North, albeit the more travelled and well-mapped Mackenzie River route to the Arctic, and contains northern photographs and ethnographic descriptions of indigenous groups that can be compared to Hubbard's. These three contemporaneous books are all more light-hearted than Hubbard's very serious narrative. The difference lies both in the tragic pre-text for Hubbard's trip – the narrative of her husband's death – and in the fact that of these four women travellers, she was the only one who was not a professional writer, who ventured into territory previously unmapped by European Canadians, and who did not use established or scheduled means of travel. The model she follows is not so much that provided by women such as Duncan or Cameron but her own image, as presented in an article written by her husband about an earlier, less rigorous wilderness trip they took together. In that article, Leonidas Hubbard authorized a limited role for her as explorer by writing that when their guide commented, "Madam can not go, of course. No white woman has ever seen this lake," the restriction "fired every bit of Madam's latent explorer spirit. If no white woman had been there, she was going" ("Off Days" 721). Mina Hubbard appropriated and extended this characterization of herself as woman explorer when she authorized her later journey into Labrador.

In 1905 the Ontario-born Hubbard undertook the arduous 576-mile canoe trip upstream along the Naskaupi River in Labrador (with

2.2 "A Magnificent Trophy," frontispiece, *The New North* (New York: Appleton, 1909). Courtesy of the City of Victoria Archives, PR14–1474

Newfoundland, then a self-governing British colony), through Lake Michikamau and Lake Michikamats to the height of land, and then downstream along the George River in the Ungava District of Canada's Northwest Territories (now northern Quebec). Like journeys by Binnie-Clark and the women writers whose work is explored in other chapters of this book, Hubbard's trip was fundamentally relational in that it was provoked by the previous actions of another person – in this case, her husband, an American adventure writer. Two years earlier Leonidas Hubbard, his friend Wallace, and guide Elson from James Bay, in Ontario, had tried to make the same journey following incomplete maps of the Geological Survey of Canada, supplemented by hand-drawn maps from information supplied by local trappers. The three men had taken the wrong route almost from the beginning, struggling up Susan Brook instead of the much larger, nearby Naskaupi River, which they thought they were navigating. With too few supplies and too little time to complete the journey, the party had turned back in late September. Wallace and Elson survived, but Hubbard died from starvation exacerbated by intestinal illness.

As a signed agreement in the Centre for Newfoundland Studies Archives indicates, Mina Hubbard commissioned Wallace to write the book that her husband had been planning (Agreement, 1 Oct. 1904). Using Leonidas Hubbard's travel diaries and the services of a ghost writer (Davidson and Rugge 179), Wallace produced a compelling tale called *The Lure of the Labrador Wild: The Story of the Exploring Expedition Conducted by Leonidas Hubbard, Jr* (1905).[9] Mina Hubbard believed that the book represented her husband in a negative light, and indeed, although *The Lure* depicted Hubbard as a good-hearted and often heroic friend, it also showed him making bad decisions; focused much more on his mental health than on that of its author, often characterizing Hubbard as depressed; and referred to the thirty-one-year-old expedition leader as a homesick boy (172). Early in 1905, at the same time as Wallace was planning a return journey to Labrador, Mina Hubbard decided to make the trip herself and to produce her own narrative of the journey, which would include an edited version of her husband's diary so that, she claimed, his story could be told in his own words.

Hubbard's book is thus the story of a rivalry that is never overtly expressed in *A Woman's Way*, although it is an explicit part of the journal upon which the book is based. The most candid entry from her diary reads: "All at pretty high tension to-day, wondering whether

2.3 "The Arrival at Ungava," *A Woman's Way through Unknown Labrador.*
Courtesy of Betty Ellis

our rivals had reached Seal Lake and the Nascaupee" (17 July 1905).[10]
Wallace's second book, *The Long Labrador Trail*, published the year
before Hubbard's, also never mentions her parallel expedition. Indeed,
although they saw each other before and after their wilderness expeditions – they met aboard the steamer *Harlaw* on the way to North West
River Post in June 1905 and again at the end of their respective canoe
trips while they awaited the ship *Pelican* at George River Post, near
what is now Kangiqsualujjuaq on Ungava Bay – they never encountered
each other on their canoe travels. Each subsequently made distinct
claims to primacy. Hubbard, who arrived at the end of August, claimed
to be the first white woman (and indeed, the first white person) to travel
and map that particular route, to meet with two groups of Innu, and
to see the caribou migration. Wallace, who arrived seven weeks later
after a much more arduous and dangerous journey during which he sent
his Ojibwa guide and two other travelling companions back, claimed
that he and his one remaining companion were the first white men to
make the trip without the help of Native guides and the first to make
the long journey back by dogsled. By focusing on her race and gender

and, like Wallace and other explorers before her, eliding the experiences of both her travelling companions and the Innu men and women she encountered, Hubbard was able to accurately claim to be "first" to travel this route. By taking metaphorical possession of the land in the name of empire, she was able to represent herself as "first" to map it. Where and how Hubbard situated herself, the indigenous peoples she met, and the geography of Labrador is a "politics of location" (A. Rich 215) that encompasses discourses of both colonialism and gender.

"AT HOME" IN LABRADOR AND THE STRATEGIC POWER OF NAMING

It seemed to me fit that my husband's name should reap the fruits of service which had cost him so much, and in the summer of 1905 I myself undertook the conduct of the second Hubbard Expedition. | Mina Hubbard, *A Woman's Way* 50

With this comment, Hubbard announces that names will be crucial to her venture. She is undertaking her expedition because she carries her husband's name, and his name must be inscribed on her success. In making her exploratory journey, Hubbard countered implicit criticism that she was acting in a way unbecoming a woman. As an early twentieth-century woman, her place was understood to be in the home.[11] Only two years earlier Hubbard's husband had considered the interior of Labrador an unsuitable place for her to venture; instead, he set off with Wallace and Elson, leaving her behind. Twelve years earlier the Royal Geographical Society in Britain had reaffirmed its disapproval of woman explorers in general by renouncing its brief decision to elect women as members.[12] After Hubbard sent her first telegram stating that she had successfully completed her expedition, several journalists refused to believe that a woman could have made such a journey. The writer for the *North Adams Evening Transcript* maintained that "she cannot have carried out her original intentions" because those would have taken her "on a much longer journey than she has apparently made" ("Mrs. Hubbard Safe").[13]

Hubbard does not directly counter these societal, personal, and institutional barriers to her participation in wilderness exploration. Instead, she sidesteps them and, in the process, validates her venture by apparently embracing the ideology of women's place. First, she constantly reiterates the fiction that the expedition is in fact her husband's, one that she is completing only for his benefit and in a way that could never meet his exacting standards. Second, she makes strategic claims about home: once her husband is dead, home can be anywhere, but especially in the Labrador wilderness where he is still metaphorically present.

Hubbard's constant invocation of her husband's name helps to perpetuate her claim that this is his journey. Some women writers who were her contemporaries, such as Charlotte Perkins Gilman, signed their work by incorporating their maiden names or their mothers' family names into their own. Others, such as Sara Jeannette Duncan, used both their husband's names and their original family names on their written work.[14] Instead of employing "an accumulation of names that reflected compound identities and preserved a lineage that would otherwise be lost," Hubbard harked back to earlier Victorian women writers such as Mrs Gaskell, Mrs Oliphant, and Mrs Jameson, who "established their allegiance to marital respectability" by calling themselves "Mrs" (Gilbert and Gubar 241). Her name is thus given as "Mrs Leonidas Hubbard" on the cover of the book and "Mrs Leonidas Hubbard, Junior" on the title page, emphasizing not her own patronymic but her husband's.

"Mrs Leonidas Hubbard" is the conventional, self-effacing name for a wife and widow, but for Mina Hubbard it can also be considered in some respects a pseudonym. Sandra Gilbert and Susan Gubar argue that "by the late nineteenth century the male pseudonym was quite specifically a mask behind which the female writer could hide her disreputable femininity" (240), as did Duncan when she used the pseudonym Garth Grafton and her friend Lily Lewis when she called herself Louis Lloyd. Hubbard hides behind her husband's name not to disguise her own femininity – the Mrs instead points to it, as does the book's title, A Woman's Way – but instead to justify it.[15] If Mina Hubbard travels and writes in her husband's name, then the trip is really his and she is not participating in an activity unsuitable for a woman. LaFramboise claims that by positioning herself "within the discourse of late Victorian widowhood," Hubbard appropriates her husband's "protective sanction to her potentially transgressive enterprise" ("Just a little" 20), but she is doing more than using her husband's name as protection. While she is outside her home exploring, writing, and publishing, she metaphorically takes on her husband's name and identity in order to validate her venture. In thus naming herself, she makes strategic use of the convention that a husband and wife are in fact one person, and that person is the man. If she *is* her husband, she cannot be accused of inappropriately usurping his role. She is not just undertaking this journey to honour her husband, as she explicitly claims; she *is* her husband, and thus there can be no impropriety, either social or sexual, in her making this journey, even in the company of four men.[16]

At the same time, Hubbard is unable or unwilling to completely efface her own identity. She signs her preface "Mina Benson Hubbard" (xi), thus providing at least one record of both her first name and her family name.[17] Likewise, although the chapter that introduces her narrative describes only her husband, his father, and his maternal grandfather, Hubbard mentions her husband's mother's name in the dedication and in chapter 1, ensuring through these brief references that his maternal lineage also will not be forgotten.

The 211 pages of Hubbard's own narrative begin and end with reference to her metaphorical conception of home – her relationship with her dead husband. Chapter 1 is titled "Leonidas Hubbard, Junior" and describes his family, his work history, and his decision to take an expedition to Labrador. That chapter functions to introduce Hubbard as the loving wife (and not as the former teacher or competent nurse, which she also was), who is completing the journey in her husband's name to ensure that name will not be forgotten. Thus she writes that she undertook what she calls "the second Hubbard Expedition" in order that the work she was doing "would for ever associate my husband's name with the country where he hoped to begin his explorations" (114). Her determination that Leonidas Hubbard's name be remembered was evident at Lake Michikamau, when she wrote on a stone with a piece of flint, "HUBBARD EXPEDITION, / ARRIVED HERE, AUGUST 2ND, 1905" (143), and at the height of land, when she named the lake that serves as the source of the George River, Lake Hubbard. In her book and diary, she repeatedly bemoans her inadequacy in comparison with her husband. She writes that she has "not his spirit, not that of the true explorer" (MH Diary 10 July); that she feels "wretched and mean and unbeautiful" when she compares herself to him (14 Oct.); that no matter how she tries, she "could never be so generous and self-forgetful as he" (WW 234). Perhaps the strongest statement of this feeling appears toward the end of her book: "We were like Light and Darkness and with the light gone how deep was the darkness. Once I had thought I stood up beside him, but in what a school had I learned that I only reached to his feet" (235). As a result of this undermining of her own worth, the reader is encouraged to forget that her expedition succeeded where her husband's had failed.

Throughout the book, Hubbard situates herself primarily as a wife; she even quotes her husband as calling her not Mina but "Wife" (33).[18] The names that she calls others and that others call her further locate her in her social and cultural context and provide evidence of hierarchies of gender, class, and race. According to both her account and Elson's, he and Chapies, Iserhoff, and Blake invariably called her Mrs Hubbard (or, in Elson's journal, occasionally M.B.H.), while she called them by their first names. In contrast, she refers to non-Native men by their surnames, either with a respectful title (such as Mr McKenzie) or without (Wallace). Hubbard and Elson were not alone in using forms of address as markers of race and class. Indeed, in both his diaries and his books about the 1903 and 1905 expeditions, Wallace calls his First Nations guides by their first names (George, Pete, and Duncan) and his white companions, even friends, by last names alone (Hubbard, Stanton, Easton, Richards). While he clearly viewed his companions as equals, his guides were not only of another race but also essentially his servants and thus to be addressed less respectfully.[19] On the occasions in his book about the 1903 expedition when he refers to Leonidas Hubbard as "the boy" (LLW 144, 172), Mina Hubbard perhaps rightly interpreted this naming as a sign of his lack of respect for her husband; while she calls her husband "Laddie" in her diary, in her book she always refers to him as "Mr Hubbard."

She also explicitly names most of her companions in terms of race.[20] While the Scots-Cree Elson is introduced in her book only as the man who had "loyally served" her husband in the earlier expedition, she calls Job Chapies a "pure blood Cree Indian," Joseph Iserhoff a "Russian half-breed," and Gilbert Blake a "half-breed Eskimo boy trapper" (51).[21] As this passage indicates, she also categorizes Blake in terms of age, calling him "a bright-faced, merry-hearted boy" (52), "a merry, happy-hearted boy" (94), a "great kid" who was "very proud of his company" (MH Diary 1 July), and a "very funny little kid" (2 Sept.), even though at the time of the journey he was nineteen years old and married, with one child.[22] Hubbard provides the first and last names of the men in this introductory section of her book. Although some reviewers such as Munson Havens in the *Dial* followed her lead, others such as the anonymous reviewer for the *Western Mail* identify Elson only as "an Indian hunter" and the other men as her "three servants" ("Through Unknown Labrador").

Hubbard situates herself socially by using metaphors of home, as well as through the conventions of naming. As she sets out, she stresses

2.4 "George Elson," photograph by Mina Hubbard. Courtesy of Betty Ellis

the familiarity of her surroundings: "I do not feel far from home but in reality more at home than I have done since I knew my Laddie was never coming back to me" (MH Diary 23 July; see also WW 113–14). A month later, her diary entry reads, "we have come these 2 months through this deserted wilderness and I have never felt as if I were far from home ... I think I have felt more at home here in this Labrador wilderness than I have ever done any place since I was in our home in Congers" (25 Aug.). The book makes the same assertion in a less emotional and less personal way: "The long miles which separated me from the world did not make me feel far away – just far enough to be nice – and many times I found myself wishing I need never have to go back again" (177). By repeatedly situating herself "at home," Hubbard not only assuages her grief but also helps to dispel the notion that she is in fact venturing outside women's place.

She also repeatedly downplays the hardships of the trip, in effect domesticating the Labrador wilderness. She writes that she "slept as comfortably as if in the most luxurious apartment" (60) and, in her diary, that she finds herself "feeling astonished that Labrador can be so kind and so beautiful" (29 June). Although a canoe had capsized, almost killing Chapies and sending some crucial equipment to the bottom of the river (79–80), and although blackflies and mosquitoes kicked and struggled until they made their way through her veil (85), covered her plate of food (93), and bit her neck and ears until the blood streamed (126–7), Hubbard writes, "I had encountered none of the real stress of wilderness life, everything had gone well with us, everything was made easy for me; I had had no hardships to bear" (114; see also MH Diary 23 July). Later in the book, she again reduces adversities to nothing more than fatigue and discomfort: "Weariness and hardship I had looked for, and weariness I had found often and anxiety ... but of hardship there had been none. Flies and mosquitoes made it uncomfortable sometimes, but not to the extent of hardship" (177). For Hubbard, the word "hardship" is clearly reserved to describe experiences that are more directly life-threatening.

The effect of these statements is to make a powerful claim that she is not in fact travelling outside women's sphere. Because she is making this trip for her husband, in his name, in a place that is no less comfortable than her own house, her actions are not unsuitable for a woman. Thus there can be no impropriety in the fact that she makes this journey accompanied only by men. At the end of the nineteenth century and the beginning of the twentieth, more and more women were making unchaperoned travels, but "unchaperoned" often simply meant without a husband or an older female companion. Duncan, for example, travelled with a friend who was five years younger; Cameron was a mature woman herself and was accompanied by her niece; Binnie-Clark travelled with a sister. Of these four women, Hubbard is the only one to journey with male companions alone. She thus has more need to justify her actions, and strategies of naming and claims about home become crucial to her narrative.

BEGINNINGS AND ENDINGS: FRAMING THROUGH MASCULINE NARRATIVES

Hubbard's beginnings and endings are also strategic. Her published narrative covers only the two months her group spent on the rivers and lakes of Labrador; it omits the planning of the trip, the voyage to North West River Post, and at the end of the canoe journey, the nearly two months spent waiting at George River Post for the arrival of the long-delayed Hudson's Bay Company ship from London and the subsequent trip back to southern Ontario. In fact, she left her parents' home in Bewdley, Ontario, on 5 June 1905 and did not return to Montreal until 21 November. Her "before" and "after" narratives thus take up large sections at the beginning and end of her diary. Her book, however, simply introduces her husband as her reason for launching the expedition and then skips to her arrival at North West River Post on 25 June 1905 and her official departure by canoe two days later. It ends with her journey down the George River and arrival at George River Post exactly two months later on 27 August, wrapping up in one paragraph the seven weeks she spent at the post and the four weeks of her return journey via several steamships. This elision of the journeys "to" and "from" is conventional; many writers of travel narratives, including Jameson, make the same choice in order to focus on the part of the trip that they perceive as of most interest to readers.[23] In Hubbard's case, as in Jameson's, such narrow focus fills a secondary and more personal function. Just as it allows Jameson to avoid mention of her marital difficulties, so it permits Hubbard to avoid discussion of Wallace's expedition. Another effect of the curtailment of Hubbard's narrative is to cut short both her initial impressions of the four men who will be travelling with her and her reassessment of them in light of several months spent waiting for the ship. Instead, she can write about them only as they appeared on her journey – as the competent and even heroic men who brought her swiftly and safely on her chosen path.

The shortening of her narrative allows Hubbard to bookend her text in several ways, a bookending presaged by the cover illustration on the 1908 Murray edition of a canoe carrying a woman framed by caribou antlers, with a man paddling in front and back (fig. 1.1). Her text begins and ends with references to a man: her husband, Leonidas.[24] Her opening chapter tells readers in much more personal detail about her husband than it does about herself. The final chapter, "The Reckoning," justifies his failure by downplaying her own success. In it she claims that "if the season of unprecedented severity, in which my husband made his journey, could have been exchanged for the more normal one, in which I made mine, he would still have returned safe and triumphant" (236), and she suggests that the final entries in his diary in the hours before he died "turned his defeat to a victory" (237).[25] Hubbard thus begins and ends by purposefully undermining her own achievement. What she did, she writes, was for her husband's memory, and even his failures are more important than her successes.

As well as bookending her own narrative by references to her husband, his goals, and his previous journey, the British and Canadian first editions of Hubbard's text are framed by narratives written by three men. American autobiographical theorist Sidonie Smith uses an apt metaphor when she suggests that women's narratives were sometimes placed between "the initiating words" of one man and "the concluding words" of another because women's words, like women, "cannot be officially allowed to travel on their own" (13). In Hubbard's case, these initiating and concluding words take up more than a third of the 338 pages of the book and give it the sort of multiple authorship that is uncommon in men's travel narratives. The introduction is a 29-page disquisition by outdoor adventurer William B. Cabot, who describes Labrador, defends Leonidas Hubbard's expedition, and only briefly outlines Mina Hubbard's accomplishments when he focuses on her map and on the novelty of "a woman, slight, young" making such a trip with only "four Indians" as companions (28).[26] At the end of the book are 46 pages of excerpts from the diary Leonidas Hubbard kept on his trip in 1903 and 47 pages of a retrospective journal by Elson outlining Hubbard's last days and the recovery of his body. Mina Hubbard's inclusion of these masculine narratives bolsters her own authority; both her husband and an expert on Labrador travel (Cabot) endorse her tale by lending their words to introduce and frame it. Hubbard's book is also purposely relational, providing an outlet for both her husband's voice and one seldom heard, that of a Métis man.[27] Finally, the inclusion of both of the latter narratives emphasizes what she has been trying to convince readers of all along: that she is a stand-in for her husband, that this book is really about his earlier expedition, and that her narrative is in fact a post-mortem account of his success.

The fiction of joint authorship for Mina Hubbard's narrative cannot be kept up throughout the book, and the text indeed demonstrates repeated tension between her need to have the expedition interpreted as her husband's and her equally pressing need to have her writings recognized as authoritative enough to be influential in changing negative public opinion about him. Hubbard is more in control of the narratives of Elson and her husband than she lets on. Although the final narrative from Elson reads like a journal from 1903, she in fact asked him to write it early in 1905, in order to have an account, other than Wallace's, of her husband's final days and the recovery of his body, and thus she may have had the opportunity to edit it before publication.[28] As Sherrill Grace points out in her introduction to the scholarly edition of Hubbard's book, Hubbard also appears to have suggested changes to Cabot's introduction, including asking him to reduce mention of Dillon Wallace (235n20).

The choices that Hubbard makes in including her husband's diary in her book show a similar control. She states that her motive is "to complete my husband's unfinished work, and having done this to set before the public a plain statement, not only of my own journey, but of his as well. For this reason I have included in the book the greater part of Mr Hubbard's diary, which he kept during his journey, and which it will be seen is published exactly as he wrote it" (ix). To give her husband belated authorship, she incorporates most of his diary, and she states unequivocally that the diary is published "exactly as he wrote it." In fact, Leonidas Hubbard's diary was heavily edited for inclusion in his wife's book, in both length and content.[29] The editorial changes are as much designed to create a particular character for Hubbard's husband as her own writing is designed to situate herself. Her version of his diary begins with several lines that are not in the diary on the date claimed (LH Diary 7 July), but which represent him as romantic and eager: "Last night moonlight and starry and fine. This morning the shore of Labrador spread out before us in the sunshine. It calls ever so hard, and I am hungry to tackle it" (WW 239). Although Hubbard may have been metaphorically hungry to tackle Labrador, the physical hunger he encountered on his expedition is much more prominent in the diary. His words reveal him as obsessed both by what he is going to have at his next meal and by what he will eat once he returns home – not surprising in a narrative of starvation.[30] The deletion of many of these references to food softens the emotional impact of Leonidas's narrative and at the same time presents him in what might be a more flattering light. In effect, while Mina's narrative domesticates her own journey, alterations to her husband's narrative elide from his at least one aspect of the domestic.

The version of Leonidas Hubbard's diary in *A Woman's Way* was one of two published versions. The first, printed in March 1905 in *Outing*, the magazine for which Hubbard worked when he undertook his expedition, also shortens the diary, but in sometimes similar and sometimes remarkably different ways. While *Outing*'s version, edited by Caspar Whitney, omits many of the passages in which Hubbard dreams about eating, Mina Hubbard goes further and excises arguably interesting descriptions of food the men actually killed, cooked, and ate on the trail. She especially deletes references to food that may have seemed "uncivilized" but that was essential for the maintenance of health in subsistence conditions, such as guts of fish, caribou, and birds (LH Diary 24, 27 Sept., 11 Oct.). While *Outing* includes Hubbard's retrospective lists of the supplies he realized he should have taken on the trip (10, 14, 28 Sept.), *A Woman's Way* omits these lists and thus bolsters Mina Hubbard's assertion that his difficulties were caused by a "season of unprecedented severity" in which game was scarce (WW 236).

Other parts of her husband's diary that Hubbard deletes include those that might trivialize his journey or make him appear overly sentimental or less than heroic. Thus while *Outing* includes his references to his frequent illnesses, *A Woman's Way* omits those of 14 August and 31 September. And while *Outing* excises virtually all references to Hubbard's family and friends (11 Sept., 31 Aug., 4 Oct.), *A Woman's Way* consistently omits only positive references to Wallace (for example, 10 Oct.), while retaining those about Elson (20 July, 24 Aug., 5 Oct.).[31] That version also retains references to Mina and to the home she and Leonidas shared, such as this entry: "Have thought a good deal about home. It seems to me I'll never be willing to leave it again. I don't believe I'll want any more trips too hard for M. [Mina] to share. Her companionship and our home life are better than [the glory of] a great trip" (WW 273, LH Diary 18 Sept.).[32] By omitting the words "the glory of," which were present in the original diary, Mina Hubbard emphasizes her husband's joy in his relationship with his wife, while downplaying his hunger for recognition.

When she includes diary passages referring to food that Whitney omits from *Outing*, these passages almost invariably demonstrate Leonidas's emotional connection to his wife. Thus *A Woman's Way* includes the words, which *Outing* excludes, "I'd like to be home to-night and see my girl and the people, and eat some bread and real sweet coffee or tea or chocolate" (WW 254; LH Diary 15 Aug.), and "Dreamed last night came to New York, found M. [Mina] and had my first meal with her" (WW 282; LH Diary 15 Oct.).[33] Hubbard is cautious, however, about the extent of personal detail that she is willing to reveal. Of her husband's last diary entry, when he describes holding in his hand a can of mustard she gave him, she follows *Outing*'s lead in including the words "I sat and held it in my hand a long time thinking how it came from Congers & our home, and what a happy home it was," but omitting the phrase that follows: "& what a dear, dear girl presided" (18 Oct.).[34]

While Hubbard's professed goal is to allow her husband's own voice to be heard and thus to assert his authority over both their expeditions, her editing of his diary constantly undercuts that very goal. Instead, she suppresses part of her husband's voice in order to present a version of him as someone whose project is worthy of her sublimation of her own interests. Hubbard professes an implicit belief in the need for men's narratives to legitimate her own, but she then subverts her own beliefs by taking control over several of those narratives.

SAYING "I": PRIMACY AND THE LANGUAGE OF EXPLORATION

Hubbard's treatment of her husband's diary is one example of the negotiations she makes to justify her activities and downplay their unconventionality, while at the same time asserting the control over her journey and her texts that is necessary if her narratives are to be accepted as credible by the reading public. LaFramboise suggests that the changes made in the transition from diary to book represent "a careful textual negotiation of the discourses of exploration, femininity, and race, in order to produce and maintain the authority of the expedition's leader" ("Just a little" 18). Hubbard must indeed justify herself as a woman undertaking such a venture, but her book is called *A Woman's Way*, and much of the public interest in it is assumed to come because such a journey is an unusual venture for a woman. Indeed, many contempo-

2.5   *The Author*, frontispiece drawing by J. Syddall, *A Woman's Way through Unknown Labrador*. Courtesy of Betty Ellis

rary reviews stressed her gender in their analyses of her writing style, in effect praising her for writing like a woman. A 1908 review in the *Times Literary Supplement* praises her "restraint and modesty" and her "unpretentious method" ("Through Unknown Labrador"), while the *Western Mail* notes that her story is "charmingly told" and "filled with the unsophisticated wonder of it all": "These little womanly touches add infinitely to the charm of the story" ("Through Unknown Labrador"). For contemporaneous reviewers, it was important that Hubbard not only write like a woman but also appear to act like one even while participating in a potentially unladylike venture: "Mrs. Hubbard is not one of those semi-masculine ladies who astonish the reader by their courage in face of difficulties and the strength and perseverance with which they carry out their plans. We judge from her writings that she is timid and feminine to a degree; but the beauty of the book is that one can see how, in spite of the weakness of her sex, she, buoyed up by the great love she bore her husband, was enabled to carry her project to a triumphant issue" ("Country Life"). The *Evening Standard*'s reviewer also praises her for managing to "remain more woman than explorer": "She never seems to have been hardened as so many explorers, huntresses, and adventurers of her sex become hardened by these extraordinary toils" ("Love's Labour").

In only one of the four magazine articles Hubbard wrote and published before and concurrently with her book does she address the barriers placed in her way because of her gender. Each article is a draft of or excerpt from the book, tailored to meet the needs of her various audiences.[35] Her articles in two general-interest magazines, *Harper's Monthly Magazine* and *Windsor Magazine*, are the most similar in tone and wording to her book, although necessarily less detailed. These magazines catered to middle-class audiences interested in non-scientific accounts of travel, the main market for her book. While the *Harper's* article provides details of her meetings with the two groups of Innu, the *Windsor* account ends with her arrival at the headwaters of the George and Naskaupi Rivers, less than halfway through her journey, thus emphasizing the attainment of that goal. Both include photographs of the landscape and of herself in it, while the *Harper's* article contains a preliminary map of her party's route. Her article for the more specialized *Bulletin of the American Geographical Society* (an article reproduced with a change of title in the *Journal of the Manchester Geographical Society*) gives a much more detailed account of the topography of Labrador, including its lakes, rivers, and mountains, as well as its flora, fauna, and weather systems. This essay is accompanied by photographs of the landscape and the geographical features of Labrador, as well as by the detailed map later reproduced in her book. Her final article, in the *Englishwoman's Review*, is aimed specifically at women readers and thus personalizes her trip, especially in terms of what it meant to be a woman contemplating such a journey. Of the "dark days" that followed her husband's death, she writes: "I suppose no one will ever quite know with what a sickening sense of limitation I longed to be a man, so that I might go away and do the work to which my husband had given his life, and which his death left unfinished. But I was a woman, and it did not occur to me that I could do anything till that January day, when, as I sat looking out of the window, aching with a sense of my own littleness and impotence, suddenly something thrilled through my whole being ... [I]t came like a sudden illumination of darkness, and it meant, 'Go to Labrador' " ("Through Lonely Labrador" 82).[36] An almost religious "thrill" and "illumination" have allowed her to overcome the strictures of gender, which until this time have led her to characterize herself as both little (in the figurative as well as the literal sense) and powerless. She is not embarking on this journey of her own volition; instead, forces outside herself compel her to step outside gender barriers to lead the expedition.

Yet gender difference continued to play a part in her Labrador journey, as both the article and the book make clear. Typical is one incident that Hubbard details when, concerned about her safety as she overlooked the rapids, Elson told her that if she did not obey him and stay away from the river, "we will just turn round and go back to North-west River" ("Through Lonely Labrador" 85). Hubbard's response – "We had no further disputes on this subject" ("Through Lonely Labrador" 84) and "That settled the matter" (*WW* 70) – shows her initial concession to the restrictions placed upon her because of her gender. *A Woman's Way* goes on, however, to detail her eventual frustration with such strictures. "It began to be somewhat irksome to be so well taken care of," she writes after Elson, wary of a bear attack while they were portaging the supplies, told her to "sit right down there by the rifles" instead of fishing (85, 84).[37] Later, as in the *Englishwoman's Review* article, Hubbard several times wishes ineffectually that she were a man and thus had the right to participate in exploratory activities (87; MH Diary 9 Aug.).

Early in the book, Hubbard describes in detail the gear and food purchased and packed for the journey and her own mapping and record-

2.6 "Breakfast on Michikamau," *A Woman's Way through Unknown Labrador*. Courtesy of Betty Ellis

ing equipment, which included two cameras, a compass, a sextant, an artificial horizon, a barometer, and a thermometer. This passage indicates both that she was making essential decisions about the well-being of the expedition and that she hoped to accomplish the crucial work of measuring and mapping. Immediately following is a description of what she wore on the journey, down to her underwear, and of her inclusion of an air mattress, comforter, pillow, and hot water bottle in her luggage (53–4). The *Englishwoman's Review* article avoids reference to mapping equipment, but describes her sleeping gear in detail. These inclusions and omissions thus emphasize for her readers that she has taken the appropriate gear for a *woman* traveller. Later in the journey, she writes, "I ... wondered how I looked; but I was rather glad that I had no mirror with me, and so could not see" (88). Contemporaneous reviewer Munson Havens comments on the "naive femininity" with which Hubbard describes her dress and the comforts she brought with her (286), but the inclusion of these descriptive passages is in fact anything but naive. As Alison Blunt demonstrates in her book on Mary Kingsley's travels, conduct books such as Lillias Campbell Davidson's *Hints to Lady Travellers at Home and Abroad* (1889) "attempted to inform women how to maintain respectability while violating the codes of society by traveling beyond the domestic sphere" (68). Advice on what to wear made up a large part of that maintenance of respectability. Thus while Hubbard may be the leader of her expedition, like any respectable woman she must be well-dressed and comfortable. Her text stresses her femininity as a way of reassuring readers that she is not moving far from "home," her place as a woman.

Such reassurance is necessary in a narrative written by a woman travelling unchaperoned through "unknown" territory. Contemporaneous northern traveller Agnes Deans Cameron, by contrast, took a trip that was less challenging of norms (on a more established route and accompanying another, younger woman) and thus allowed herself to dress and act more daringly. While photographs in her book show that she wore a Mountie look-alike hat and jacket over a long, dark skirt, photographs of Hubbard show her in an ankle-length pleated skirt, a sweater over a high-necked blouse, and a floppy hat with a veil to keep out the insects (facing 142, fig. 2.6).[38] Similarly, while the frontispiece of Cameron's book is a photograph showing her holding the severed head of a moose she had killed, which was being butchered for her group to eat (fig. 2.2), Hubbard's frontispiece is a pen-and-ink drawing by J. Syddall that shows her in typically feminine and "civilized" pose and

2.7 "My Premier Moose," *The New North*

attire – her neck long and shoulders sloping; her face, in profile, remote and unsmiling; her hands (the capable part of her body) unformed; her clothing flowing and feminine, with a string of pearls around her neck, a brooch at her breast, and a flower at her waist (fig. 2.5). Cameron looks directly at the viewer, a position that photography theorists have suggested gives her power in her relationship with the viewer (Maxwell 13–14), while Hubbard's face is in complete profile and her eyes gaze toward the side of the page.[39]

Cameron feels comfortable enough with her position as woman traveller to portray what was considered a masculine pleasure associated with travel. A second photograph of the results of her hunting, labelled "My Premier Moose," shows a serious (and masculine-looking) Cameron holding a gun over the dead animal, while her smiling niece and three of the men of her party look on (347, fig. 2.7). Although it is clear from her narrative that she wanted to experience hunting, she represents necessity as her excuse for usurping this masculine role. In response to an imagined reader who might accuse her of cruelty, Cameron writes: "'Cruel!' you say. Well, just you live from mid-May

2.8   "Skinning the Caribou," photograph by Mina Hubbard. Courtesy of Betty Ellis

to mid-September without fresh meat" (348). Although Hubbard, in contrast, tells readers that she was carried away by the thrill of the chase to shoot at a bear (59), she never actually killed any of the food she ate, except an occasional fish (144, 147). The photographs of dead animals in her book, including ducks and a caribou, show them being handled by the men, not Hubbard (facing 94, 112; fig. 2.8). In her book, she tells readers that she did not like her first taste of porcupine (60) and that her "heart sickened" and she covered her eyes when a caribou was killed (112). Only in her diary does she note that she liked porcupine and even caribou gut on subsequent occasions (30 June, 8 July, 12 Aug.). Hubbard thus consciously creates a public persona of a woman explorer who may participate in adventure but always maintains her femininity and respectability.

That Hubbard experienced a personal as well as a rhetorical struggle between adventure and femininity is most evident in her representation of one episode when she was so discouraged by gender restrictions that, as she writes in the chapter titled "Scaring the Guides," she "ran away."[40] The running heads in the British and Canadian first editions indicate that Hubbard is relating a series of actions which began with frustration at rules that disallowed her the role of explorer and that culminated in an assertion of that role. Hubbard had earlier referred to her inability to assume the position of explorer by describing an occasion when Chapies assured her that a hill the men had just climbed "was altogether too steep and slippery" for her: "It seemed such an ignominious sort of thing too, to be an explorer, and have one of my party tell me I could not do something he had already done, and was about to do again, just for the mere pleasure of it" (109–10; see also MH Diary 21 July). The emphasis in this passage is on a putative explorer who was prevented, by her assumed weakness and delicacy, from conducting her explorations. Not only did the head guide, Elson, feel it his prerogative to control her behaviour for her own safety; so too did other members of the expedition. She earlier writes: "A new thrill came with this being up among the hill-tops, and I began to feel like an explorer" (101; see also MH Diary 13 July). The effect of this care and control is to diminish the "thrill" that initially propelled her into Labrador as an explorer.

In "Scaring the Guides," Hubbard writes that she proposed to walk alone up a mountain that the group had climbed earlier in the day, to take photographs while the others made one of their numerous portages around rapids. As frequent references in her diary and book indicate, an important part of her work was to provide a pictorial record of her trip; nevertheless, she writes, Elson agreed to her proposal only reluctantly, "with the manner of one who is making a great concession" (122). Hubbard set off equipped with "two kodaks, note-books, revolver and cartridges, bowie knife, barometer and compass" (122), and she went farther than she had promised she would venture. Her sense of challenging boundaries is evident in the metaphors she uses to characterize herself: first as a naughty child and then as an animal, both of whom have escaped from the walls and fences that enclose them. She set off, she writes, "with something of the feeling a child has who runs away from home" (124). She continued her explorations even though she knew that the men were searching for her: "I meant to go just as far as I could, before I was rounded up and brought into camp" (126). During her escape from the men, the flies were biting so hard that her ears and neck were wet with blood, but, she says, "what did flies matter when you were *free*" (127). Hubbard quotes Elson as reinforcing these characterizations of herself as child or animal loosed from house or corral by saying that as he watched her on the mountain, she looked "as busy as a Labrador fly" and "just like a little girl that was playing at building something" (130). The comment about the fly is also noted in Hubbard's diary, but the description of her as a "little girl" is either added from memory or inserted to emphasize her own characterization of herself as a child (28 July).

Several pages later in the book, Hubbard implicitly compares her own position to that of her guides when she also calls them children. She describes watching the men discuss a wood chip that they had found and writes, "How much a seeming trifle may mean to the 'Children of the Bush,' or for that matter to any other 'children,' who see the meaning of things" (141). Here, Hubbard is not just repeating a common trope, but also directly quoting her husband, who titled one of his essays "The Children of the Bush." Although she never uses the equally common expression "noble savage," she does emphasize an inclination toward poetry in such representations when she looks at a gravesite and asks, "Who could doubt that romance and poetry dwell in the heart of the Indian who chose this for the resting-place of his dead" (159).[41] In Hubbard's narrative, race is thus represented as being both similar to and different from gender in its restrictions and freedoms. Hubbard is like her male First Nations guides in that all are as children; she is different from them in that their childishness allows them, unlike her as a woman, to be inherently free.

When Elson and Chapies finally "catch" her (or, as the running heads announce, "Freed from My Guard" [123], "I Run Away" [125], "Recaptured" [129], and "I Am Admonished" [131]), she quotes the following bargain with Elson: "If I can have some one to go with me whenever I want to climb a mountain, or do anything else that I think it is necessary to do in my work, without any fuss about it, I promise not to go away alone again" (130). Hubbard finally acknowledges in this passage that she considers her work of measuring, mapping, and recording to be as important as or more important than her guides' work of canoeing, navigating, portaging, setting up camp, preparing meals – and protecting her. Before she can assert this view, she must first acknowledge restrictions and then negotiate their relaxation. In forcing this compromise, Hubbard is different from the usual woman traveller, as is evident from the comment she quotes Elson as making (transcribed almost word for word from her diary): "The men ... said they had been on lots of trips before, and where there were women too, and they said to me they never were on a trip before where the women didn't do what they were told" (130–1; see also MH Diary 28 July).

If gender forms a large part of the tensions in Hubbard's narrative, so too do race and class. Her negotiation of these issues often involves indicating to the reader by the use of the word "I" at key points in the narrative that, although inferior in gender, she is superior in race and class to the men she employs. In particular, when Hubbard wants to assert her primacy or her related figurative solitude, the "we" and "our" of the shared journey, as expressed in her diary, are converted in her published narrative to the "I" and "my" of the traditional explorer. Although Elson may be "the trusty hero whose courage and honour and fidelity made my venture possible, and who took from my shoulders so much of the responsibility" (55), it is "*my* plans and *my* directions and desires," she writes, that he will communicate to the other men (55; italics added). As my analysis of Jameson's *Summer Rambles* indicates, such representations of female solitude while travelling with male, First Nations companions are not uncommon. Indeed, when Cabot writes in his introduction to Hubbard's book that "she set forth, with her two canoes, from Hamilton Inlet" (26–7), he almost makes it appear as though she took her two canoes solo through the wilderness.

Both race and class enforce this metaphorical separation of her from the other members of her group. Exploration narratives by definition require such separation, since explorers can only claim primacy if they elide the presence of others, often of another race, who accompany or precede them. Hubbard thus can claim in her book to be the "first" only if she writes, and is written about, as though she is alone. The "firsts" that are described in her diary, in contrast, are less calculated, more genuinely emotional, and more accurate. She writes, for example, "I think I am getting some good pictures and am really enjoying the thought of the fact that I am the first to photograph the points of interest along this river as well as the first white woman to see it " (25 July) and, when she thinks of her husband, "I have to keep reminding myself all the time that I am the first of my kind to see it and I don't get any thrill out of it at all except only as I can make it honor him" (10 July). When the group reaches Seal Lake, her diary entry uses the first-person plural pronoun to include her companions: "we have seen the Nascaupee flowing out of [Seal Lake]" (17 July). In the book, "we" becomes "I" to describe not only her feelings but also the accomplishments of the expedition: "I had, too, not only seen Seal Lake, I had seen the Nascaupee River flowing out of it; ... and, best of all, there came the full realisation that *I* was the first in the field, and the honour of exploring the Nascaupee and the George Rivers was to fall to me"

2.9 "Where Romance Lingers," photograph by Mina Hubbard. Courtesy of Betty Ellis

(107). As her italicized "*I*" indicates, while her companions serve and accompany her, she is the first person – or, more accurately, the first person who counts – to act as explorer of this particular "field."

When Hubbard's narrative describes the group reaching the height of land where the waters, which have been flowing south, begin to flow north, what has been a team effort again becomes an individual one. Her companions are insignificant to the project because of their race and their gender, and thus their presence is elided. She writes herself as alone in the wilderness, as the differences between her accounts in diary and book of reaching this landmark show. In her diary, she records: "At 5 P.M. we embarked on a beautiful lake beyond it [the height of land] and at 6 we were at the head of a stream flowing N. The men were as much excited as I. When our little canoe touched shore just at the head of the stream, Job jumped out and ran down a piece to make really sure which direction the water was flowing and came back shouting 'Hā hā Jordan seepee'" (10 Aug.).[42] The published narrative, in contrast, removes all reference to the men's excitement and to Job's role in determining the direction of flow and identifying (in Cree) the stream as the beginning of the George River. Instead, Hubbard writes: "It was just 5 P.M. when, three hundred miles of my journey into the great, silent wilderness passed, I stepped out of the canoe to stand at last on the summit of the Divide – the first of the white race to trace the Nascaupee River to its source" (174; see similar wording in "Exploring Inner Labrador" 561). The strategic use of "my" and "I" makes it appear as though she is alone; because she is "the first of the white race," only her accomplishments matter.

"We" also becomes "I" after Hubbard experiences another milestone, the caribou migration. While in both diary and book she writes about the delight of the whole group in encountering the massive herds (MH Diary 8 Aug.; WW 164), the corresponding passage in A Woman's Way adds the claim, "I alone, save the Indians, have witnessed the great migration" (167). The "save the Indians" is the key point, of course, as is attested by her earlier description of her companions' joy and by the words of Mary Jane Pasteen, an Innu woman also known as Miste Mani-Shan. In an oral narrative made in 1976 and later transcribed, translated, and published, Pasteen, who was about Mina Hubbard's age and who lived in the area of the Ungava District that Hubbard visited, speaks of routinely killing caribou on their annual migration across the George River, to which she gives the Innu name Mushuau-shipu, or Barren Grounds River: "Whenever the caribou crossed the Mushuau-shipu and there were no men around, we women had to chase caribou by canoe. I would be in the front of the canoe with a spear. It was no problem to kill a caribou. A lot of women killed caribou in the water with spears or guns" (36). Hubbard's claim thus is accurate only if she includes her disclaimer about race, since not only had contemporaneous Innu women seen the caribou migration, but also they considered it "no problem to kill a caribou."

Throughout the book but more prominently toward its conclusion, the "we" of the companionable traveller turns into the "I" of the decision-maker. Hubbard writes, for example, about "anxious" hours and "sleepless" nights "as I tried to make my decision whether, in case it should become evident we could not reach Ungava in time, I should turn back, leaving the work uncompleted, or push on, accepting the consequent long winter journey back across Labrador ... and the responsibility of providing for my four guides for perhaps a full year" (178). Her decision, she says, was to "go on to Ungava whatever the consequences might be" (187). In reality, Elson and the other men continued to make decisions such as this one, several of them contrary to Hubbard's wishes. As she records in her diary, she wanted to return down the Naskaupi River, should they be forced to turn back, while the four men preferred returning by the more well-travelled Grand (or Hamilton) River route. Hubbard quotes her conversation with Elson verbatim, a conversation only obliquely alluded to in her book (197): "'Now if you refuse to take me back I cannot compell [sic] you to do it and I shall not try but you will record in my diary that I asked you to do so and you refused and state your reasons which you think are good.' He replied, 'Yes and I will be very willing to do that.' I said 'Alright. You can talk it over with the men and make your decision and let me know what it is.' To-night the decision is to make a big try to get down to Geo R. Post in time to catch the Pelican" (MH Diary 17 Aug.). As LaFramboise notes in her analysis of this passage, Hubbard needs to assert discursive authority in her book ("Just a Little" 41); on the journey itself, however, she cannot compel her experienced male guides to take a route they think unsafe. But she can manipulate gender codes by asking Elson to sign a document in which he admits that he is less daring than she is. At the same time, the decision, a compromise that the group will push forward rather than turning back, is left to him.

As another way of asserting her primacy on the expedition, Hubbard also downplays her worries, expressed in her diary, about the men's competence. Her concerns about Iserhoff's cough (17 June) and about the fact that the men once pitched her tent on a bear trail (15 July) and her worries that the men were not travelling fast enough and were taking too many breaks (6, 25, 26 July) do not find their way into the published version.[43] She does include a description of the near disaster when both Chapies and much of the equipment were nearly lost after a canoe capsized (79–81) because it provides cautionary excitement in an otherwise apparently safe trip and determines part of the subsequent route, including a stop at two trapping cabins (one belonging to Gilbert Blake's brother) to borrow supplies to replace those lost. She makes a joke of other potentially troubling incidents when the men, given the brandy bottle so that they "might have a bracer ... drank it all!" (132), and when she was angry at them for stretching out the last few minutes of the journey: "my strong desire was to take them by their collars and knock their heads together *hard*" (230). Hubbard suppresses most of her doubts; instead, she emphasizes her admiration of and confidence in her four guides. She writes: "They were gentle and considerate, not only of me, but of each other as well" (94), and "When you saw these men in the bush you needed no further explanation of their air of quiet self-confidence" (92).[44]

At the end of the book, the men who have been her companions are transformed into employees who must be protected and led by her. Hubbard's account of the group's arrival at George River Post initially emphasizes that her race and gender place her "first"; she writes that Mrs Ford, the blue-eyed factor's wife, greeted her with the words "You are very welcome, Mrs Hubbard. Your's is the first white woman's face I have seen for two years" (233–4). Only after Hubbard has walked to the house (or, according to her diary entry of 27 August, actually entered the house) does she consider the men who have been her companions and guides for the past two months, still waiting in the canoes. She writes: "Suddenly I realised that with our arrival at the post our positions were reversed. They were my charges now" (234). With the return to a settled community, Hubbard must assert her position as employer; gender hierarchies become unimportant, and class and race differences that seemed less significant during the journey must again restrict her behaviour and that of her companions. Hubbard was housed with the Fords – as were Wallace and his remaining white travelling companion, Clifford Easton, once they finally arrived – but Elson and his crew pitched their tents outside. While she expressed some regret about this separation ("As I watched them from the post window busy about their new camping ground, it was with a feeling of genuine loneliness that I realised that I should not again be one of the little party" [235; see also MH Diary 27 Aug.]), she recognized its essential correctness. As her diary indicates, she visited the tents only a few times, although she brought the men a hot water bottle and books, and occasionally they were invited to the house. On the voyage back in early November, she even enlisted their help in "rolling the barrels" aboard ship, thus reiterating that they were sometimes viewed as servants. If, as Terry Goldie writes, "the balance of power" often weighs in on race over gender (81), Hubbard's narrative indicates that it sometimes also clearly weighs in on class.

SEXUALITY AND VIOLENCE AS "STANDARD COMMODITIES"

By taking a trip accompanied only by men, and by men not of her own race or class, Mina Hubbard placed herself outside the bounds of cultural and social rules. According to Goldie, literature about indigenous peoples often represents them as possessing "an innate, natural sexuality, unbounded by the necessary restraints of civilization" (83). Hubbard was certainly aware of this representation, and her book employs several strategies that help to allay potential suspicion that sexual impropriety occurred during her trip, including paradoxical reference to what Edward Said calls the "standard ... commodity" of indigenous sexuality (190) and what Goldie identifies as the supplementary commodity of violence (15).

Speculation about a romantic relationship between Hubbard and Elson began before any of her published accounts appeared. Annie Wallace, Dillon Wallace's sister, wrote in a letter of 22 November 1905 that the "general opinion of people seems to be that Mrs H. & Geo. will get married. Whatever she may think, I feel sure that is what Geo. has had in mind" (A. Wallace, Letter). None of the contemporaneous reviews of Hubbard's book contain such speculation, however; instead, they focus on Hubbard's dedication to the memory of her dead husband. Conjectures about an intimate relationship between Elson and Hubbard became widespread after Pierre Berton began researching their trip in the 1970s. In a chapter of *The Wild Frontier* (1978), in his forward to the 1981 reprint of Hubbard's book, and in a 1985 film he narrated (*The Revenge of Mina Hubbard*), Berton speculated that Elson was in love with her. Since then, James West Davidson and John Rugge have reproduced and expanded upon Berton's speculations in their popular history of the Hubbard and Wallace expeditions, as have Clayton Klein in his fictional version of Elson's life and Randall Silvis in his dramatized portrayal of Mina Hubbard's expedition, while archival researcher Anne Hart believes that the two may have had a mutual love affair that did not survive the return to settled society.[45]

Certainly, Elson and Hubbard had a relationship that included the intimacy of a close friendship and collaboration. But much of the interest in that friendship by researchers today probably lies in a desire to convert the narrative of a woman's travel into a more traditional and acceptable narrative of heterosexual romance. Another aspect of that fascination is the taboo and even miscegenistic nature of such a relationship, which would have crossed barriers of class and race as well as offending contemporary morality. Because of these taboos, such a romance was unlikely, but the texts themselves also provide little evidence for such speculation. Hubbard's book in fact follows the pattern set in her diary by stressing her continued romantic obsession with her dead husband, which would have precluded any possibility of a new romance. The book's more subdued tone can be attributed both to a reticence about exposing such intense feelings to public scrutiny and to the fact that by the time it was published, Hubbard had travelled to England and met Harold Ellis, her second husband.

In her diary, Hubbard repeatedly notes that she "honored" and "almost worshipped" Leonidas Hubbard (23 July); that she was "lonely," "hungry," and "homesick" for her "sweetheart" (10, 26, 30 July); that only her work on the expedition kept her from being "utterly desperate" (5 July); and that she was not sure how she could live her life without her husband (5, 26 July, 25 Aug.). She writes in both book and diary that she wondered if "even in the larger higher life to which he has gone" (29 July), "sometimes he wished to be with me" (134), and she notes that she had trouble fishing because it reminded her of her husband (1 Aug., 137). Even in the last pages of her diary, when she has reached George River Post and any romance with Elson would have been well under way, she says that remembrances of life with Leonidas "filled my heart with that awful sense of loss and lonliness and longing. Oh what days they were [and] how beautiful all the world seemed then. Love & Hope grew round us then" (28 Aug.).[46] More than a month after her return to her temporary home in Williamstown, Massachusetts, she writes: "Stars so beautiful. Heart so hungry so hungry Oh so hungry. How his eyes would shine if he could stand by me now to tell me how proud he was of my success. Oh Laddie, dear precious beautiful Laddie I want you Oh I want you this beautiful Christmas eve. I love you" (24 Dec.).

Hubbard does not sound at all like a woman in love with another man, and thus researchers such as Berton and Davidson and Rugge speculate that the attachment was one-sided on Elson's part. The textual evidence from Elson's diary to support such an argument is, however, either inconclusive or absent. Elson describes Hubbard as "bright" and "smart" (GE Diary 17, 28 July), "a dear little Lady" (23 Aug.), a "[d]ear little woman" (30 Oct.), and "nice" and "good" to him and the other men (17, 28, 30 July). He also says she is like a "sister" (28 July, 23 Aug.), a "good friend" (28 July), and even "my best friend in the world" (30 Oct.). A typical entry reads: "Mrs Hubbard is doing well, and I like her so very much. She is really nice to us. I cannot speak enough good things about her. Oh I do wish I will be able to bring her out safe again" (30 July). None of these descriptions smacks of explicit sexual or romantic interest, and Davidson and Rugge therefore speculate that Elson wrote his most personal feelings in several pages that were cut out of his diary and in another notebook, to which he repeatedly refers with the notation "see other book." Elson gave his primary diary to Mina Hubbard for use in drafting her book, and he may indeed have concealed or removed personal sections; certainly, a number of pages are missing from the diary. Since the "other book" has never been found, evidence of a relationship between Hubbard and Elson remains speculative.

Several quotations from Elson's diary that Davidson and Rugge claim point most definitively to Elson's infatuation with Hubbard (322–3) are reproduced in their book without contextual material that might put their theory into question. They quote Elson as writing that he and Hubbard were "talking about some things [of] great importance," and that he "could not sleep" because he was "thinking lots of new plans": "What a happy life if it would really happen. New plans. So good of her to think of so kind thoughts of me" (7 Sept.). They do not indicate that Elson has written vertically in the left-hand margin beside this passage that "this is something about Margrette." He had written in his diary the day before, "Mrs Hubbard and I were wondering if Margrette was still in Congors [sic]" (6 Sept.), and Roberta Buchanan, who has edited Hubbard's and Elson's diaries for publication, speculates that "Margrette" or Margaret may have been a servant girl from Hubbard's marital home in Congers, New York, whom Elson met when he visited Hubbard (Buchanan, Interview). Thus Elson may have been considering the possibility of marrying Margaret, or of Mina Hubbard promoting such a match, when he wrote: "I would like now to get married this fall, if I was lucky enough. What if I could strik [sic] luck and could get a white girl that would marry me, and especially if she was well learnt we then could write some nice stories, because she would know lots more then I would. [B]ut not likely I will be so luckly [sic]" (31 Aug.). A marriage between Elson and a servant girl would at least not have offended class sensibilities or contemporary notions of morality, as would a relationship with Hubbard. Of course, it is also possible that Elson wrote in the margin "this is something about Margrette" in order to mislead Hubbard (who, he knew, would be reading his diary), when she was in fact the "well learnt" woman he was thinking of marrying. Certainly, Hubbard took an interest in his childhood stories, which she believed might make the basis for a boy's adventure book (MH Diary 20 July).

That Hubbard feared speculation about a sexual liaison with one of her guides is evident in the cautious wording of her book. Descriptions in her diary of personal time spent with Elson are often absent from the published version of the journey: Elson taking her hand to help her up or down a hill (2, 3, 8 Aug.; 163), giving her flowers (9 July), paddling alone with her in a canoe or kayak or climbing hills with her (21, 25 July, 8 Aug, 9, 19 Sept., 2, 7 Oct.), teaching her to speak "Indian" (6 Aug.), and talking about his childhood diaries (20 July). In contrast, Hubbard retains mention in the published version of the fact that Gilbert Blake brought her a dandelion (13 July; 100). Because she has repeatedly characterized him as a child, she can include reference to his kindness without provoking speculation about a relationship between the two of them. Yet she omits from her book the fact that Job Chapies also often did kind things for her, "and in such a pretty way" (MH Diary 6 Aug.). Although it is possible that the omission of interactions with Elson might be evidence of a romantic relationship that she is trying to conceal, it seems more likely that Hubbard omits innocuous kindnesses on the part of Elson and Chapies purposely to preclude conjecture.

The closest she comes to expressing personal feelings about Elson is when she writes in her diary that she is disappointed in some of his actions and hopes that he will live up to his "possibilities" (21 Sept., 15 Oct.). Hubbard was especially unhappy when she learned that dogs had taken the caribou skin, left in Elson's keeping, which was her only "souvenir" from the more northerly Innu camp: "Felt awfully bad about it and do yet ... The one thing I had from the Nascaupees but the loss of the skin does not bother me near so much as what that and a lot of other things indicate in him. Did not sleep much more than half the night last night thinking about them. He has in him such great possibilities but am afraid he is not going to come up to them" (21 Sept.). Hubbard was not only concerned about what she perceived as Elson's lack of responsibility; she was also suspicious that he was planning to write his own account of the trip, as the next day's entry makes clear. She considered asking him "to sign an agreement not to write anything about the trip without my written consent and approval" (22 Sept.). The last part of the diary, written while she waited for the ship at George River Post, is much more taken up with the difficulties of writing an account of her journey than with details about her friend-ship with Elson. A typical entry reads: "Writing to-day. Slow. Hard to decide what to write about. Afraid of writing what people are not at all interested in and being thought silly or rather a bore. Wish I knew a bit better what public is interested in. Suppose best way is to write everything and then cut out" (31 Aug.). Hubbard in fact mentions that she is writing, or trying to write, and worries about the quality of her prose and her methods of writing, in at least every second diary entry while at George River Post.[47]

Throughout both book and diary, she consistently describes Elson through her husband's eyes, writing, for example, that "George was always the gentle, fun-loving, sunny-tempered man my husband had admired" (WW 94–5). The men in general she represents as her "brothers," as well as people she thinks about in terms of her husband: "no one, except Laddie, was ever more thoughtful and kind to me than they have been" (MH Diary 10 July). And she often describes Chapies in almost as glowing detail as she does Elson. Elson may have been "Great Heart," but Chapies, who was the expert in whitewater canoeing, was "Eagle" (MH Diary 7 Oct.). According to Hubbard, he had "wonderfully fine eyes," was "quick, clever" (92), "brave and full of energy," "capable," "gentle and courteous and thoughtful" (3 Aug.), and "wonderful" (22 Aug.): "Job is a whole host in himself. We have come thus far under his guidance and have as yet not made a single mis-step" (5 Aug.).

As she does with Elson, Hubbard considers her relationship with Chapies in terms of how her husband would have thought of him; she writes: "He grows more wonderful to me every day. How Laddie would have admired and liked him" (23 Aug.). Her representation of him is also linked to notions about race current at the time. Chapies was the only "pure blood Cree Indian" of the group, the only one who did not speak much English, and thus to Hubbard he was naturally closer to nature and more able to navigate his way through it. She respected those navigational skills; she writes, "He loved to pole up a rapid or hunt out a trail just as an artist loves to paint" (73), and that while shooting down a series of rapids on the George River that were as steep as a toboggan run, "[h]is eyes fairly blazed ... And yet he loves it as all men or most of them love to do things that are hard to do which they can do well" (22 Aug.).

Hubbard provided herself with a disclaimer that there was no sexual relationship between herself and her male companions by requiring them to sign a statement to that effect at the end of her diary and by herself signing a similar statement at the end of Elson's diary. Although the passage in Hubbard's diary, dated 16 September, is in Elson's handwriting, Hubbard probably drafted it, since she notes in her diary entry of the previous day that she had asked the men if they would be willing to make such a declaration. The statement is not explicitly worded, but its intention is clear; each man declares that he "at all times treated Mrs Hubbard with respect" and that "Mrs Hubbard was always treated with respect by the other men of this Party." Each also promises that he will "never by look or word or sign lead any human being to believe that during the trip there was anything in the conduct of Mrs Hubbard and her party towards each other which was unbecoming honorable Christian men and woman." Using very similar wording, Hubbard wrote in the back of Elson's journal that "he at all times treated me with respect and as an honorable Christian man," and she promises that she "will never by word or look or sign lead any human being to believe that he ever otherwise treated me." Since Hubbard kept both her diary and Elson's, she possessed sworn statements denying any sexual impropriety.[48] Thus she had documentation for anyone who might have suspected that she carried what Karen Lawrence has called "the female traveller's particular baggage [which] includes the historical link between female wandering and promiscuity" (16n18).

That the four men also recognized the explicitly sexual aspects of intersections of race and gender is evident not only in the fact that they signed the statement but also in their concern that she return unscathed from this journey. After she has "run away," Elson tells her that if she had been killed, none of the men would have been able to go back to their homes (131). The unstated implication is that if she were to die, the public presumption might be not just that her four guides were incompetent but also that they might have raped and murdered her.[49] Both she and her guides understood the trope of white women's fear of indigenous male sexuality and, in fact, discussed it obliquely when they were about to meet a group of Innu. Her stereotypical and thus fearful views of unfamiliar First Nations peoples (and the almost equally fearful views of her companions) are evident in her descriptions of the group's preparations for meeting the Innu, which at first puzzled Hubbard (182). She quotes Blake (who, she writes, was familiar with the Innu) as saying that the more northerly Innu "would not kill you, Mrs Hubbard. It would be to keep you at their camp that they would kill us" (183; see also MH Diary 14 Aug.). She is again reminded that should she be killed on the trip, her guides would be blamed; she writes that "remembering their agony of fear lest some harm befall me ere we reached civilisation again, I realised how the situation seemed to the men" (184).

Even Hubbard's indigenous and Métis guides recognized that sexuality and violence were components of the standard representations of First Nations peoples. Hubbard reports that the men were afraid because the groups they might encounter were strangers, and they feared a repeat of incidents they had read and heard about, such as the "Hannah Bay massacre," which had occurred in 1832 in the area where Elson, Chapies, and Iserhoff lived.[50] In her book, Hubbard quotes her assertion to the men that she was willing to engage in battle against these unknown but presumably dangerous peoples: "You do not need to suppose that because I will not kill rabbits, or ptarmigan, or caribou, I should have any objection to killing a Nascaupee Indian if it were necessary" (183).[51] She emphasizes her responsibility for the expedition (and the narrative) by expressing her willingness to meet violence with violence, an assertion that is absent from her diary entry describing this conversation.

The alterations in the wording of this incident from the diary to the British and Canadian editions of her book and to the American edition serve to justify this fear and proposed violence. The diary entry of 14 August notes only that Hubbard was oiling her gun "ready for encounter with Nascaupees if there is trouble." The identical Murray and Briggs editions of 1908 assert that she was "turning over in my mind plans of battle in case we should meet with treachery" (184), while the McClure edition published later the same year concludes with the words "in case the red men proved aggressive" (152).[52] This change in wording is significant, since Hubbard was, for her time and place, remarkably non-stereotypical in her descriptions of First Nations peoples. Her texts can be contrasted with those of her husband, who in his published writing makes use of terms such as "squaw" and "red man" ("The Children of the Bush" 536–7); Wallace, who uses expressions such as "red man" (LLT 1), "squaw bread" (39), and "savage" (215); Duncan, who writes in her fictionalized travel account of a "brave of the tomahawk" whose "countenance was not noble, aquiline, or red, but basely squat" and who was probably called "Left-Wing-of-a-Prairie-Chicken" or "He-Who-Stands-Up-and-Eats-a-Raw-Dog" (Social Departure 27–8); and numerous other writers whose use of terms such as "dusky" and "tomahawk" is "immediately suggestive everywhere of the indigene" (Goldie 10).[53]

Hubbard did stereotype Cree and Innu in one obvious way, by referring to their languages by the common term "Indian." She in fact knew that her three James Bay guides and the people she encountered in the Ungava District came from differing cultural groups, and that although their speech was of the same language group (Algonquian), it had some differences. Occasionally she even quotes the three older men speaking in Cree – "*Ma-losh-an!* (fine! fine!)" (60); "*Tanta sebo?* (Where is the river?)" (190) – and she includes a list of Cree and Innu words and phrases at the end of her diary. When referring to the people themselves, rather than to their languages, Hubbard often does make cultural divisions. She follows the lead of previous and contemporaneous ethnographers (such as Cabot, Introduction 10) in dividing the Innu into two separate groups, calling the more southerly ones "Montagnais" and the more northerly "Nascaupee." In fact, the geopolitical division of the territory in which they lived and subsequent ethnographic categorizations of the two groups had enforced an inaccurate cultural separation, as Hubbard partially acknowledges when she writes that "the two camps are friendly and sometimes visit each other" (192). A little more than twenty years after Hubbard's visit, anthropologist William Duncan Strong observed that the Montagnais and Naskapi were in reality one people with one language, of the same language group as Cree, so that Elson, Chapies, and Iserhoff could understand both Innu groups when they spoke. Instead of using the (arbitrary) names given by earlier British and French Canadian travellers, Strong locates these people geographically, calling the more southerly group the Davis Inlet band and the more northerly the name they called themselves, the Barren Ground People (57).[54]

For Hubbard, then, the alteration of the unspecified "trouble" that she fears from the Naskapi, as noted in her diary, to the more politically charged "treachery" and to the general pejorative aggression of "red men" must be a specific strategy either on her part or on that of her editors to emphasize the threat of violence. Fear of violence is common in literature about indigenous peoples; Cameron, for example, is fascinated by reports of cannibalism (276–8, 363–5). Hubbard's text shows that the first Innu group she met themselves feared violence from outsiders; the group was composed mostly of women and children, who were terrified of Hubbard's party. The previous fears of Elson, Chapies, Iserhoff, and Blake thus were completely unwarranted, and Hubbard's inclusion of those fears in her narrative paves the way for an element of comedy in her description of that meeting.

While her diary entry notes only that the women screamed and shouted in fear (17 Aug.), her published version of the incident quotes their words – "'Go away, go away,' they shrieked. 'We are afraid of you. Our husbands are away'" (189) – and Elson's reply: "We are strangers and are passing through your country" (190). Because she could not

2.10 "Indian Women and Their Home," photograph by Mina Hubbard. Courtesy of Betty Ellis

understand what was being said, Hubbard relied on observations in Elson's journal:[55] "When we got near the shore they sung out Who are you? go way go way we are afriad [*sic*] of you waving some things they had in their hands. Our husbands are all away. All the men are off, and we are afriad [*sic*] of you. I sung out to them, dont be afriad [*sic*] we are only travelling about we will not hurt you. We want you to tell us something about this river" (GE Diary 17 Aug.). Hubbard emphasizes in her narrative that at the end of the visit, the women were no longer fearful, by referring to the trope of the naturally sexual indigene. In a detail that is absent from both her diary and Elson's, and also from the description of the meeting published earlier in *Harper's*, she writes in her book that the Innu women "were anxious to have the visit prolonged, and every inducement was held out even to offering them wives, temporary, if they would remain" (194–5). According to Hubbard's account, the men refused the offer, and the implication is that this refusal was on moral as well as practical grounds: not only were they Christians, but also they had to push on as soon as possible to meet the ship at George River Post. They were flattered by the offer, however; as they left the camp, Hubbard writes, Chapies stood in the canoe, took off his hat, bowed, and called out, "Good-bye, good-bye, my lady" (195).

Several brief Innu accounts of the first meeting with Hubbard's party exist, gleaned from oral reports made in 1927 and 1967 and first published in 1994 and 1969 respectively. In the report from 1967, Shushep (Joseph) Rich repeats the story of Mrs Hubbard as told to him by his mother. This account of the meeting coincides with at least the first part of Elson's and Hubbard's accounts:

> During their journey they met many Indians, but the Indians never did any harm to them. They went deep into the bush and came to a place named Kamu-shuast [or Kamushuasht, which Hubbard called Montagnais Point]. Missus Hubbard met my mother there.
>
> There were no men in the camp, only women. All the men had gone to Davis Inlet. My mother said that Missus Hubbard called out to them.
>
> "We were afraid of them," my mother said, "but they called out to us, 'Don't be afraid. We are human.'" ...
>
> Missus Hubbard passed by and went down the [George] river and they came to other Indian camps. They were taking photographs of the Indians and the Indians didn't do any harm to them. (78)[56]

In the Innu account of the meeting, Elson not only told the women not to be afraid but also said, "We are human." The women may not have been reassured to hear, as Hubbard wrote, that her group consisted of "strangers," but they would have been heartened to hear that these were "humans" – in other words, people like them.

Another account of the meeting, paraphrased by Strong in his 1927–28 journals (unpublished until 1994), also notes that only women and children were present: "The Cree Indians with Mrs. Hubbard were able to converse with the Davis Inlet women and according to my informants, these guides were very anxious to find out what sort of reception they might expect from the Naskapi farther to the north. Skwish, the mother of Shū'shebish [Joseph Rich], told them that the Naskapi would not hurt them and, after the brief visit described in Mrs. Hubbard's vivid account, they went on" (56). In this account, the fear experienced by Hubbard's group is emphasized more than the fear felt by the Innu women. Strong also writes that although Hubbard indicated that the Naskapi, once she did meet them, told her that they could not move south to hunt for caribou because it was not their country, "no sooner had Mrs. Hubbard gone on than the entire band moved south to where the Davis Inlet band were then camped and lived with them through September and October" (56). He thus notes the inaccuracy of Hubbard's assumption that these were two separate, if friendly, cultural groups. Rich's narrative points out the same inaccuracy, since his mother apparently learned of the activities of Hubbard's party after they left Kamushuasht by speaking to members of the other Innu group.

Nowhere in either Innu account is the offer of "wives, temporary" mentioned. According to Sara Mills, it would have been "improper" for a woman travel writer such as Hubbard "even to allude to sexual matters" (22). Hubbard may have included this "improper" detail to divert readers from consideration of her own potential sexual activity and toward consideration of more socially acceptable sexual liaisons, since according to the ideology that lumps all indigenous groups together, such liaisons would at least be intra-racial. In Hubbard's account of the meeting, the commodities of potential violence and sexuality add popular interest and serve as possible substitutes for subjects that Hubbard would prefer not to broach. The subjects that she intends to broach, meanwhile, are evident not only in her text but in the accompanying photographs.

HUBBARD'S PHOTOGRAPHIC PROJECT AND THE DISCOURSES OF ETHNOGRAPHY AND LANDSCAPE

The forty-nine mostly full-page photographs included in Hubbard's book provide a striking complement to the written narrative of her Labrador journey and to the unwritten narrative of relations of power that can be read between the lines of her book. These photographs have been studied only briefly for their contribution to the "structural multiplicity" of her text (Grace, "A Woman's Way" 196; see also Grace's introduction to WW lv–lix). Hubbard intended the photographs, taken with a folding pocket Kodak and a panoramic Kodak, to serve as a record of her journey and as concrete evidence of the topography of the countryside through which she travelled and the ethnography of the peoples she encountered. The portable Kodak, invented by George Eastman in 1888, just seventeen years before Hubbard's journey, made it possible for travellers to carry cameras with them on arduous trips. Although Hubbard's were not the first photographs of Innu people, they were the first from that part of the Ungava District. Mills writes that women travellers, like men, often included photographs and maps in their travel narratives in order to prove that they did indeed travel where they claimed to have gone (113). Hubbard's images provide such proof regarding the landscape, the First Nations people she met, her four guides, and herself.

When she first saw the developed photographs several months after the return of the expedition, Hubbard was delighted with their quality. She wrote in her diary: "My pictures came to-day and they are wonderful. Feel all excited about them they are so fine. I have never seen such pictures anywhere as some of them are. I think there are none in existence can equal some of them. So glad so glad they are good" (25 Dec.). Several contemporaneous reviewers also praised the photographs, and indeed, they are of much higher quality than most travel photographs of the era. The *Geographical Journal* called them "excellent" ("Labrador" 614); the *Spectator* claimed that they were "as beautiful as they are rare" ("A Woman Explorer" 473); and the *Western Mail* noted that "the only keen regret that the book causes us [is] that amongst the many admirable photographs there is none of the caribou migration" ("Through Unknown Labrador"). Hubbard herself lamented, "I haven't half as good pictures [of the caribou] as I might" (MH Diary 16 Aug.). She also wrote that her "great regret concerning pictures is that they cannot give the color" (19 July). Her photographs do provide "color," however, by offering a complex picture of the social relationships that were part of her journey.

Although Hubbard is never directly credited, she is implicitly represented as the author of all the photographs. Elson notes in his diary, however, that he "took Mrs Hubbards [*sic*] picture" (6 Aug.) and a few days later that he "took her pictur [*sic*] three times" while she was doing her washing (9 Aug.). Wallace's publishers note whenever photographs were taken by his "white" companions,[57] but Hubbard's publishers never credit her Métis companion as author of the seven images of her that appear in the book. Elson is thus both an acknowledged collaborator in *A Woman's Way*, through his retrospective 1903 narrative, and a doubly unacknowledged collaborator in the 1905 portion of the narrative: Hubbard used his diary and his interpretation of Innu words to flesh out her own notes, and she published his photographs. Her book thus elides part of his contribution to the process of describing and illustrating the 1905 journey, although it also indicates the fascinating intimacy of the collaborating pair, an unconventional relationship further complicated by the triangulation of their separate relationships with Hubbard's husband.

Hubbard's contribution even to photographs in which she appears was of course substantial, since she probably set up most of those scenes and thus retained control over the way she was portrayed. The photographs of her illustrate two conflicting characterizations with which her book also grapples: that her behaviour on the journey was properly feminine and that she was "first" in terms of her guides and the First Nations peoples she met in Labrador. In order to make those points, the images, like the text that surrounds them, must assert both Hubbard's femininity and her control over the expedition. Thus the photographs of Hubbard show her alternately in feminine, domestic roles and doing the work of explorer, mapper, and expedition leader. Hubbard is portrayed in three photographs engaged in typical womanly activity – washing clothing in a basin (facing 78, fig. 2.11); sitting in the centre of a loaded but stationary canoe, her face covered by mosquito netting (facing 100); and cooking before a fire, even though she seldom cooked (facing 142, fig. 2.6). These photographs complement and reinforce the frontispiece portrayal of Hubbard as delicate and feminine. In contrast, two other photographs stress her active part in the expedition – striding along the trail carrying what appears to be a rifle (facing 88, fig. 2.1) and standing in a wind-blown camp while the men recline at her feet (facing 152). None of the photographs of Hubbard show her in as masculine a role as the image of Cameron holding a gun over a moose (347, fig. 2.7), in part because Hubbard's unchaperoned status means that she must be more guarded in her self-representation. But her book does include two photographs that emphasize attainment of two of her "firsts": her contact with the Innu (facing 210, fig. 2.12), and her arrival at her planned destination, George River Post (facing 232, fig. 2.3).

The photograph of arrival at the post corresponds exactly with the written description in *A Woman's Way*. Hubbard is pictured, as the narrative describes, wearing her waterproof sealskin boots, using a paddle as support against the treacherous mud, and being helped out

2.11 "Washing-Day," *A Woman's Way through Unknown Labrador*. Courtesy of Betty Ellis

of the canoe by the agent, Mr John Ford. As her text also indicates, all four of her travelling companions are still in the two canoes. But unlike the spontaneity implied by the narrative and by the caption, "The Arrival at Ungava," this seemingly spontaneous scene has been carefully orchestrated. As Elson notes in his diary entry of 7 September, their arrival on 27 August was restaged eleven days later

2.12 "With the Nascaupee Women," *A Woman's Way through Unknown Labrador.* Courtesy of Betty Ellis

in order that a photograph could be taken. (He writes, "fine day got our picture taken as when we arrived.") During that restaging, the men are shown waiting in the canoes while Hubbard is the first to set foot on land at their destination. She must be seen to be not only the first white woman but also the first of her expedition to step on the ground.[58] Although she was short of film, she had earlier made a point of saving one exposure so that she could document this occasion (MH Diary 26 Aug). Again, the photographer of this scene is not credited, but must have been someone from Ford's household or contingent.

The one photograph of Hubbard with the Innu also represents a first, although of a different kind. It pictures her standing on a rock, her hand raised and her index and middle fingers pointed, apparently lecturing to (or at least talking to) the Naskapi women. Again she is first: not only the first white woman to speak to the Innu of this area but also, in this photograph, dominant in terms of her physical position. She stands above them; her raised hand and pointed fingers indicate that she is saying something of import. Contact and communication with First Nations peoples is an essential part of her work and, the photograph implies, such contact and communication was successful. Her narrative, in contrast, indicates that communication was difficult and incomplete, since she could not understand or speak Innu-aimun. She writes, "I could make almost nothing of what they said, and when I called George to interpret for me they seemed not to want to talk" (211).[59] Hubbard was unsure how to approach the women and decided on an overture that she viewed as universally socially acceptable: admiring a baby. As a result, she writes, "[a]lmost immediately ... I was surrounded by nearly the whole community of women who talked rapidly about the babe and its mother" (211).

Hubbard spent only a few hours with each of the two Innu groups, but her book includes twenty pages of description of them and nine photographs. Although most reviewers applauded the information she was able to provide, Millais in *Nature* deprecated the dearth of "ethnological notes," calling the book unsatisfactory because it did not provide "firsthand observations of [the] ... ways of the wild races" (402). Contrary to this criticism, Hubbard's textual and pictorial ethnographic records do illustrate the two Innu groups' dress, dwellings, and way of life. Many of these records focus on women, however, which may be the source of Millais's discontent. Photographs of the first group show women and children (facing 194, 312), tents (facing 188), and what one caption identifies as "A Montagnais Type" (facing 320, fig. 2.13) wearing what Hubbard describes as a traditional head scarf, with a large crucifix around the neck. In contrast to many ethnographic photographs of "types," this person is pictured looking directly at the camera, as are several other people in the background. Thus, although the viewer is invited to gaze, the pictured person is allowed to gaze back. This reciprocal effect is uncommon in ethnographic photography (Maxwell 13; see

2.13 "A Montagnais Type," photograph by Mina Hubbard. Courtesy of Betty Ellis

also E.A. Kaplan 9–10). More typical is Cameron's photo of "A Slavi Type" in which a woman is framed as in a portrait, but gazes to the left of the frame rather than at the viewer (184, fig. 2.14).

Australian photography theorist Anne Maxwell contends, "Most of the photographs of colonized peoples produced in the late colonial period ... empowered Europeans by upholding the binary opposition of civility versus savagery" (14). Hubbard's photographs are less rigidly divided in that they show a traditional way of life – caribou skin clothing

2.14 "A Slavi Type from Fort Simpson," photograph by Agnes
Deans Cameron

and tents – existing simultaneously with encroaching civilization in the
form of trade and religion – cloth kerchiefs and crucifixes. Photographs
of the second group of Innu present the men wearing skin clothing and
holding a wooden paddle (facing 10, 202) and the women and children
wearing cloth and skin clothing and standing in front of a caribou-skin
tent (facing 24 [fig. 2.10], 214). Hubbard's textual descriptions of the
Innu often pivot on intersections of civilization and savagery, however,
evidenced by matters of dress, grooming, cleanliness, and display of
religious artifacts. The women's clothing is described as being "of a
quite civilised fashion" (190), while both women and children, although

"not scrupulously clean ... were not dirtier than hundreds of thousands to be found well within the borders of civilisation, and all, even the little children, wore the crucifix" (191).

Like other ethnographers, Hubbard is interested in manners and customs. She writes that one woman looked different from the others and speculates that she had come as a bride from another cultural group (210). She notes that the old women "were apparently important people in the camp" (210). She relates that the Naskapi chief absent-mindedly examined his daughter's head for lice while saying goodbye – "Apparently it was as much a matter of course as eating" (214) – and that even the old women smoked tobacco (207). When one of the young men seemed to want her to notice his red leggings, she wrote: "Even in barren Labrador are to be found little touches that go to prove human nature the same the world over" (208). [60]

Hubbard, like other writers about indigenous populations, "types" the Innu by representing them as both childlike (195) and "animal like" (191). She writes that "the types were various as those to be found in other communities ranging from the sweet and even beautiful face to the grossly animal like" (191). She portrays the Naskapi men as having "markedly Indian faces" and describes them alternately as noble savages (although she never uses that exact phrase) – "tall, lithe, and active looking, with a certain air of self-possession and dignity which almost all Indians seem to have" (203) – and as a collective and stereotyped "mind" – "I could not know how far the Indian mind had been influenced, in gauging the distance [to George River Post], by a desire to reduce to the smallest possible limit the amount of tobacco the men would need to retain for their own use" (212–13). Hubbard also occasionally "types" the Innu by reference to the picturesque and beautiful of landscape discourse, because for her, as for other explorers, indigenous peoples are in some respects part of the landscape. She writes of the Innu women, "Both the manner of wearing the hair and the *tuque* were exceedingly picturesque" (190).

Hubbard's description of the Innu can be compared to Wallace's account of those he met: "It was a picturesque group ... the women quaint and odd" (*LLT* 134). Wallace then takes this typing several steps further by repeating something he has heard: "The women are generally squatty and fat, and the greater a woman's avoirdupois the more beautiful is she considered" (136). In Cameron's book about her trip north, she also includes ethnographic descriptions and photographs that document what she perceived as a disappearing way of life. She photographs Inuit and Indian crafts, clothing, and tools (106, 235, 245, 247, 338); a tent with a moose hooked to a sled in front of it (121); modes of transportation such as a dogsled (115), birchbark canoes (125), and kayaks (254); and "The World's Last Buffalo" (147). Her descriptions of people are presented as testing "text-book" accounts, which she finds wanting: "'The Eskimo is a short, squat, dirty man who lives on blubber,' said text-books we had been weaned on, and this was the man we looked for. We didn't find him" (212). Her description of Inuit thus can be contrasted to Wallace's: "If some of the men that I saw in the North were dressed like Japanese or Chinese and placed side by side with them, the one could not be told from the other – so long as the Eskimos kept their mouths closed" (*LLT* 217).

Not all of Hubbard's photographs of people are ethnographic records; some demonstrate the work necessary for the success of such an expedition. Thus she includes photographs of Elson, Chapies, Iserhoff, and Blake canoeing, traversing rapids, skinning caribou, smoking meat, cooking bannock, and portaging canoes and supplies. One portage photograph, ironically labelled "The White Man's Burden" (facing 18), is placed in Cabot's introduction to illustrate a claim he makes that large amounts of provisions are necessary when white men, but not First Nations men, travel. A similar photograph by Cameron, in comparison, is titled simply "Portage at Grand Rapids Island" (63). While Hubbard's text has earlier named the four men who accompany her and has identified their cultural origins, her photographic portraits of the men give them faces as well as names (although the caption under Elson's portrait is the only one that includes his family name). Grace comments that the portraits "are remarkable because they grant visual presence and individual importance" to Native men ("A Woman's Way" 196). Elson and Chapies in particular are pictured looking directly at the camera, again conferring on them some power in the encounter with the viewer. Even the portraits, however, show the men in relation to their work: Elson sitting among a pile of portaged supplies (facing 54, fig. 2.4); Chapies paddling the canoe, his pipe clenched tightly in his mouth (facing 60, fig. 2.15); Iserhoff holding freshly killed game (facing 94); and Blake laughing as he throws a piece of wood on the fire (facing 172).

The final category of photograph, of the landscape through which she travelled, least satisfied Hubbard because it could not show the "color" of her natural surroundings. These photographs illustrate the changing geographical features she describes in her narrative, from bush to barrenlands. Thus while "On into the Wilderness" shows a trail leading

2.15 "Job," photograph by Mina Hubbard. Courtesy of Betty Ellis

into a thick stand of pines (facing 38), "Deep Ancient Valleys" presents a wide watercourse strewn with boulders and surrounded by barren hills (facing 4). A number of Hubbard's photographs also illustrate the waterways her expedition navigated. "Up the Fierce Nascaupee" and "Shooting the Rapids" demonstrate the challenges provided by the Naskaupi and George Rivers for both navigation and mapping (facing 28, 220), while "Solitude (Seal Lake)" and "Great Michikamau" picture the wide expanses of water that sometimes had to be crossed (facing 106, 266). The landscape photographs help to make concrete Hubbard's relationship with the landscape, which can perhaps best be explored by comparing her textual descriptions to those of her contemporaries and to conventional portrayals of landscape.

Hubbard's descriptions of the landscape are more vivid than accounts from the three contemporaneous men – Leonidas Hubbard, Elson, and

Wallace – who travelled through the same area. Buchanan suggests that Mina Hubbard engages with the Labrador landscape as a sympathetic observer, while corresponding narratives by Leonidas Hubbard and Wallace in particular contain much briefer descriptions that represent the landscape as an obstacle to be "forced, penetrated, combated and subdued" ("The Langscape before Her" 10). According to Buchanan, although the men may have other things on their minds than describing the scenery, including successful completion of the venture and avoidance of starvation, Mina Hubbard's descriptions of landscape differ from theirs in other fundamental ways. One difference is that she makes more explicit use of the language of landscape aesthetics, descriptively framing her scenes by using directional phrases such as "[o]n either side" and "[e]astward" (102) and employing terms such as "picturesque" (74, 153, MH Diary 30 July), "beautiful" (74, 75, 102, 177), "desolately grand" (75, 197), "wild" (177), and sometimes "pretty" or "charming" (99, 152). (While "charming" might seem an inaccurate word to use to describe Labrador, Hubbard employs it exclusively in descriptions of her campsites and thus lends a further air of "homeyness" to the wilderness.) Romantic, picturesque landscapes initially contained elements of both the beautiful – the calm and pleasing – and the sublime – the wild and rugged. Like Jameson's sketches of Niagara Falls, however, Hubbard's photographs of Labrador more often show what might be termed the sublime. Frequently, scenes she pictures are ones that provoke awe and fear: craggy cliffsides (facing 124, 304 [fig. 2.16], 332) and roiling waterfalls and rapids (facing 70, 116, 124, 134). The beautiful is also in evidence; one photograph, titled "Where Romance Lingers" (facing 46, fig. 2.9), pictures a rippled lake with partially submerged snags in the foreground, two men in a canoe in the middle distance, and trees and mountains in the background. In another photograph, the winding Naskaupi River is framed by trees on either side, with rocks in the foreground and hills in the background (facing 280).

Buchanan claims that Hubbard's position as a woman allows her a fundamentally different approach to nature than her male contemporaries, one that represents nature as "a source of spiritual renewal and inspiration" (10). Indeed, Hubbard writes of Labrador, "[H]ow beautiful it had been, with a strange, wild beauty, the remembrance of which buries itself silently in the deep parts of one's being. In the beginning there had been no response to it in my heart, but gradually in its silent way it had won, and now was like the strength-giving presence of an understanding friend" (177). This linkage of the sublime landscape to

2.16 "A Rough Country," photograph by Mina Hubbard. Courtesy of Betty Ellis

spirituality occurs not just because she is a woman; she is also influenced by Romantic literary tradition. Romanticist Anne Mellor notes that according to eighteenth-century philosopher Edmund Burke, when a sublime landscape is viewed, "the human mind first experiences terror or fear and then – as our instinct for self-preservation is gradually relaxed – astonishment, admiration, reverence and respect." Through this process, the viewer is "led to a sensible impression of the Deity by whose power such magnificent scenes are created" (86). Mellor goes on to point out that Romantic poets Samuel Taylor Coleridge and William Wordsworth transformed Burke's notions of the sublime "by insisting that the experience of infinite power is attended, not by fear and trembling, but rather by a deep awe and a profound joy" (89). In her book and her diary, Hubbard specifically associates sublime landscapes with a Christian God who invokes awe and joy rather than fear. In the wild and beautiful Labrador landscape, the spiritualization of nature provides friendly solace for the loss of her husband.

Just as Hubbard deliberately presents Labrador as "home" to justify her presence away from women's traditional sphere, in a related narrative effect she revises Romantic conceptions of landscape by further personalizing it. She conflates her feelings about her husband, including the sense that he accompanies her on this journey and thus makes Labrador "home," with a spiritualization of the landscape. At the end of chapter 1, before Hubbard has even begun to describe her journey, she refers to the hypothetical landscape of a dreary November day, when "the hills are solemn and sombre" and "the lake black and sullen," to evoke her husband's continuing presence and to connect it with the unseen presence of God. She writes that when the sunshine breaks through briefly and then disappears, "you do not forget the *Light*. You know it still shines – somewhere" (48). Light and shadow, hills and lake, provide a metaphoric way for Hubbard to indicate her husband's spiritual presence on this journey.

In both diary and book, the scenes through which she passes cause Hubbard to reflect on the pain of her loss. After Elson points out "the ridge of mountains away to the south-west which he had crossed with Mr Hubbard" (102–3), she comments in her diary that "the grander and more beautiful it grows the more I hunger for the one who made all things beautiful so much more beautiful by the spirit which he breathed into them" (16 July). Often, passages in her book are more metaphoric than those in her diary in order to be less directly personal and thus make more use of the landscape as a means of expression. She writes, for example, that "the sun came out again, throwing a golden glow over all. Clouds lay like delicate veils along the hill-sides, sometimes dipping almost to their feet ... It was very wild and beautiful, but as an exquisite, loved form from which the spirit has fled. The sense of life, of mystery, and magic seemed gone, and I wondered if the time could come when beauty would cease to give me pain" (95). Hubbard's diary entry for the same day, 10 July, deals more explicitly with her feelings about her husband, his death, and her subsequent assumption of his mantle: "It is all so wild and grand and mysterious and how his heart would beat hard with pride and joy in it all if he could be here. Along the edge of the bank I watched it for some time thinking, thinking. So very, very beautiful yet lacking that which completes and perfects. I have not his spirit, not that of the true explorer." Hubbard's feelings of inadequacy in comparison to her husband and of sorrow at his loss are often connected to descriptions of the landscape. Again, such links are less explicit in *A Woman's Way* than in the diary. Thus while Hubbard writes in the book that "the great hills rose rugged and irregular, and farther away in the blue distance the range lying beyond Seal Lake, all touched to beauty by the evening light" (102), her diary entry notes that she looked at this scene with "so many thoughts crowding my mind and making me sick with longing that the one who so much more deserved it and who could have so much more appreciated the privilege might have seen what I saw" (16 July).

Descriptions of landscape in Hubbard's book often stand in for her feelings about her husband, which are expressed through her person-alization and spiritualization of the landscape. Thus personalized, the barren landscape becomes less threatening and more the home that Hubbard implies can be found in the metaphorical presence of her husband. The people she meets and photographs, while also some-times portrayed through Romantic landscape discourse or the colonial discourse of civilization versus savagery, at other times, like the young Innu man waiting for his red leggings to be noticed, remind her of the familiar features of home.

MAPPING THE UNMAPPED: POSSESSION THROUGH NAMING

The full title of Hubbard's book, *A Woman's Way through Unknown Labrador: An Account of the Exploration of the Nascaupee and George Rivers*, implies that she will inform readers of a lone female explorer's journey down two "unknown" rivers in Labrador. Even before publica-tion of the book, Hubbard's articles had already demonstrated a typically masculine attitude toward the land: in *Harper's* she named Labrador "terra incognita" (813), while in the article published in the American and Manchester Geographical Society journals she called it "virgin field for the explorer" (530; 170). Her exploration efforts were recognized by contemporaneous Canadian reviewer Jean Graham of the *Canadian Magazine*, who wrote that Hubbard's book was a "vivid account of a Canadian explorer's work" (471). As Hubbard's own article for the two geographical journals notes, "The map which this article is intended to accompany sets forth the work I was able to accomplish" (531, 171). Throughout her trip, she took measurements for that map using her compass, sextant, and artificial horizon and made detailed notes on topography. In fact, she berated herself in her diary for her trouble with equipment or failure to take observations (30 June, 1, 5, 24 July) and for the inaccuracy of her measurements (17 July, 29 Aug.).

The geographical knowledge that helped "to legitimate and to perpet-uate" imperial power was long perceived as a masculine prerogative (Blunt and Wills 196). For that reason, women seldom participated in

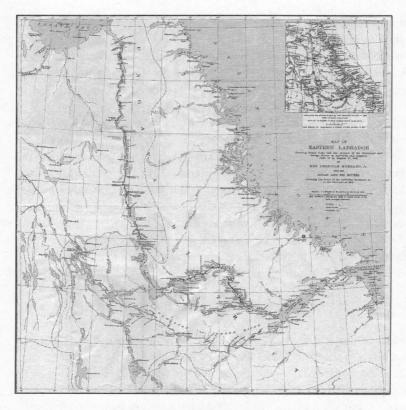

2.17   Map, *A Woman's Way through Unknown Labrador*. Courtesy
of Betty Ellis

the measuring and mapping that would stake an imperial claim to an
area. Hubbard was unique in that the map she produced with the help
of the American Geographical Society was the first detailed and accurate
chart of that area of Labrador. The *Geographical Journal* of the Royal
Geographical Society carried two reviews of Hubbard's book, the first
of which noted that the map "makes no claim to be other than the result
of pioneer work," mainly because Hubbard took no observations for
longitude but only some for latitude "as cartographic guiding-points"
("Recent Crossing"). The second review, however, pointed out that "an
examination of the map ... shows the value of her work, especially in
the extraordinary divergence between her observations of the course of
the Nascaupee and its course as previously conjectured" ("Labrador").

Meanwhile, W.H.W. in the *Journal of the Manchester Geographical Society* called the map "excellent" and the book a "splendid addition to the knowledge of Labrador" (133) and "of great geographical value" (134). He even gave Elson a sort of backhanded credit, as having a "name, which while it can never figure in the list of those who have directly added to the geographical knowledge of the country, must, so long as Mrs. Hubbard's work lasts, and longer, command the admiration of all" (133). (Presumably, Elson could not be given direct credit because he did not write the book or draw the map, although his work did allow Hubbard to do so.) One review, in the *Western Mail*, used Hubbard's cartographic work as a metaphor for her accomplishments in general: "The map of the interior of Labrador needs to be differently drawn in future. Where men have died of starvation in that dread interior, it has yielded its secrets to a woman whose expedition was steadfast and plucky and, withal, pleasant " ("Through Unknown Labrador"). Gentle feminine efforts thus had coaxed the "secrets" from Labrador and resulted in its map being "differently drawn." Almost the only dissenting opinion was in the *Nation*, whose reviewer maintained that Hubbard's "topographical results were of slight value."

The fact that Hubbard delivered two lectures to the Royal Geographical Society in London (in the summer of 1907 and the winter of 1908)[61] and that her article and map were published in the journals of both the American and Manchester Geographical Societies indicates that she was taken seriously by geographical authorities. Later writers about Labrador, including Strong (15) and Cabot (Introduction 27–8; *In Northern Labrador* 10), considered her maps of the Naskaupi and George Rivers to be major accomplishments since they showed "what geographers had supposed were two distinct rivers, the Northwest and the Nascaupee, to be one and the same" (WW 236).

From a contemporary perspective, Hubbard's achievement does not just rest on her measurement, location, and description of topographical features such as rivers, lakes, waterfalls, and mountains but on her naming of them. Her book is sprinkled with offhand references such as "away ahead were the blue ridges of hills with one high and barren, standing out above the rest, which I named Bald Mountain" (84) and "George pointed out the ridge of mountains away to the southwest ... and I named them Lion Heart Mountains" (102–3). At times she emphasizes her act of naming, but at others she simply includes her own names for geographical features in her narrative, such as on the page in which she describes the Bridgman Mountains and Helen

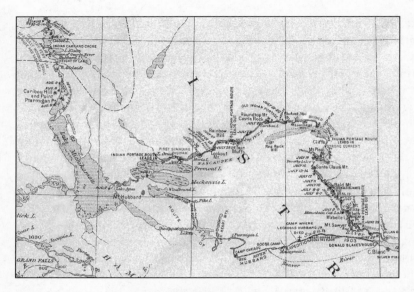

2.18   Detail of map, *A Woman's Way through Unknown Labrador*.

Falls (226), but does not indicate that she has chosen those toponyms in honour of publisher Herbert L. Bridgman and his wife, Helen. Her diary entry of the day she passed by those geographical features indicates that she was thinking of her friends; she writes, "The Bridgmans will be delighted with my success" (25 Aug.).

As the 18-by-20-inch map that accompanied her book shows (fig. 2.17, and detail, fig. 2.18), Hubbard's toponyms honour many other friends and acquaintances. Mount Sawyer and Point Lucie in Labrador are named for her minister, James Sawyer, and his wife, Lucy. Elson Lake in Quebec is named for George Elson, Cabot Lake for the man who wrote the introduction to her book, and Ford River and Ford Island for the George River Post factor. She also repeatedly inscribes her husband's name and his earlier expedition on the landscape. In what is now Quebec, she named Hubbard Lake. In Labrador she repeated the memorialization of her husband begun by his travelling companion, Wallace, by including on her map his Disappointment Lake, Windbound Lake, and Mount Hubbard. She changed the name of Wallace's Kipling Mountains to Lion Heart Mountains to honour her husband's courage.[62] She labelled other geographical features according to their appearances, often in terms of her own cultural knowledge. In Labrador she named not only Bald Mountain but also Santa Claus Mountain ("the outline of its rugged top looked as if the tired old fellow had there lain down to rest" [105]), Mount Pisa ("distinctly leaning towards the east" [106]), and Lookout Mountain (the "view from the mountain top was magnificent in all directions" [121]). In Quebec she named Slanting Lake (which "appeared to dip ... from one side to the other" [221]), the Hades Hills (which looked to her like the entrance to the Greek mythological underworld [220–1]); and Pyramid Mountain ("It reminds me of an Egyptian pyramid" [223; see also MH Diary 24 Aug.]). All of Hubbard's toponyms listed above are on current topographical maps produced by the government of Canada, except Point Lucie and the Lion Heart Mountains (Labrador, Labrador-Quebec, and Quebec, Maps 13E, 13F, 13K, 13L, 23H, 23I, 23P, 24A, 24H, 24I, 24J). The largest of those mountains appears today under Wallace's original name, Kipling Mountain.[63]

Remarkably, Hubbard recorded the names of a number of women friends and family members by writing them onto the land, distinguishing the women from their husbands or fathers by using first names. By labelling features of the landscape with women's given names, she was tackling what Gilbert and Gubar call the problem of "woman's patronymically defined identity" (237). Women often disappeared from historical records because they were known only by their husbands' or fathers' names. Hubbard lists herself on the title page of her book as "Mrs Leonidas Hubbard, Junior"; she never provides Mrs Ford's first name, although she stayed with her for almost two months; and even in her diary she refers to friends as Mrs Krafft, Mrs Bartlett, and Mrs Bridgman. While it is often difficult to identify with certainty whom Hubbard was honouring, two geographical features that she almost certainly named for friends are Helen Falls and Point Lucie. In her 1920 book *Within My Horizon*, Helen Bridgman asserts that the falls were named after her (81), and Point Lucie follows Hubbard's practice of naming a large geographical feature for a male friend (Bridgman Mountains and Mount Sawyer) and giving a nearby smaller geographical feature the first name of his wife (Helen Falls and Point Lucie). On the day Hubbard's group travelled past a high sandy point of land and a nearby mountain, Hubbard wrote in her diary, "Named it Pt. Lucie and [the mountain] Mt. Sawyer" (29 June).[64]

Anne Hart has identified a number of lakes and falls that Hubbard named in honour of her nieces, including Dorothy, Marie, Orma, and Agnes Lakes and Gertrude and Maid Marion Falls.[65] Hubbard probably also named one lake after herself – Adelaide Lake, just south of Hubbard Lake, commemorating what on her birth certificate is listed as her second name.[66] She thus inscribed her matrilineage on the landscape, eschewing the patronymic for both herself and her young female relatives. Other geographical features on her route that she may have named for unidentified women friends include Mabelle Island, Mount Elizabeth, and Isabella Falls. The only one of these geographical features that Hubbard mentions naming, in her diary, is a "beautiful evergreen covered island ... which we named Mabelle I." (1 July), but she does not identify the source of the name. Indeed, her use of the first-person plural pronoun indicates that "Mabelle" may have been connected to one of her travelling companions. Such wording also suggests that, contrary to the impression given by her use of "I" in her book, the choice of toponyms was not always hers alone, but at times was a joint project with her companions.[67] Again, all except the island, which is no longer marked, Gertrude Falls, which is now identified simply as "Falls," and Lake Agnes, which was subsumed in the Smallwood Reservoir, are names used on topographical maps today.

In honour of International Women's Day in 1999, the Quebec toponymy commission published an Internet article lauding Hubbard for being one of the few women to have had such an effect on the mapping and toponymy of the province (Richard). The pride that accompanies a recognition of her courage and audacity in appropriating the masculine role of naming the physical environment, and of her lasting influence, as shown by the subsequent official adoption of these names, must be tempered by a recognition of the imperialistic implications of her actions. Alison Blunt and Jane Wills suggest, "The most tangible relationship between imperial power and geographical knowledge was through exploration and so-called discovery, charting territory that was often thought to be unknown and mapping and naming apparently 'new' places" (194). Although Hubbard made no explicit claim to be part of the British imperial project (unlike Binnie-Clark, who recruited even the sidewalks in the "great cause of Imperialism" [*Summer* 28]), the mapping and geographical naming in which she engaged place her squarely within that project. She mapped parts of both a British colony and a Canadian territory. London, England, was the home port of the Hudson's Bay Company trading ship that was to pick her up at George River Post. Hubbard's book was published in England, Canada, and the United States, and her book tour roused much interest in England (where she met Harold Ellis, the man who would become her second husband and the father of her three children).

As she compiled her map, Hubbard made use of the names of topographical features established by previous imperialist explorers and traders. Occasionally, the established names were Innu ones, such as Lake Michikamau and Lake Michikamats. At other times, Hubbard included English translations of Innu names in her book and on her map, such as Barren Ground Water (which she transcribed in her book as "Mush-au-wau-ni-pi" [201]) for Indian House Lake. Most often, though, the established names honoured English-speaking explorers or historical figures, such as George River instead of the Innu Mushuau-shipu (or river of the barrens [Byrne and Fouillard 13]) and Mealy Mountains rather than the Innu Akamiuapishk^u (Andrew 232). When Hubbard had no established names of geographical features to go by, she occasionally chose aboriginal names; when she learned from her one local guide, Blake, for example, that the region they were traversing was "great marten country," she writes, "I named the tributary stream we followed, Wapustan River" (96; *wapustan* is the Cree word for marten). For the most part, though, Hubbard inscribed either the names of friends and family members or her own allusive fancies onto the landscape. Like other explorers, she assumed that because the names of topographical features were unknown to her, these features were unnamed. Geographical theorist Paul Carter claims that the naming of places is a form of "spatial punctuation, transforming space into an object of knowledge, something that could be explored and read" (67). In making her maps, Hubbard participated in this compression of a three-dimensional world into two dimensions, thereby making it appear both knowable and manageable for herself, her readers, subsequent geographical researchers, and Canadian politicians.

In an oral account recorded in the mid-1990s and published in 2000, Mary Adele Andrew, also known by the Innu name Mani-Aten, spoke of the Innu toponymy of what is now called Labrador and northern Quebec. She said: "There are thousands of Innu names for the lakes, rivers, mountains, peninsulas and other geographical features of our land. These names have been here and are still used by us, the Innu, after thousands of years. Today, the maps drawn by the Europeans carry the names of these geographical features in English, for example: Churchill Falls for Mista-paustuk, Churchill River for Mista-shipu and Mealy Mountains for Akamiuapishk^u. These are only a few, and the names I give you in Innu are the proper ones" (231–2). Examples of geographical features that had established Innu names before Hubbard and Wallace renamed them are the lakes Nisukaka, Atshuku-nipiss, and Keshikashkau (Orma, Namaycush, and Disappointment Lakes).[68]

The practice of renaming places as a way of taking possession of them was and is a precursor to and accompaniment of physical possession. The land around Lake Michikamau, which Hubbard mapped and where Andrew speaks of living with her family (232), was possessed in a particularly irreversible way in the 1970s with the completion of the Churchill Falls hydroelectric project and the creation of the Smallwood Reservoir. Maps literally changed overnight – places were not just renamed; they disappeared entirely, including two dozen lakes that were subsumed in the reservoir (Labrador and Quebec, Maps 13E [1952 and 1989], 13L [1968 and 1990], 23H [1964 and 1990], and 23I [1953 and 1983]). Elizabeth Penashue (Tshuaukuish) writes: "My late father, Stakeaskushimun (Simon Gregoire), was always very emotional when he talked about how his belongings, including his canoes and traps, were flooded over when the Mista-shipu (Churchill River) was dammed. He was not the only one to lose all his belongings. Many others also lost all the basic things they used to survive in *nutshimit* [the country]. My father lost everything, even his hunting land. He mentioned this many times, over and over again. He was so troubled about what had happened. Mista-paustuk [the great rapids or Grand Rapids, now known as Churchill Falls] no longer exhaled the mist, which was a landmark that helped us find our way from afar" (158). In *Colonialism and Landscape*, Andrew Sluyter discusses the "pristine myth," which "erroneously characterizes precolonial landscapes as having lacked dense populations and productive land uses" (6). Hubbard's map promoted this myth of an unused landscape, a myth that later paved the way for flooding without consultation. Since the popularization and romanticization of Hubbard's trip by historians such as Pierre Berton, several people have tried to canoe all or part of the route her party took. An attempt in 2000 by British adventurer Alexandra Pratt and Innu guide Jean Pierre Ashini (Napes) failed very early in the journey, in part, Pratt claimed, because the creation of the reservoir reduced the flow of the Naskaupi River to make it, too, unnavigable.[69] According to geographical researcher Linda McDowell, places are "constituted and maintained by social relations of power and exclusion" (4). Thus the Innu, excluded from official mapping and naming of the territory in which they lived, hunted, and trapped, could sixty years later also be excluded from decisions about the destruction of that territory through flooding.

Hubbard understood the importance of naming geographical features. In her book and on her map, she called the small waterway on which her husband had lost his way the Susan River, even though it was known locally as Susan Brook. (Wallace also called it Susan River, and it is still listed as a river on topographical maps.) Giving the waterway its common designation would have meant admitting that her husband's judgment was poor, because he had mistaken a brook (the Susan) for a river (the Naskaupi) and continued to portage and struggle up it long after he should have recognized his error and turned back. Nikolas Huffman notes that "Native American maps very accurately reflect the topology of river networks" (260). Local sources had identified the Naskaupi River as the only one coming out of Grand Lake. If the map Leonidas Hubbard drew using those sources reflected the utility of waterways, it was accurate, since the Naskaupi was indeed the only navigable river.

Mina Hubbard's mapping enterprises also elided some of the contributions of First Nations men. In her diary, Hubbard repeatedly refers to the "Indian maps" that Elson acquired for her at North West River, which helped guide them through the first part of the journey (23, 25 June, 18, 23, 24, 26 July, 1 Aug.), but in her book she mentions only one map of a portage, which she calls "crude" (62). Not only did her four Métis, Cree, and Inuit companions, Elson, Chapies, Iserhoff, and Blake, take her through the territory she subsequently mapped, but also Elson estimated the distances they travelled each day and drew the initial route map of the 1903 expedition (a drawing she credits in her preface [x]). In her diary, Hubbard notes that she also consulted him in making the first draft of her map of the 1905 journey (20 Sept.). At Elson's request, Blake mapped Grand Lake, which, far from pleasing her, caused her to suspect that Elson was planning to write his own version of their journey (22 Sept.). She recognized at least part of Elson's geographical contribution to her journey, however, by naming a lake after him.

Women traditionally have been excluded from geographical investigations, as their historic exclusion from the Royal Geographical Society attests. Thus, in terms of gender, Hubbard's involvement in recording, photographing, and mapping are noteworthy achievements. In terms of race and colonialism, however, these achievements must be examined with a more critical eye, since her work not only posits her as "first" but also excludes Innu toponymy and elides some of the contributions of Cree, Métis, and Inuit men. When one re-examines the title of her book, *A Woman's Way through Unknown Labrador: An Account of the Exploration of the Nascaupee and George Rivers*, its inaccuracy becomes apparent. Hubbard was neither alone nor did she travel through "unknown" territory, but she needed to give the illusion of both in order to be seen as a legitimate explorer.

The word "mapping" is often used as a metaphor for taking possession of a body of knowledge. Hubbard literally named, mapped, and located Labrador, but she also figuratively named, mapped, and located herself and the people and landscapes she encountered. As Duncan and Gregory point out, "Travel writing is often inherently domesticating": it takes what is unknown and locates it both as familiar and as suitable for reading at home (5). Hubbard took "unknown Labrador" and domesticated it for herself and her British, Canadian, and American readers. Its location may have been far from home, but it was metaphorically well within her private domestic sphere. Her book maps issues of both gender and race in its purported authorization of her trip through the use of masculine names and narratives, its diversionary use of sexuality and violence, its claims to primacy, and its pictorial and textual representations of indigenous landscapes and peoples. In making her trip and publishing her book, photographs, and map, Mina Hubbard made a subtle assault on the divisions between private and public space. By renaming Labrador as home and by giving public geographical features names that, at least initially, had only private meaning, she took the public and the outside and turned it into the private and the inside.

chapter three | "I WAS AGAINST IT" | Margaret Laurence and British Imperialism in Somalia

I believed that the overwhelming majority of Englishmen in colonies could properly be classified as imperialists, and my feeling about imperialism was very simple – I was against it. | Margaret Laurence, *The Prophet's Camel Bell* 25

When Margaret Laurence wrote *The Prophet's Camel Bell*, a book about her experiences in the British Somaliland Protectorate in the early 1950s, she titled the first chapter "Innocent Voyage." This title is ironic, of course, since Laurence was well aware that the blamelessness implied by such a heading and its implicit corollary of the innocent voyager is unattainable when one begins one's travels from the privileged subject position of the Western visitor. As Laurence wrote in her 1963 travel memoir and in the essay "The Very Best Intentions," she only gradually came to realize how implicated she was in the British imperialist project during her time in Africa. *The Prophet's Camel Bell* and the translations, critical material, and fiction that stemmed from her six years in Somaliland and the Gold Coast demonstrate her questions about the success of her negotiations with imperialism and gender and, at the same time, map her rigorous and complex attempts at such negotiation.

In an essay published in 1978, Laurence linked her "feelings of anti-imperialism, anti-colonialism, anti-authoritarianism" to her "growing awareness of the dilemma and powerlessness of women, the tendency of women to accept male definition of ourselves, to be self-deprecating and uncertain, and to rage inwardly" ("Ivory Tower" 24). She concluded that the situation of "peoples with colonial mentalities, was not unlike that of women in our society" (23). Despite this conscious linkage, Laurence's feminist principles are sometimes at odds in her African texts with her anti-imperialist beliefs. She struggles with what Linda

3.1 "The bungalow at Sheikh," *The Prophet's Camel Bell*. Courtesy of David and Jocelyn Laurence

Alcoff calls "The Problem of Speaking for Others." Her dilemma is to find a way to discuss issues of gender in Somalia, while maintaining an awareness of cultural difference and of the unequal power relations that stemmed from her position as a Western outsider. Laurence wrote about colonial structures and about women's lives during a time when the terms "postcolonial" and "feminist" were not in common use and when the theoretical language to discuss such issues was just developing. Her mapping of issues such as compulsory early marriage, bride price, polygyny, spousal abuse, compulsory maternity, prostitution, and female genital mutilation reveal conflictual efforts to write about women's lives in the context of imperialism. But her travel memoir and her other African works are neither especially sensitive in their cultural commentary nor noticeably flawed in the way they appropriate Somali and Ghanaian voices or universalize African experiences. Instead, they provide a tentative map for the reconciliation of tensions between anti-imperialism and feminism.

Laurence travelled to the British Somaliland Protectorate in late 1950 and lived there from early 1951 to mid-1952. Her husband, Jack, was an engineer in charge of building desert reservoirs to collect runoff from rainwater, a project of the British colonial government that was both well-intentioned and paternalistic.[1] Margaret and Jack Laurence spent some of their time in camps in the Haud desert and the remainder travelling across British and French Somaliland and living in the communities of Sheikh and Hargeisa. *The Prophet's Camel Bell*, the book that marks the starting point for this chapter, provides an account of the Laurences' life and travels during those eighteen months. It includes a description of the planning and construction of the reservoirs; several chapters of character sketches, mostly of Somali men but also of people Laurence refers to as "the imperialists"; and a chapter about the Somali oral literature she worked on translating. The translated and transcribed stories and poems were published by the protectorate government in 1954 as *A Tree for Poverty*, after she and Jack had moved to the Gold Coast (now Ghana). Her Somali travel memoir, called in Canada and Britain *The Prophet's Camel Bell* and in the United States *New Wind in a Dry Land*, was first published in 1963, eleven years after the Laurences left the area and three years after Somaliland joined a neighbouring, formerly Italian colony to form the independent Republic of Somalia.

The Laurences lived in the Gold Coast from late 1952 to early 1957. There Jack worked as an engineer in the construction of the new port of Tema, and Margaret looked after their two young children and wrote fiction. She had started an unfinished novel and written several short stories while she was in Somaliland (including "Uncertain Flowering," set in Somaliland and published in 1953). In the Gold Coast she wrote more stories and another unfinished novel and began drafting *This Side Jordan*, a novel about the end of colonial rule that was published in 1960. Her collection of short stories set in Ghana just before, during, and after the country's independence in 1957 was published as *The Tomorrow-Tamer* in 1963, the same year as her travel narrative.

Laurence's last African work, a book of criticism about Nigerian novelists and playwrights, originated from her deep interest in writers such as Chinua Achebe ("Books that Mattered to Me" 246). She did not travel to Nigeria, as she had to Somaliland and to the Gold Coast, but instead researched at a distance through the literature of the country. *Long Drums and Cannons: Nigerian Dramatists and Novelists, 1952–1966*, first published in 1968, outlines the burgeoning production of novels and plays in Nigeria during the 1950s and 1960s. As Laurence points out in her introduction, her analysis would have been less optimistic had the book not been researched before the outbreak of the Nigerian civil war and the Biafran war of independence. While Laurence's last African book was published eight years after Nigeria's independence, her first four were researched, written, and published during the years when a break with the colonial past was occurring in Somaliland and the Gold Coast. Her African writings demonstrate an enduring engagement with the British, French, and Italian colonial legacies in Africa and an interest in the effects on women's lives of both pre-existing patriarchal structures and colonial situations. In particular, Laurence examines issues of gender and heterosexuality in the African colonial context.

The first three of Laurence's Manawaka books, *The Stone Angel* (1964), *A Jest of God* (1966), and *The Fire-Dwellers* (1969), were begun during the early to mid-1960s; thus her Canadian fiction does not mark a distinct temporal break from, but instead overlaps with, her African texts. Several critics of her work have indeed identified thematic connections between her African and Canadian works, including a continuing focus on what Konrad Groß calls "freedom and dependence or dominance and subordination" (78). *The Prophet's Camel Bell* and her other African writings launch her later, more explicit feminist commitment toward exposing the conditions of women's lives and revising and expanding their roles in literature, evident throughout her subsequent work.[2] Laurence's comments on gender and sexuality are significant in that they provide initial discursive treatment of a subject for which she had few practical or theoretical models. Her preliminary observations about women's lives are sometimes muted, however, by her avowed need to avoid making judgments about an unfamiliar culture. Laurence is able to begin a reconciliation of tensions between her feminism and her anti-imperialism only by examining the material details of women's and men's lives that provide evidence of power relations in colonial and postcolonial situations.

Like a memoir, *The Prophet's Camel Bell* presents the author's retrospective account of events and relationships during a finite period in her life.[3] Like a travel narrative, it is structured around travels to the British Somaliland Protectorate, within the colony, and to neighbouring French Somaliland (now the Republic of Djibouti). Laurence's book can be compared to two contemporaneous memoirs: *To My Wife – 50 Camels* (1963), by British writer Lady Alys Reece, wife of the governor of Somaliland during the Laurences' stay there, and *Brazilian Journal* (1987), Canadian poet P.K. Page's account of her life in Brazil during the late 1950s. Reece travelled to the same area of Africa as Laurence and

is mentioned in her text, although not by name, when Laurence notes their common interest in writing and in translation of African poetry and folk tales (*PCB* 257).[4] Page travelled to a different continent but is, like Laurence, a female Canadian author writing about experiences of travel during the 1950s. All three women look back on a stay in another country that was then many years in the past – ten for Laurence, fifteen for Reece, almost thirty for Page. Each of the women travelled because of her husband's work – Page from 1957 to 1959 in Brazil with her ambassador husband, Arthur Irwin; Reece from 1936 to 1948 in northern Kenya, where her husband, Sir Gerald Reece, worked before he was sent to Somaliland as governor. Laurence, meanwhile, gives as her motive for travelling Jack's need to do "a job that plainly needed doing" (*PCB* 11). In keeping with the relational nature of their books' origins, each author dedicates her book to a male family member – Laurence and Page to their husbands, Reece to her son Andrew (although the title of her book comes from a will her husband made before their marriage and thus points to her role as wife). Rather than just accompanying their husbands, however, Reece, Laurence, and Page turned their stays in Africa and South America into examinations of the cultures they visited and their own places within those cultures.

To My Wife is a useful comparative text not only because it describes experiences of the wife of a British government official in northeastern Africa but also because it presents photographs that have similarities to (and marked differences from) those in Laurence's book. Page's book, in contrast, offers an alternative perspective by another Canadian woman writer abroad in very different circumstances during the 1950s. While Laurence lived in the back of a Bedford truck in the desert, Page managed an ambassador's residence with a pink marble staircase, a swimming pool, six bedrooms, and four bathrooms. Like Reece and Laurence, she took on a project outside her own writing; while in Brazil, she temporarily abandoned poetry and instead turned to drawing and painting under her married name, P.K. Irwin. Page suggests, in fact, that she was abandoned by the poetic muse, writing that notes for her journal had included a "complex note, an attempt to understand my poetic silence, this translation into paint" (195). Thus while Laurence's book is illustrated with photographs taken by her and by the former information officer for the protectorate government, Page's is illustrated with her own drawings and paintings of scenery, still lifes, and the interiors and exteriors of buildings.

Each of the three travel memoirs is a rewriting and retelling based to greater or lesser extent on journals kept by the women or, in Reece's case, by her husband (73, 84). Reece's book is purposely descriptive rather than analytical; the "Author's Note" ends with the self-deprecating disclaimer that the book "does not attempt to ask or answer any questions, and is merely a record of life from a woman's point of view" (11). (Indeed, the book mentions only in passing Britain's war with the Italians in Africa, which occurred while the Reeces were in Kenya.) Page, meanwhile, bases her book not only on her journal but also on letters to her family. While she notes that to produce the book, she has "clarified" and has occasionally "fleshed out what were merely notes" (Foreword, np), she retains the feel of a journal by naming her book *Brazilian Journal*, by dating each entry, and by maintaining the language of relatively unreflected immediate response. That the journal form of Page's book does not reveal all about her life and feelings is evident when she notes, "I rarely write of things that distress me" (194).

Laurence quotes directly not only from what she calls her "note-books" (journals she subsequently destroyed, probably during an attempt to lighten her load when moving from one country to another [King 78, 315]) but also from observations she made about Somali culture in the introduction to *A Tree for Poverty*. Her alterations to that introduction and her comments about her diary entries indicate that she is reinterpreting events and opinions from the standpoint of ten years' more life experience, including a subsequent reading of books about other colonial situations that helped her come to a retrospective understanding of Somaliland and her role within it. Often, Laurence's references to her notebooks demonstrate to readers the naïveté or lack of understanding she now identifies in her earlier opinions. She quotes, for example, a comment from her diary about the ease with which one could gain the respect of Somalis (200–1); the reference is to the Laurences' driver, Abdi, whose subsequent difficult relationship with them she then explores in detail. Laurence in fact had reinterpreted that section of her journal much earlier, probably while she was still in Somaliland. She writes that she had added "in heavy lead pencil one word – *Bosh*" (201).

AN ANTI-IMPERIALIST PERSPECTIVE

From the beginning of *The Prophet's Camel Bell*, Laurence positions herself as one traveller among many. She refers to herself in the second person, relating the way in which, weighed down by "notebook and camera" (9), she and other travellers set out burdened also by naive, preconceived expectations of discovering the exotic: "Nothing can equal in hope and apprehension the first voyage east of Suez, yourself eager for all manner of oddities, pretending to disbelieve in marvels lest you appear naive, but anticipating them just the same, prepared for anything, prepared for nothing, burdened with baggage – most of it useless, unburdened by knowledge, assuming all will go well because it is you and not someone else going to the far place (harm comes only to others), bland as eggplant and as innocent of the hard earth as a fledgling sparrow" (9).[5] The remainder of Laurence's narrative is a revision and complication of this earlier position as an unreflective traveller.

A large part of that revisionary project rests in her rigorous and self-conscious examination of colonial systems and of her own place within those systems as traveller, wife of a colonial official, and writer.

Both because of her involvement with the "old Left" of North Winnipeg during and just after her college years and because of the era in which she travelled – the tail end of British imperialism – Laurence is by far the most self-conscious and self-analytical of the travel writers discussed in this study. She introduces the issue of colonization in her accounts of her journey to Somaliland even before she begins her description of the colony. In three paragraphs, her narrative moves from a critical description of 1856 writings on Somalia by Richard F. Burton, who believed that "his footsteps were the first that really counted"; to a mention of the Somali war for Ethiopia against the Portuguese; to a description of Somalia as a place where "the Arab slave routes had emerged at the sea, and from there the dhow-loads of slaves had once been shipped across the Gulf of Aden to be sold in the flesh markets of Arabia"; to a discussion of the early twentieth-century independence fighter "Mohamed Abdullah Hassan [sic], the so-called Mad Mullah of Somaliland, [who] had fought the British for years and was defeated only when at last his forts were bombed" (12–13).[6] In this brief passage, Laurence explicitly links travel writing – an activity in which she, as well as Burton, engages – with other, more blatant aspects of imperialism, including invasion, slavery, and the crushing of struggles for independence from colonial rule.

To ensure that the connection between European imperialism and the discourse surrounding travel is unequivocal, Laurence then records her ship's stop in Genoa, the birthplace of Christopher Columbus. She never mentions Columbus or his connection to the beginnings of European imperialism on another continent, but as in her short story "The Perfume Sea," set in an unnamed African country (modelled on Ghana) as it gains independence from British rule, the allusion is implicit.[7] In that story, as Arun Mukherjee argues, references to Genoa and Columbus raise the global history of imperialism at the same time as the story focuses on an apparent manifestation of the end of colonial rule. Just as changing human relationships in "The Perfume Sea" highlight Laurence's exploration of neo-colonialism, her mention of Genoa in *The Prophet's Camel Bell* highlights what will be an equally strong focus on imperialism in Somaliland.

Laurence's own subject position is crucial to her representation of colonial structures. She is directly linked to the British colonial government through her husband's work and also through a brief period when she worked for Chief Secretary and Commissioner for Native Affairs Philip Shirley, during the time when he was striving, as Laurence writes, "to prepare for the country's independence by a gradual transfer of power" (246).[8] As a Canadian in Somaliland, however, her initial position is an anti-colonial one. She is aware that her status as a "colonial" makes her inferior in the eyes of many British people abroad – she even quotes one man who calls her a "bloody colonial" (229) – and her disdain toward that condescending attitude is clear (25). She notes that while the British may be biased against her, and while Burton may have been biased against Somalis before he arrived, thinking them "stupid, dirty, and most damning of all, poor Muslims" (25), she is biased in another direction. As she writes, mocking what she now perceives as a naive attitude, "I believed that the overwhelming majority of Englishmen in colonies could properly be classified as imperialists, and my feeling about imperialism was very simple – I was against it" (25). Laurence's subsequent descriptions of "the imperialists," whom she initially defines as people who work in the interests of the British Empire and who believe in the superiority of that empire, are often scathing. She writes that although she had imagined that "if I ever wrote a book about Somaliland, it would give me tremendous joy to deliver a withering blast of invective in their direction," she is unable to do so because it would be "like mutilating a corpse" (226): "I have never in my life felt such antipathy towards people anywhere as I felt towards these pompous or whining sahibs and memsahibs, and yet I do not feel the same anger now. Their distortions have been presented in detail often enough, both fictionally and journalistically, in almost every tale of colonial life" (228).

One of the fictional representations of colonial distortion to which Laurence may be referring is her own *This Side Jordan*. Her first published novel is presented through the alternating viewpoints of two men – one from England, the other from the Gold Coast – but enters more deeply into the thought processes of the African character, Nathaniel Amegbe, through the use of interior monologues. The language Laurence employs when quoting his speech and that of other Ghanaians is almost stilted, and this formality of language serves as a marker of translation when the character she represents is, in the context of the novel, speaking a language other than English (a technique Ashcroft, Griffiths, and Tiffin call "code-switching" [72; see also Rimmer 7–8]).

As Laurence wrote nine years after the novel was published, "I actually wonder how I ever had the nerve to attempt to go into the mind of an African man, and I suppose if I'd really known how difficult was the job I was attempting, I would never have tried it" ("Gadgetry or Growing" 82). Mary Rimmer suggests that although Laurence was indeed "making wild guesses about her characters' language and speech," she chose "to make speech and dialogue central elements" in order to enact "personal and cultural power struggles, particularly for low-status speakers" (4). Laurence allows the Ghanaian characters in her book more of an opportunity to speak than is common in Western literature about Africa, and she thus assigns them some power in the colonial situations she describes, a courageous but risky venture in the literary milieu of the late twentieth century, considering the potential for charges of appropriation of voice.[9] The emphasis on her Ghanaian protagonist's inner voice makes him a much more sympathetically drawn character than his European counterpart, the overtly racist and sexist Johnnie Kestoe. As *The Prophet's Camel Bell* does with Somaliland, Laurence's novel reflects on the prejudices of imperialists in the Gold Coast such as Kestoe.

In her travel memoir, Laurence is even more critical of some aspects of English, French, and Italian colonization of Somalia. Part of that tripartite colonization included the division of what had been one people, with one language, into three distinct territories, each with its own language of colonization. Although most of Laurence's invective is directed at the "sahib-type English" in British Somaliland (226), she also comments critically on that colonial government's historical suppression of dissent. In French Somaliland (which Laurence visited), she is critical of a colonial enterprise that included Catholic mission schools, where children were fed during famines "at the price of relinquishing Islam" (127), and of the practice of recruiting policemen from Senegal, because "if the police ... did not have tribal or family connections in the country where they worked, they would have no objections to strong-arm tactics in dealing with the locals" (128).

In contrast to Laurence's analysis of colonial practices, Reece takes a relatively uncritical approach to the established systems she entered in Kenya. The language she uses to describe the people she met also evinces an unselfconsciousness about difference. She describes workers as "monkey-like" (53) or "like a baboon" (172), and she writes that one man had an "expressionless" face (38) and that she was surprised by the sympathy another expressed at the death of a horse, "because Aden's face had seemed as blank and uncaring as any" (184). Page, too, is less determinedly analytical about cultural difference than is Laurence, in part as a function of the much less edited nature of her narrative. She comments repeatedly about the difficulty of communicating with others in a language other than her mother tongue, but while Laurence analyzes her position in terms of theories of colonization, Page's more unmediated, diaristic book includes a comment that having only servants who do not speak English "is exactly like having a house full of monkeys" (17). (Page subsequently took lessons in Portuguese so that she could speak the language of her host country, and she noted her dismay about the poverty she encountered on her travels throughout Brazil.)

Laurence is also sometimes unable to recognize all of her own biases. Even when she is proclaiming her lack of racism, she repeatedly types Somalis as "expressionless" (24, 201), "timeless" (115), and "inscrutable to the last" (207). She also writes that Somali men who were disturbed by a robbery in the camp "darted hither and yon like swallows, gabbling at the top of their voices" (107); language that is not understandable to her is thus represented as a kind of non-language spoken by non-humans. Simon Gikandi contends that for Western writers, "even when you speak against the culture of colonialism, you speak its language because it is what constitutes what you are" (142). Indeed, Laurence's use of language is influenced by her heritage as a white North American, while her actions were sometimes determined by her position as the wife of a colonial official. Thus although she initially resisted having servants and being called memsahib, "a word which seemed to have connotations of white man's burden, paternalism, everything I did not believe in" (23), she eventually capitulated to the use of the title and deferred to her husband's insistence that "[y]ou don't tote your own luggage here. It just isn't done" (23).[10] When Laurence writes that she was distressed by her cook Mohamed's comment, "Memsahib – must be you step carefully-carefully" (23), her dislike of the term is clearly based as much on the gender restrictions it imposed as on the imperialism it implied.

Reece, too, writes that she disliked the word "memsahib," but her distress stemmed from the fact that the term suggested "a caricature of the British matron abroad" (52) – the kind of caricature that Laurence refers to and at times perpetuated. Page also comments disparagingly about the role her position enforced. She notes that when she dressed for an ambassadorial function, she felt "that the whole thing is make-believe and that I am dressed up in my mother's clothes" (29), and she

3.3 "Hargeisa town," photograph by C.J. Martin. Courtesy of C.J. Martin

bought jewellery that she did not want because "some ambassador's-wife role I seem to be playing at the moment ... finds them necessary" (173). As she later, revealingly, writes, "It will be hard to turn my back on luxury. I expect never to have so much again" (238). Laurence, meanwhile, writes about the months spent living in the back of a truck: "Only those who have never experienced anything except comfort think that physical comfort is unimportant" (137).

At times, as Laurence's narrative indicates, her attempts to be unlike the memsahibs caused her to act in a manner that upset Somalis' sense of propriety. When she describes walking to the market accompanied only by Mohamed, which resulted in an uproar among local residents and police, she first quotes from her notebook the comment "much ado about nothing" (34). She then notes her subsequent revision of that assessment, pointing out that she had been unable to recognize the hostility around her because she "did not then know how much the Somalis resented the Christian conquerors" (34).[11] In other passages, she complicates her initial blatant anti-British bias by emphasizing her often peripheral, but nevertheless real, position among the colonial administrators' contingent. Her description of members of the colonial government and their families gathered to celebrate the queen's birthday places her both outside and inside the group. She describes the preparations and clothing worn by others (including the strange ostrich-plumed hat of the governor) with the ironic voice of an outsider, but includes herself in the group through the use of the first-person plural pronoun: "We all had to behave ourselves" (225).

She also introduces readers to people connected to the colonial government who belied her own stereotypical notions of the "full-blown imperialists" she had expected to meet (228). One was the public works foreman who, despite great obstacles, succeeded in having roads repaired and lorries serviced; Laurence describes him as having "a kind of heroic quality" (29). Another was Mary Shirley, the wife of the chief secretary of Somaliland, who worked in a camp for refugees of the drought (245).[12] A third was a district commissioner who ate poisoned bran to show Somali camel herders that the grasshopper bait would not hurt their camels and who collected books on Somaliland: "He was the only Englishman in government service, as far as we could discover, who spoke really fluent Somali, and one of the few who understood the complexities of tribal organization and tribal law" (241). Laurence was particularly impressed not only by this man's determination to speak to Somalis in their own language but also by his analysis of his own and other Europeans' positions in Africa, which she summarized in this way: "he wondered if it would not be better if all Europeans left Africa, for he was discouraged at the number of people who had political or religious motives for their work. If only Europeans could work there simply because various technical skills would be needed until African countries developed enough technically educated men of their own" (244). Laurence clearly shared this opinion – and indeed, included her husband among the government employees who worked in Somaliland only until technically educated Somalis were available – just as she admired this man's understanding of Somali language and law.

REPRESENTING SOMALI CULTURE

Laurence carefully situated herself as someone who was also trying to learn the Somali language and who appreciated Somali literature. In contrast to the memsahibs she describes, who spoke "very loudly to Somalis, as though a greater volume of sound would be bound to pierce the language barrier," and who "persisted in the belief that the Somalis were of an inferior mentality because they did not speak English" (*PCB* 52), Laurence writes that she took daily Somali lessons from the translator in her husband's work camp, Hersi Jama (171). She found learning the language "slow going" (51). When a group of men came to talk about the reservoirs, she writes, "[i]t was not to be wondered at, that I had failed to get across anything to them. My grasp of Somali was too limited, and so was my understanding of the country" (70). Because few Somali women could speak English, her interactions with those women were often mediated through male interpreters. It is thus with evident relief that she writes of a visit by two young women during her last months in Hargeisa: "My grasp of Somali was not good, but it was good enough now to enable me to talk with them without the inhibiting presence of an interpreter" (255). The difficulties of teaching and learning another language were brought home to Laurence when she tried to teach Mohamed to read and write English. Her ironic description of that experience provides a satirical reinterpretation of previous imperialist accounts of instruction in another language: "I have read, in many books about Africa, of Europeans who taught their servants how to read and write. *Under my tutelage, Ali made very rapid progress and was soon able to write down his market accounts and to read the correspondence in The Times.* I wonder how they managed it" (183; italics in original).

That Laurence learned at least the rudiments of the Somali language is demonstrated by her inclusion of Somali words (such as *balleh* for reservoir) in her narrative. Such words are highlighted using italics, but instead of defining them in the text, Laurence often either indicates meaning through context or forces readers to look up the words in the glossary at the end of *The Prophet's Camel Bell*. Again, as Ashcroft, Griffiths, and Tiffin argue, this "use of untranslated words as interface signs seems a successful way to foreground cultural distinctions" (66). Since, as Laurence notes, there was at that time "no official orthography for the Somali language" (261), she uses phonetic spellings of the Somali words. In the glossary, she also provides the spellings recommended in 1961 by the Somali Ministry of Education, which became part of the official orthography adopted in 1972. Thus although her text uses the spelling *balleh*, she notes in the glossary that according to Somali orthography, the word is *balli*.

Laurence's interest in Somali culture is demonstrated through her repeated references, both in *The Prophet's Camel Bell* and in letters written in 1951 to her friend Adele Wiseman (*Selected Letters*), to her task of transcribing and translating the Somali oral poems and stories that until that time had been kept alive mostly through poetry-singing gatherings. Laurence's were the first systematic translations into English, although as Lidwien Kapteijns points out in *Women's Voices in a Man's World*, German and Austrian scholars had begun recording Somali oral literature even before the turn of the twentieth century (209). The title of the book that resulted from Laurence's investigations, *A Tree for Poverty*, is taken from a Somali *gabay* (which she spelled *gabei*), a long alliterative poem. The poem is about drought, but Laurence uses the line to refer figuratively to Somali oral literature as an antidote to perceptions of cultural drought. The publication of the translations became possible after Laurence took a job with Chief Secretary Shirley in early 1952. When she showed the manuscript to him, he decided "it should be published by the government," if only because one passage described Somali tribesmen's "harrowing and precarious life in the dry *Jilal*" (*PCB* 247). Prefiguring her debunking of her own stereotyping of the British, Laurence writes of her surprise "that it would be an 'imperialist' who would make the publication of these translations possible" (*PCB* 47).

Throughout her travel memoir, Laurence refers to her research on her book of translations and borrows directly from it. Research into Somali oral literature was one of her primary creative activities during her year and a half in Somaliland, as is evident from her repeated, sometimes self-deprecating references to that work. "I had found what I would like to work at, here," she writes (*PCB* 46), and when asked by Governor Reece what she did with her time, "I had stammered over a reply, hesitating to tell him that I spent most of my time in attempting to translate Somali poems and folk-tales" (*PCB* 98).

Laurence discusses the life history of one well-known poet and resister of British colonialism, Mahammed 'Abdille Hasan, in the first chapter. Midway though the book, in a section on Somali attitudes toward love and marriage, she describes Somali love poetry, quotes several poems, and discusses poet Elmii Bonderii (101–6).[13] Toward the end of the book, she then summarizes her findings about the country's literature in one chapter that she excerpts directly from *A Tree for Poverty*, which is given the same title. In that chapter, Laurence comments approvingly on the Somalis' "large body of unwritten literature, containing such a high degree of dramatic sense, vivid imagination and wit" (212; see also *TFP* 47). She mentions that there are ten different types of Somali poems, but talks mostly about two: the *balwo* (which she spells *belwo*), "a short lyric love-poem" whose name literally means "a trifle" or "a bauble" (211), and the *gabay*, "the highest literary form," whose most common subjects are love and war (211). Laurence includes translations of four *balwo*, excerpts from two *gabay*, and two complete tales.[14]

Like Jameson, Laurence was more rigorous in her recording of the language and oral literature of her hosts than the superficial cultural examinations in which many contemporaneous travellers and writers engaged. She was also more self-effacing about her task; she realized "how impossible it was to blow in from the sea and size up a land's centuries in a few months" (247). She points out the limitations imposed by her lack of knowledge of the Somali language, and she gives credit to those who collaborated with her on the projects. For the poems, those collaborators were B.W. (Guś) Andrzejewski, a Polish poet who was visiting Somaliland to research the region's language and who later provided his own more detailed transcriptions of Somali poetry, and the Somali man who helped Andrzejewski, Musa Haji Ismail Galaal, whom Laurence describes as "something of an orator, and ... a well-known poet in the Somali language" (45).[15] Laurence represents Musa as at first discouraging about her work; she writes that he believed Somali poetry would only be "mangled in translation" (46). Part of his difficulty working with her, she suspected, was that he "was not accustomed to women who talked as much as I did" (113). Nevertheless, Laurence depicts him as swayed to help her with her project by her suggestion "Think of all the English here who had no idea that the Somalis had ever composed poems – think of showing them some of the epic *gabei*, the lyrical *belwo*" (46). She describes her collaboration with the two men in detail: "It was a three-way process. Musa knew a great many *gabei* and *belwo*, and had a wide knowledge of the background and style of Somali poetry, but while his command of English was fluent, he had to discuss the subtler connotations of the words with Guś in Somali. Guś and I then discussed the lines in English, and I took notes on the literal meanings, the implications of words, the references to Somali traditions or customs. I would then be able to work on this material later, and attempt to put it into some form approximating a poem, while preserving as much as possible of the meaning and spirit of the original" (113). As the poems in *A Tree for Poverty* demonstrate, Laurence attempted in her translations to retain a sense of poetic form, rather than just of literal meaning. Thus while she translated one *balwo* as "All your young beauty is to me / Like a place where the new grass sways, / After the blessing of the rain, / When the sun unveils its light"

(*PCB* 213; *TFP* 50; *Selected Letters* 64), Andrzejewski later interpreted the same poem in a much more literal fashion: "You are like a place with fresh grass after a downpour of rain / On which the sun now shines" (Finnegan 112). More recently, Kapteijns and Maryan Omar Ali translated the song in this way: "Your beauty is radiant like the rays of the sun / falling on the lush green grass, washed by the rain" (180). Like Andrzejewski's translation, these words are literally correct; like Laurence's, they are also poetic.

Laurence notes that once she finished translating the "several *gabei* and perhaps a dozen *belwo*" (114) she obtained from the two poets, she began collecting Somali tales, some of Arabic origin, from two other collaborators: her husband's employees, identified in *The Prophet's Camel Bell* as "Hersi and Arabetto" (138) and in *A Tree for Poverty* as Hersi Jama and Ahmed Nasir (21). Hersi Jama, the camp's translator, "was not only an orator but a poet" (*PCB* 170), and Ahmed Nasir was a cosmopolitan Somali Arab truck driver and mechanic. Laurence writes that while it took Hersi many months to trust her enough to tell her stories, he not only eventually told her "the stories he knew himself – he also went to considerable trouble to gather tales from various elders in the town and in nearby camps in the Haud" (176). One problem, though, was that he "edited, of course, and would only tell me such tales as he considered suitable for my ears" (176). He also acted out the plot lines, which Laurence said "compensated to some extent for the fact that I was not hearing the stories in Somali" (177). She distinguishes in *A Tree for Poverty* between the "paraphrased Somali stories" she heard mostly from Hersi and Arabetto and the "directly translated stories" she obtained from Musa Galaal and Andrzejewski (21).

The Somali language was "well suited to poetry," Laurence claims, because "so many of its words were of the portmanteau variety, containing a wealth of connotations." She gives as an example a word that describes "a wind that blew across the desert, parching the skin and drying the membranes of the throat" (*PCB* 45). Because of her Western literary background, she uses Western categories to describe these poems, as is evident in her adoption of the terms "lyric" and "epic." Her translations also represent mostly what she can understand, as she makes clear when she relates a story about a stink ant which puzzled her but which the Somalis considered "uproariously funny" (*PCB* 142–3).

In her 1978 book, African writer Micere Githae-Mugo stresses the cultural sensitivity of *A Tree for Poverty*, suggesting, "Out of respect and fear of maligning another's culture [Laurence] stretches her 'feelers' only so far" and thus "succeeds in leaving her translations as Somali as possible in content and flavour" (12). Fifteen years later, in her introduction to the 1993 republication of *A Tree for Poverty*, Donez Xiques quotes from a letter written by Andrzejewski, who cautiously praises Laurence's work, suggesting that "in spite of the language barrier she developed such empathy with the Somalis that even though her translations are sometimes not very close to the original she conveyed their spirit and atmosphere with a high degree of accuracy" (12). Kapteijns, meanwhile, includes Laurence in her bibliography but credits Andrzejewski and I.M. Lewis with "the first scholarly edition of Somali oral literature in English and Somali" (211). David Richards provides the most critical assessment of Laurence's translations; he claims that the fact that the book is "so accessible to a non-Somali reader" can be attributed to Laurence's tendency to Westernize and thus ignore the specific characteristics of Somali culture (28). Richards suggests that "the admittedly unrepresentative selection seems to have been chosen for its proximity to western literary criteria with little sense of these poems' status within the society which created them" (28). His criticism seems harsh, especially if one notes that Laurence included in both *A Tree for Poverty* and *The Prophet's Camel Bell* the story of the stink ant, which she admitted fell outside both her individual comprehension and broader Western literary standards. The continuing relevance of Laurence's translations is evident in the fact that Somali Canadian filmmaker Deeqa Omar used the poems in *A Tree for Poverty* to pave the way for her own return visit to Somalia. Indeed, the title of Omar's film project, "A Nation of Poets," is taken from Laurence's comment that "the Somalis are a nation of poets" (*TFP* 23).[16]

PROVIDING A COUNTER-NARRATIVE

One of Laurence's purposes in *The Prophet's Camel Bell*, as her translations indicate, is to provide a counter-narrative to previous imperialist discourse about Africa. If British colonizers believed the Somalis were without culture, Laurence proves them wrong by demonstrating the existence of a rich Somali literature threatened by colonialism. Similarly, in *The Tomorrow-Tamer* and *This Side Jordan*, she provides details about Ghana's pre-colonial history and culture, and in *Long Drums and Cannons* she focuses on the renewal of indigenous literature during and after the dismantling of colonial rule in Nigeria. In that last book,

Laurence argues that the scars of colonialism "can be seen outlined with bitter clarity in the novels of such writers as Chinua Achebe" (*LDC* 12). She notes approvingly that much Nigerian literature of the postcolonial era is an attempt to recover some of that society's history and culture. In a passage that Achebe later endorsed, Laurence writes, "No writer of any quality has viewed the old Africa in an idealised way, but they have tried to regain what is rightfully theirs – a past composed of real and vulnerable people, their ancestors, not the figments of missionary and colonialist imaginations" (178).

In *The Prophet's Camel Bell*, Laurence directly and explicitly counters a previous example of "colonialist imagination": Richard Burton's *First Footsteps in East Africa*. By referring repeatedly to his account of his travels in Somalia during the mid-1800s, Laurence undoubtedly acknowledges that the travel narrative "derives its authority from its pre-texts as much as from original observations" (Gikandi 97). At the same time, her account purposefully counters Burton's racist and Eurocentrist narrative, which refers to Somalis as "a barbarous people, who honour body, and degrade mind to mere cunning" (1894: 1: 33). Laurence points out that while Burton believed, as the title of his book and her chapter ("Footsteps") indicates, that "his footsteps were the first that really counted for anything in East Africa," he had in fact "come late in the roster of explorers" of that region (12). Her own narrative provides a history of the area which shows that a complex society flourished long before Burton's visit. She follows directly in his footsteps when she visits the mosque in Zeilah (Saylac), where he boasted that, in the disguise of an Arab merchant, he had preached so skilfully that he was commended for his knowledge of the Koran; she then undermines his self-important comments by telling her readers, "No one here had ever heard of Burton" (119).

Laurence later quotes other, more recent authorities in order to undermine their biased or superficial descriptions of Africa (*PCB* 249): James Thomson, who journeyed to East Africa because he loved "wanderings" (Hunter and Mannix 61); John Hunter, a game hunter who perceived Kenya as "a desert island" (Hunter and Mannix 158); and Graham Greene, who wanted to regain "the Africa of the Victorian atlas, the blank unexplored continent the shape of the human heart" (*In Search of a Character* 123). To Africans, Laurence points out, the continent was never a desert island or a blank space on the map (*PCB* 252). In her writings, she fills in the traveller's and explorer's metaphorical empty

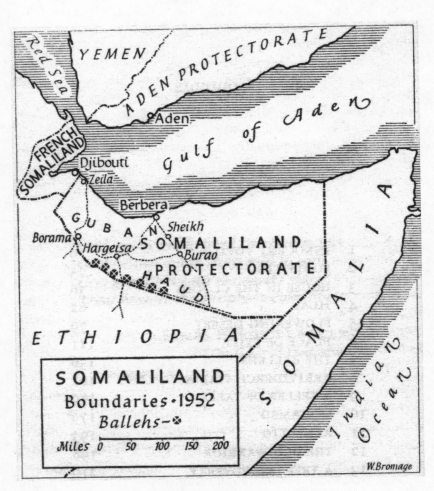

3.4   Map of Somaliland, *The Prophet's Camel Bell*

space with people who come alive through descriptions of them as "A Teller of Tales" or "The Old Warrior," and whose language and literature are represented as worthy of attention.

Paradoxically, while Laurence's narrative works to fill in blank spaces, the map of northeastern Africa that appears at the front of her book reinscribes metaphorical emptiness (fig. 3.4). It focuses on her experience of Somalia by showing mostly the communities she lived in or visited and prominently displaying the locations of the water reservoirs Jack was in charge of constructing. The rest of the British Somaliland

Protectorate, French Somaliland, and Somalia are conspicuously blank. One possible reason for this discrepancy is that although the dust jacket of the British edition notes that the map was "specially drawn" to illustrate Laurence's book (a statement reproduced in the 1988 McClelland and Stewart edition, 8), the map is signed by W. (William) Bromage, and thus it is clear that Laurence was not its author. In Reece's book a map of northern Kenya on the front and back fly-leaves provides more detail but also illustrates areas important to her, while Page's narrative is preceded by a fanciful palm tree–studded map labelled "The Brazil of P.K. Page." Graham Huggan calls a map positioned as frontispiece to a text an "icon" that "supplies an organizational principle for the reading of the text: information gleaned from the text is referred back to the map for verification, so that the act of reading the text involves an alternation between verbal and visual codes" (21). The disjunction between the visual code of Laurence's map and the verbal code of her text highlights the self-conscious questioning evident in her narrative.

One Western writer about Africa whose works Laurences embraces rather than questions is O. Mannoni. She quotes at length from his *Prospero and Caliban: The Psychology of Colonization* (1950) in order to discredit notions of the "'primitive' world" that travellers such as Hunter and Greene often carry in their minds, notions that make the places they visit "less real than our own" (Laurence, *PCB* 251; Mannoni 207). Laurence read an English translation of Mannoni's psychological interpretation of the struggle for independence in Madagascar in about 1960, eight years after she left Somaliland and a year or two before she completed *The Prophet's Camel Bell*.[17] Her reading came, she writes in that book, "with the shock of recognition one sometimes feels when another's words have a specific significance in terms of one's own experiences" (208). Laurence borrowed from and transformed a discussion of the mentality of the colonizers that appeared in *Prospero and Caliban* in order to describe the people she calls "imperialists." She quotes long passages from Mannoni's analysis of colonial officials in Madagascar. Adapting his theories to Somaliland, she concludes that the Westerners she met there were "not people who were motivated by a brutally strong belief in their own superiority, but people who were so desperately uncertain of their own worth and their ability to cope within their own societies that they were forced to seek some kind of mastery in a place where all the cards were stacked in their favour and where they could live in a self-generated glory by transferring all evils, all weaknesses, on to another people" (226–7). Laurence also disturbingly echoes Mannoni's theory that women colonialists were more racist than men (Mannoni 114–15) when she quotes the "dreary complaining" by wives of the colonial administrators and merchants in Somaliland (162).

In *The Prophet's Camel Bell*, Laurence admits that during her stay in Somaliland she gradually became conscious of her inability to interpret African culture except through her own cultural biases. As she writes after a long quotation from Mannoni, "This was something of an irony for me, to have started out in righteous disapproval of the empire-builders, and to have been forced at last to recognize that I, too, had been of that company" (251). Despite her best efforts to the contrary, she writes, she too, like Thomson, Hunter, and Greene, sought "a mythical kingdom and a private world" (251). In the years after she wrote *A Tree for Poverty*, Laurence certainly became more attuned to the possibility of cultural self-absorption in writing about an unfamiliar society. Her chapter on Somali oral literature in *The Prophet's Camel Bell* is taken almost directly from *A Tree for Poverty*, but the minor changes she makes reflect her desire to avoid homogenization of Somali religious beliefs with Western Christian beliefs; for example, as Fiona Sparrow notes, she replaces all references to "God" in the earlier book with the word "Allah" in the later one (Sparrow, *Into Africa* 146).

The pervasive influence of imperialist attitudes on Laurence's writing is evident in her adaptation to the Somali context of Mannoni's theory that colonized peoples have a prior need to be dependent. As he writes, "colonization has always required the existence of the need for dependence. Not all peoples can be colonized; only those who experience this need" (85). Thus the coming of Europeans, he argues, "was unconsciously expected – even desired – by the future subject peoples" (86). Mannoni's concept of a "dependence complex" has been refuted by theorists beginning with Frantz Fanon in 1952 (*Black Skin, White Masks*) and Aimé Césaire in 1955 (*Discourse on Colonialism*), but Laurence probably did not read either book while preparing her travel memoir, since they were first translated into English in 1967 and 1972 respectively. Fanon argues persuasively that dependence is not innate but is instead the result of "the arrival of white colonizers on the island" (108): "Let us have the courage to say it outright: *It is the racist who creates his inferior*" (93; italics in original).

An example that Mannoni provides to support his theory is of a Malagasy employee who, once offered a reward over and above his pay, demanded more and more from his employer. Mannoni attributes such behaviour to a transference of the Malagasies' reverence toward and dependence on their ancestors onto the colonizers who employed and protected them. While he points out that the Malagasies referred to both their ancestors and their colonial employers as "the father and also the mother" (61), Laurence writes that Jack's Somali employees referred to the two of them as "like my mother and my father" (189) and like a king and queen (200, 209). Reece, too, writes that as district commissioner in Kenya, her husband repeatedly heard the phrase "You are my father and my mother," sometimes as a reproach because "the District Commissioner appeared to be forgetting what was due to a well-loved son," and sometimes in gratitude because he had made a decision "to the speaker's advantage" (41). Reece calls it an "overworked phrase" and says that it meant that, in the opinion of the speakers, "everything that concerned the welfare of the people in his [Gerald Reece's] district was his responsibility" (41). She also reports that she was called "Mumma" by "all and sundry" (52), including a man she said was almost three times her age.

While Reece describes without comment the practice of using the nomenclature of parenting as a term of respect, Laurence suggests that in characterizing her and Jack as parental figures, the Somalis, like the Malagasies Mannoni describes, could feel they had allied themselves with "strong" and "capable" protectors (209). Laurence adopts Mannoni's ideas as a retroactive and revisionary way of theorizing interactions with their employee Abdi, who was at first friendly and protective toward them but who, when they failed to give in to what they saw as his increasingly outrageous demands, bitterly rejected them. She now reinterprets his identification of them as "king" and "queen" (209), which she had taken as a compliment, as an attempt to convince himself that his dependence on them was justified. She quotes from her "notebooks": "If we are sahib and memsahib, Abdi can do his job, and be polite, and try with a clear conscience to get as much as possible from us, secure in his basic hatred of us" (205, 206). She then writes that she has revised that viewpoint in light of Mannoni's dependence complex: "Seen from a distance, the details in my notebooks begin to take on a new meaning" (208). As she rereads the situation in 1963, Jack had entered into "a tacit agreement to act as a kind of protector to [Abdi] and his family ... His later and increased demands, which seemed so outrageous then, seem in retrospect to have been a frantic effort to prove that the bond still existed" (PCB 208).

Laurence was so convinced of the accuracy of Mannoni's theory that, as she writes in "Books that Mattered to Me" (244), she again adapted it outside its original cultural context when she used it as the basis for

3.5 "Hersi, Jack, Abdi," photograph by Margaret Laurence.
Courtesy of David and Jocelyn Laurence

her story "The Voices of Adamo." In that story, a young Ghanaian man whose family dies and whose community is destroyed by illness attaches himself to the British colonial army as a drummer. When, through a misunderstanding, he is discharged from the army, he kills his British captain because he is unable to face independence. Laurence's story is a melodramatic and, at the same time, textbook rendition of a theory that resonates with imperialist overtones.[18]

A more nuanced examination of the effect of a colonialist inheritance is illustrated in Laurence's "The Perfume Sea." Commentators have described it as a story of unusual love and of success in adapting to change: Craig Tapping calls "The Perfume Sea" "a gentle, compelling, ironic, and wry study of expatriate life" (78), while Jane Leney suggests that its main characters, two Europeans in a town in an unnamed African country modelled on Ghana, "are neither dominating nor dominated" and "do not attempt to exert power" (78). Those two protagonists, Mr Archipelago and Doree, run a beauty shop that flounders when they lose their European clientele after independence. With help from their African landlord and his daughter, they eventually admit African women as clients, thus safeguarding both their fragile relationship and their marginal position in the changing society. The story is indeed hopeful, but an unspoken undercurrent is that in using makeup and straightening their hair, African women have adopted the mores of the colonizers and in that way perpetuate their own colonization. As Arun Mukherjee points out, the new role of Archipelago and Doree is "to help the African bourgeoisie slavishly imitate the values of its former colonial masters" (33). She suggests that because the two main characters "have no known national identities – both of them keep changing their stories," they "represent the whole white civilization." Mukherjee contends, "The story thus underplays the lives of individuals in order to emphasize these larger issues: the nature of colonialism as well as its aftermath when the native elite takes over without really changing the colonial institutions except for their names" (33). Laurence's fictional beauty salon thus reveals the cultural methods through which colonialism is extended into the postcolonial era.

That an author's work can both be anti-imperialist and show evidence of an imperialist inheritance is not surprising. In *Long Drums and Cannons*, Laurence has been accused, as she was with *A Tree for Poverty*, of continuing the imperialist tradition of universalizing human experience, an accusation that may have some justification. Richards suggests that Laurence's "appeal to a fundamental, transcultural humanity finds refuge ... in a transhistorical comparison which collapses time, distance and cultural difference into a common pool of fundamental relationships" (28). In *Morning Yet on Creation Day*, Achebe decries the limitations inherent in the Western focus on universalism. Although he does not accuse Laurence of such a limited focus, he points out that "the work of a Western writer is automatically informed by universality. It is only others who must strain to achieve it" (9). Achebe concludes that the word "universal" should be "banned altogether from discussions of African literature until such a time as people cease to use it as a synonym for the narrow, self-serving parochialism of Europe" (9). In *Long Drums and Cannons*, Laurence indeed stresses the universality of Nigerian literature. She writes that it gives insight "not only into immediate and local dilemmas but, through these, into the human dilemma as a whole" (13); that the "best of these Nigerian plays and novels reveal something of ourselves to us, whoever and wherever we are" (13); and that a book by writer Elechi Amadi has "an unfaltering authenticity which in turn helps to extend the novel's meaning beyond any one culture" (158). As these comments indicate, Western literary notions of the importance of universality continued to be influential in Laurence's analysis of non-Western literature, indicating the power of her discursive inheritance.

DEFINING A SUBJECT POSITION

A more nuanced approach is evident in the way that Laurence's descriptions of hunting help to delineate differences in gender and culture. Like Jameson and Hubbard, Laurence positions herself as someone who, because of her gender, regards hunting as an unpleasant activity, but who is carried away by the thrill of the chase in the same way that Hubbard eventually joins in shooting at a bear.[19] In the first hunting scene in *The Prophet's Camel Bell*, Jack and Abdi are in pursuit of the fresh meat a *garanuug* or *deero* (types of gazelle, which Laurence spells *gerenuk* and *dero*) will provide. Laurence writes that from his place in the Land Rover, Jack "on wild impulse stood and took a pot shot at a fox" (65). Her own response to this gratuitous killing is not recorded, but she writes that the response of the Somali men was "fantastic jubilation! ... A good omen – now, obviously, we would get a *gerenuk*" (65). Her description of the gazelle that is subsequently shot at but missed distinguishes her from the more bloodthirsty Somali men: "I was struck, hypnotized almost, by the unbelievable grace of it. Not so the Somalis. They were too meat-hungry to consider anything else" (66).[20] Eventually, however, Laurence writes, "Even I was infected now with the spirit of the hunt, and would have seen the creature destroyed for the sheer triumph of scoring, even apart from the need for meat" (66).

Her feminine and Western sensibilities are evident in her reaction to the intimate involvement in the killing of animals for food to which she was subjected in Somaliland. She watched as the cook took away a sheep purchased to replace the escaped gazelle: "Precisely fifteen minutes later Mohamed appeared with our dinner, two steaming plates of rice with large slabs of meat at the side ... The interval between life and death, creature and meat, had been indecently slight, from my point of view" (67). The distance she attempted to place between herself and Mohamed was not only of gender but also of culture. Similarly, when Abdi shot two cheetahs, animals it was against the law to kill, she excused him by saying, "He was a hunter. He simply could not help shooting" (146).[21] She identifies her distress at the fact that the men in the camp tormented one of the still-living animals as based on cultural difference: "The Somalis thought I was foolish to want the cheetah put out of its pain at once, and I thought they were cruel to want to prolong its agony. Neither of us would alter our viewpoints" (147).[22]

Laurence later expressed distaste about the Islamic requirement that one eat meat only from animals that have had their throats slit, which led to Abdi's practice of shooting animals only to wound. She described a gazelle that he had shot running about "crazily for what seemed an eternity, bleeding thickly, half its stomach shot away" (202), and then added that she knew it was "foolish" to feel "sickened" by such a thing (202): "If I had known starvation, I would not be much concerned, either, about the death throes of a deer" (203). This passage demonstrates her desire to be sensitive to cultural difference, despite her initial distaste for unfamiliar practices.

Reece, too, describes the Islamic method of killing animals, but in a more detached and ironic way (61–2). She represents hunting as natural both to men and to Kenyans as she reports without comment that one of her husband's servants, Godana, longed to hunt a protected greater kudu with his spear. After Godana rescued a doe from the forest, she and her children made a pet of it, but returned from an outing to discover that Godana had killed and eaten the animal (179). Although Reece was initially angry with the man, she eventually disparaged her own tendency to make pets out of wild animals (180). For her, killing was a masculine activity but something she could approve of when necessary and even do herself. When a rhino charged her, she shouted to Gerald to "shoot it!" (117), and she describes feeling both "proud and ashamed" at her skill at killing snakes with a hoe (69). Similarly, Laurence writes with a kind of rueful pride that she has become "an expert scorpion-spearer" (254).

Gender and cultural difference are also evident in Laurence's treatment of the perceived dangers for woman travellers – dangers that had not changed much, apparently, if one compares *The Prophet's Camel Bell* to Hubbard's narrative of fifty years earlier.[23] Laurence outlines two incidents in which she feared for her life, both of which involved a desire by others that she use a gun to defend herself. The first perceived danger came from a group of Somali camel herders who were suspicious that the *ballehs* Jack was building might be poisoned, taken over by the British, or heavily taxed, and who as a result threatened to attack the work camp. Laurence writes that she was filled with "doubts and indecisions" about what to do about people who might "turn in their despair against the first person who happened to catch their attention, when that person might be oneself" (71). Jack had no such indecision; he decreed that because he was away surveying most days and Margaret was alone in camp (except for the cook and his ten-year-old helper), she must learn to fire the rifle. Just as Hubbard made a joke of her poor marksmanship when she tried to shoot the bear (59) and only later spoke more seriously of oiling her gun in preparation for meeting the Naskapi (WW 182; MH Diary 14 Aug.), Laurence initially described learning to shoot as a humorous incident – humorous, at least, to those watching. She "had never fired a gun of any description," but Jack loaded the .303 and told her to hold it close to her shoulder and pull the trigger. She described the outcome in this way:

Whoom! Stunningly, I found myself sprawled on the ground, the rifle beside me. In the background, the Somalis were quietly guffawing.

"For pete's sake," Jack said, trying to hold back his laughter, "I told you to hold it tightly – why didn't you."

My pride was more damaged than my shoulder. I went back to the tent by myself.

At last Jack poked his head in through the tent doorway.

"Maybe it would be safer, at that, for you to rely on your gift of the gab. You've got that in common with the Somalis." (71–2)

Their camp was never in fact attacked, and Laurence did not have to put either her lack of skill with a gun or her real skill with language to the test. The description of this incident emphasizes gender difference: because she was a woman, decisions could be made for her and she could be laughed at for incompetence with a gun. The passage also emphasizes the inherent perceived dangers for a woman "alone" in another culture where the motivations of others are difficult to comprehend. Like Hubbard and Jameson, Laurence was of course never really alone, but her cultural and gender isolation created an apparent solitude.

The second threatening incident described in *The Prophet's Camel Bell* reinforces concepts of isolation, difference, and gender-typing. After the Land Rover became stuck in mud during the rainy season in a remote area of the countryside, Jack and Abdi feared that a group of herdsmen would try to steal the rifle that was with Margaret inside the vehicle. As Abdi later informed her, "I tell them we have plenty ammunition, and I say the officer's woman, she know how to shoot very well"

(82). As a woman, Laurence might not be expected to know how to use a gun, but as a memsahib, she would. Abdi's care and her own fears in fact were unwarranted. The group of herders not only did not attack, but helped to push the vehicle out of the mudhole.[24]

ANALYZING GENDER

Laurence's critique of the status of women in *The Prophet's Camel Bell* is at times tentative, especially when compared to the more explicit feminism of her subsequent Manawaka cycle of fiction. One possible reason for this hesitancy is the gap between research and composition of the book. During that gap of about ten years, Laurence became more aware of issues relating to women's oppression, gained more access to theoretical models that would aid her analysis, and experienced the effects of gender-typing in her life. During those same years, she was in the midst of writing her first published novel about a woman's life, *The Stone Angel*, which she set aside in order to complete *The Prophet's Camel Bell*. She travelled in Somaliland when she was in her mid-twenties and childless, but by the time she wrote her travel narrative, she had had personal experience with the frustrations of trying to take care of children, keep house, and continue to write fiction. Laurence wrote to Adele Wiseman in 1956 that most of her acquaintances in Africa knew nothing about her writing: "I am a mother and housewife. Full stop" (*Selected Letters* 94). Alice Munro, who lived in Vancouver in the early 1960s when the Laurences also lived there, reported that Margaret appeared to be "someone who was trying terribly hard to do everything" – trying to fulfill a traditional housewife's role before she allowed herself time to write (qtd. in King 158). Indeed, in *Dance on the Earth*, Laurence calls Tillie Olsen's *Silences* the "best, most poignant description and analysis" of women writers who are forced to put their calling last (136).

Olsen's book was first published in 1978. During the early 1950s, when Laurence was researching her book about Somalia, she had access to few feminist conceptual models, other than Nellie McClung's early didactic feminism, which would have given her the theoretical language to write about, or even think about, women's lives ("Books that Mattered to Me" 241). In *Dance on the Earth*, she writes that she read and was influenced by Virginia Woolf, one of the first feminists to use the term "patriarchal" to describe societies based on the law of the father. Woolf's prose, she writes, "helped shape my view of life, as did her brand of feminism," but she found that Woolf's fiction lacked "ordinariness, dirt, earth, blood, yelling, a few messy kids" (130). Laurence may have read Simone de Beauvoir's *The Second Sex* (1949), which posited woman as an inessential "Other" to man's essential "One," but not until it was translated into English in 1953. In any case, de Beauvoir's book would not have been useful in her discussion of specific issues such as clitoridectomy; although the debunking of the Freudian myth of clitoral versus vaginal orgasm was just beginning at the time de Beauvoir was composing her book, she was unable to revise her thinking about sexuality enough to accommodate this change. Betty Friedan's *The Feminine Mystique* (1963) was published the same year as *The Prophet's Camel Bell*, but its frame of reference – middle-class North American women – was at such variance with the situation of women in British Somaliland that its concepts could not have been usefully applied. Books such as Kate Millet's *Sexual Politics* and Germaine Greer's *The Female Eunuch*, which provide broader feminist theoretical models and at least mention the issues of clitoridectomy and infibulation (Millet 46; Greer 260) about which Laurence also wrote, were not published until 1969 and 1970 respectively, well after Laurence began writing about women's lives in Africa and Canada. She had to create her own language to write about women's lives and had to come to her own conclusions. As she observes, the "upsurge of the new women's movement in the 1960's" simply confirmed her approach and gave her "a much-needed sense of community" ("Ivory Tower" 23).

Laurence's feminism is evident in the Manawaka books (and in her later memoir, *Dance on the Earth*) through her representation of women's lives, including their domestic lives, as a subject of fundamental interest to readers; her inclusion of descriptions of sexuality and childbirth; her rewriting of the myth of the evil stepmother; and her "writing beyond the ending" (DuPlessis 197) of the romance plot to show women as mothers and elderly women. In her African writings, by contrast, Laurence appears at first glance almost to ignore women. Only three of the stories in *The Tomorrow-Tamer* have women as protagonists – "The Rain Child," "A Fetish for Love," and "A Gourdful of Glory" – and *This Side Jordan* is told through the joint perspectives of two male characters. Most of the Somalis Laurence writes about in *The Prophet's Camel Bell* are men, and almost all the literature she transcribes and translates in *A Tree for Poverty* and criticizes in *Long Drums and Cannons* is by men (in part because very little literature by Somali and Nigerian women was available to her). Nevertheless, she does indicate in her African books at least an initial awareness of and attention to the conditions of women's lives.

In *Long Drums and Cannons*, Laurence makes few comments about Nigerian gender relations or, indeed, about the effect colonization has had on issues of gender, but her description of Nigerian literature does reveal something of women's status. As she points out, many of the works take polygyny as a given, and women are seldom protagonists of the novels or plays. Laurence notes that one of the few Nigerian novels with a woman protagonist, Elechi Amadi's *The Concubine*, "is not so much about her as about the effect she has upon the three men who involve themselves ... with her life" (158). Only one of the eleven writers Laurence discusses is female, perhaps not surprisingly, since Flora Nwapa was the only Nigerian woman who had published a book by the mid-1960s. In her discussion of Nwapa, Laurence alludes to differences between Nwapa's novel *Efuru* and the much more numerous books by Nigerian men. She notes, for example, that *Efuru* "takes place almost totally within the minds and the society of women" (169), and that the concerns of these women are with childlessness and changing customs about societal issues such as the bride price. Although comparisons between men's and women's literature are implicit rather than explicit in Laurence's criticism, and although she tends to represent gender issues in neutral terms as part of Nigeria's cultural makeup, her analysis does provide glimpses into women's lives in Nigeria.

Laurence's assessments of women poets in Somaliland and of the representation of women in Somali men's poetry provide graphic examples of the place of women within that society. She was told that some Somali women composed poems, but since Somalia was rigidly divided along gender lines, they could recite them only to other women. Because of this gender segregation and because her translators were men, Laurence could provide no examples of women's poetry. She was assured by her male informants that women's poems were never about love, the major subject of men's short poems, because "here only prostitutes sing love-songs" (TFP 27), although Laurence indicates that she doubted the truth of that report.

Women thus are depicted through men's eyes alone in the poems and stories of *A Tree for Poverty*. Many of the male poets' short love poems dwell on women's physical appearance, as in the poem quoted earlier (50). The only other poetic reference to a woman is in a longer poem in which a faithless friend is said to have a memory as "short as any woman's" about the pain of childbirth (55). In the traditional stories that Laurence includes in her travel memoir and in her book of translations, men are almost always the heroes or likable villains, although one story tells of a mother-daughter pair of cannibal women who eat their husbands, two stories recount the way in which an evil queen is outsmarted by a wise magician, and two other tales describe a wise girl who marries the sultan, whom she then outwits. In that last story, a subplot is the sexual double standard. The sultan's wife outwits him by following his impossible order – to become pregnant and bear a child during the year he is away, yet at the same time to remain faithful to him – by following him and disguising herself as another woman, whom he seduces. Her cleverness at outwitting him is the moral of the story; his infidelity is accepted and expected male behaviour (*TFP* 120). The literature that Laurence presents thus reveals aspects of Somali gender relations that include the sexual double standard and the focus on women as sexual objects. The inaccessibility of women's own literature further exemplifies their restricted place in traditional Somali society.

One counterpoint to Laurence's representation of Somali literature is supplied by Isak Dinesen, who writes that while she lived in Kenya between 1914 and 1931, she "saw few women" (179) but did interact with the Somali wife of her employee, Farah, along with several of the young woman's female relatives. Dinesen says, "Sometimes, to entertain me, they would relate fairy tales in the style of the Arabian Nights, mostly in the comical genre, which treated love with much frankness. It was a trait common to all these tales that the heroine, chaste or not, would get the better of the male characters and come out of the tale triumphant" (179–80). Dinesen's descriptions of these tales show them to be similar to a few of the stories Laurence heard. While Dinesen's use of the term "fairy tales" diminishes the impact of the stories, they have clearly been given a feminine interpretation, since the heroine can be "chaste or not" but will always be "triumphant."

A more complex analytical counterpoint to Laurence's translations is evident in a 1999 book about the representation of gender in Somali oral poetry. *Women's Voices in a Man's World*, by Lidwien Kapteijns with Somali translator Maryan Omar Ali, does what Laurence's *A Tree for Poverty* is unable to do: it examines Somali oral literature by women and comments more fully on representations of Somali gender relations as expressed through their literature. Kapteijns argues that *gabay* had the highest position in the Somali literary canon *because* they were composed by established male authors; the newer *balwo* (by younger men) and the songs by women were excluded from that canon. She notes that women sang work songs (one of which Burton refers to in his *First Footsteps* [Kapteijns 154]), but also privately composed songs called *buraanbur* with similar concerns to the *gabay*: "love, jealousy, anger, and joy" (75). (Thus Laurence's informants appear to have been mistaken in saying that women never sang love songs.) Because, as Kapteijns confirms, women's poetry was indeed only recited to a small circle of friends and family, it was not transmitted to succeeding generations in the same way as men's poetry, and much of it was lost.

Kapteijns points out that women in fact began to perform modern love songs in public in the early 1950s (the years Laurence was in Somaliland). She notes that two women who sang on Radio Mogadishu and Radio Hargeisa in 1951 and 1953 respectively were initially "targets of virulent social criticism," but they paved the way for other women's voices to be heard (104).[25] Kapteijns contends that most modern love songs "were created by men (even though they were sung by as many female as male singers)" (5). She attributes this phenomenon of male authorship in part to "a literary canon and social world defined by men" (2) and in part to reaction against colonial rule by the young male intellectuals who composed the songs. Such reaction led them to hark back to the tradition of Somali pastoral orature (109), a move that further constrained women's roles within their society.

Laurence's earliest explicit analysis of Somali gender relations is in her introduction to the orature of *A Tree for Poverty*. She writes, "Both tribal and religious traditions place women's status as infinitely inferior to that of men," and the "Somali wife is expected to be faithful to her husband, but fidelity is not expected of him" (30). She reworded that assessment for *The Prophet's Camel Bell*, but only slightly: "the status of women was low, according to both tribal and religious traditions," and once a couple was married, "[s]exual fidelity was demanded of her, but not of him" (103). That later book makes it clear that during the year and a half Laurence lived in Somaliland, she met many more men than women, in part because she accompanied her husband to desert construction camps and in part because language and cultural differences isolated her more from Somali women than from men (since the men were more likely than the women to speak some English). As does *A Tree for Poverty*, *The Prophet's Camel Bell* reflects those limitations, focusing mostly on descriptions of men, especially in the several chapters of character sketches. Laurence did meet some women, though, and her depictions of them centre on various aspects of their lives,

3.6 "Hargeisa wells," photograph by C.J. Martin. Courtesy of C.J. Martin

including marriage and child-rearing. She tells of being visited while in Sheikh by two young women, "wives of two of the local elders" (56). Of one named Hawa, Laurence writes, "I wondered how a girl her age, which could not have been more than fifteen or sixteen, felt about being married to an old man ... [T]he look of resignation in her eyes said that her life was a bitter one" (57).

Laurence notes in *The Prophet's Camel Bell* that life was difficult for many people in Somaliland in the early 1950s, but especially for the women. During her travels in the desert, she saw Somali women and children dying of thirst and starvation (77–8). She watched the women walk all day beside the burden camels and then set up the families' portable houses before they could rest (75).[26] Laurence was initially interested in education projects for Somali women, but after talking to the British wife of the director of education, she became convinced that such education had to be practical, "not the highly theoretical education which at this stage of the country's development would inevitably separate a woman from her people and turn her into a prostitute" (57). The equation of education with prostitution appears bizarre, but Laurence may have made this comparison because she adopted the opinion of a member of the colonizing culture (just as she allowed herself to be called "memsahib" even though she despised the word).

Laurence's analysis of gender includes references to the fact that Somali society was polygynous, and although Somali men often married girls of their choice, young women (such as Hawa) could be married against their wills to men old enough to be their grandfathers. A betrothed couple could spend one night alone together before marriage, Laurence writes, and although Judith Snively calls a similar practice in Kenya "mutual masturbation" (12), Laurence has a more realistic interpretation of the man's power during the encounter: "he could undress her and do anything he wanted with her, short of actual intercourse" (102–3). In fact, since the Somali girl had been excised and infibulated, only her future husband was likely to experience any sexual pleasure from the encounter. Kapteijns writes that the practice of undressing the bride was mainly to allow the husband "to verify his betrothed's virginity" and "would now be disapproved of" (29).

Laurence also reports that Somali girls changed hands from father to husband through the mechanism of a bride price. While Laurence asked tentative questions about the custom, Reece's response in her narrative about Kenya is both more explicit and more personal. She reports that after she arrived as a bride, men would often "look me over speculatively and ask how many cows I had cost" (To My Wife 66–7). She relates the story of a young Somali woman in Kenya who, when her husband died, was passed on to his brother against her wishes because she "belonged" to him (152). British complicity in this social practice became evident after the woman eloped with a man of her choice, and the British district commissioner confiscated cattle from the man's family to force him to either return her or compensate her first husband's family (154). Reece also reports her dismay when one of their servants began negotiations to "give" his twelve-year-old daughter to one of several men in exchange for ten cows. She writes that the "delightful Adie might have been a cow" herself (185). Adie's older sister, meanwhile, was married against her will to a man who had paid the bride price, because, according to the father she "was his 'mali,' his property, to dispose of as he wished" (190). Reece has no qualms about expressing her anger at such practices.

Laurence, meanwhile, learned from conversations with Somali men that wife-beating was an accepted norm in that part of Africa. When Ahmed Nasir (who related the Arabic stories to Laurence) discovered that Jack did not beat Margaret, he told her "that was carrying consideration too far" (197). Laurence notes that women did resist through their speech (which she describes as "irritable and nagging," 103), and that although they appeared meek, they were in fact "meek as Antigone, meek as Medea" (22). While Kapteijns confirms that traditional Somali poems by women "both prescribe married women's obedience to their husbands and represent women rejecting, resisting, and regretting such obedience" (44), she points out that the "very fact of contestation ... is evidence of the reality of patriarchy" (76). Laurence's depiction of violence against women is not limited to Somalis but also encompasses the British. She describes her uneasiness in a house in Zeilah, later explained by her discovery that "a British administrative officer killed his wife there and then shot himself" (125). Laurence calls her unease "implausible," "hackneyed, even" (125), but her narrative makes it clear that the murder of a British woman during domestic abuse was indeed believable.

For Laurence, purdah, or veiling of women, is a metaphor for their silencing as well as for their invisibility to her and within Somali society generally. At Port Said, on the way to Somaliland, she twice notes "women in *purdah*" (16, 17). In Somaliland she realizes that only urban women were veiled (33), "for *purdah* was never worn by those who spent their lives leading the burden camels" (75). Despite her recognition of the class implications of the veil, Laurence does not explicitly analyze its gender implications. (In a similar way, Frantz Fanon fails to recognize the patriarchal nature of the practice, calling it "a formerly inert element of the native cultural configuration" [*A Dying Colonialism* 46]). Instead, she rather flippantly describes it as a way for women to flirt more effectively using their "expressive" eyes (33). Throughout her text, though, purdah is linked to the acts of closing off, shutting away, and silencing. When Laurence describes the town of Hargeisa, she calls the cloth merchants' shops "stony hags whose angularity showed through their *purdah* of grey shutters" (33). Of one building in Djibouti, in French Somaliland, Laurence writes, "The eyes of many women in *purdah* seemed to be peering from behind these shutters, or so we imagined, peering out at a world which they were never allowed to touch" (127).

Laurence also uses the metaphor of veiling to describe the way in which she altered her own behaviour to conform to Somali gender expectations. One day when Jack was away, she invited several Somali elders who had come to talk about the water reservoirs into the house. The cook, Mohamed, later told her that "a woman alone in the house must never invite men in, not even if they happen to be about eighty years old," and that "the elders could certainly not discuss any serious matter with a woman" (41). Laurence herself could not determine their response to her efforts to explain the project (although after a subsequent meeting, she quotes another group of men as saying, "What does she know of it, the fool?" [70]). The men of this first group were certainly dissatisfied enough that they came again to talk to Jack. During that later visit, Laurence writes, she sat silently in a corner, "feeling almost as though I were in *purdah*" (41). She thus learned about attitudes toward women, and was directed to change her own behaviour, not just through observing how others lived but through the way she herself was treated.

In a parallel incident, when Alys Reece was asked by her husband to give tea to a visiting group of elders, she writes, "They would not have called on me, as I was a mere woman" (*To My Wife* 54). Reece explains that "the strain of being always on sufferance in a man's world tended to make me feel small and insignificant" (84). Although Laurence and Reece were theoretically part of the group of colonizers, their gender at times placed them at a lower status than even the colonized men; they may have been dominant in terms of race, but they were subordinate in terms of gender (Sharpe 12). Thus while Laurence writes that Jack's Somali employees openly criticized her behaviour and made fun of her ineptness with guns and her fear of geckos (39), Reece writes that even their house servants "had the customary nomadic contempt for women and regarded themselves as Gerald's servants, not mine" (92–3).

REPRESENTING VISIBILITY AND INVISIBILITY THROUGH PHOTOGRAPHS

Women's invisibility is tangible in the twenty-five photographs that Laurence and her publishers included in *The Prophet's Camel Bell*.[27] Photographs are not as integral to her narrative as they are to Hubbard's, since photography was not one of her primary activities while she was in Somaliland. Perhaps for that reason, her photographic record has received no critical attention. In her travel memoir, Laurence only once discusses taking a photograph, of a child whose nakedness had to be covered because modesty was "next to piety" for a Muslim male (55). That image is not in the book, possibly because of his mother's determined efforts to cover him. Instead, the five photographs credited to Laurence are snapshots in which adults are lined up against vehicles or buildings (see, for example, fig. 3.5). These snapshots appear designed to show readers the faces of the people about whom she writes – men who worked with her husband and who helped with her translations. Thus the men look directly into the camera and are posed with tools of their employment, including a tray for the cook, Mohamed; the Land Rover for its driver, Abdi; a book for the translator, Hersi Jama; a truck for its driver, Ahmed Nasir; and a bulldozer for the head mechanic, Gino. Two of the snapshots credited as being "supplied by the author" (Macmillan edition, "Illustrations" np) must have been taken by other people, since Laurence figures in them. Twenty photographs supplied to Laurence by C.J. Martin, the colonial government's information officer who was later in charge of the BBC Somali Service, demonstrate much more clearly the country and its people. As well as portraits of individual Somalis, Martin's photographs illustrate the Hargeisa marketplace and wells (fig. 3.3 and 3.6), the Haud desert, Somali craftspeople making baskets and sandals, nomads herding camels, the nomads' portable huts, and even the construction of one of Jack Laurence's reservoirs (fig. 3.9).

The photographs by Laurence and Martin can be compared to the fourteen photographs in Reece's *To My Wife*, which are spread over eight pages scattered throughout the book. All those in Reece's book are uncredited, but since hers is the only name on the title page, readers are led to assume that they are by her. (Again, as with photographs of Laurence and Hubbard, she cannot in fact be the author of the photograph that shows her astride a camel.) The only time Reece describes using a camera, to take photographs of a crocodile, she is disparaging of her own efforts, which she says resulted in "about fifty fuzzy outlines instead of one superb specimen" (224). The photographs in her book, while not professional, provide more details about Kenyan culture and countryside than do Laurence's about Somali culture. They show the forest, camels and an ostrich, several groups of people Reece met in Kenya (including Somali clansmen, Dubas, a Gurreh child, Ethiopian refugee children, Boran women and men, and Turkana men), and one photograph each of herself and her husband. The photographs of the

3.7   "Two Boran women at the wells with wicker water pots,"
To My Wife – 50 Camels

Boran women and men suggest that the purpose of this documentation is in part ethnographic, since they show the women in traditional dress carrying wicker water pots (facing 209, fig. 3.7) and the men wearing what the caption identifies as "phallic emblems" on their heads in preparation for a ceremony to welcome them as full members of their community (facing 224).

The photograph in Reece's book of the Boran water carriers is the only one that shows, close up and recognizably, women other than herself. A striking feature of the photographs in *The Prophet's Camel*

Bell is that the only recognizable woman in them is Laurence herself. All the portraits and activity photographs, both by Laurence and by Martin, are of men or boys, with the exception of one staged photograph of a girl weaving a basket.[28] Women appear only in the long shots, such as the photograph of the Hargeisa wells (fig. 3.6), which features a woman carrying a baby in what Laurence describes as "a sling tied around his bottom, so that his back was bent like a half moon" (55), and the photograph of Hargeisa town, in which a veiled figure in the foreground is probably a woman (fig. 3.3).

This lack of representations of women is a graphic demonstration of the invisibility of Somali women that Laurence's text implies. She writes about few women in *The Prophet's Camel Bell* because she became acquainted with few. She presents no orature by women in *A Tree for Poverty* because gender segregation made women's poetry inaccessible to her. Thus the relegation of women to the private sphere is evident as much in what Laurence does *not* write about as in what she describes, and in the photographs that she and Martin are *unable* as well as able to produce.

Textual self-representation in Laurence's and Reece's books is also mirrored in the photographs. Laurence writes that soon after she arrived in Somaliland, while she was living at a bungalow in Sheikh, a group of curious onlookers gathered to ask whether she was a man or a woman. Just as she changed her method of relating to men after being chastised by Mohamed, so her response to these comments was to conform to Somali notions of women's modesty (or at least a Westernized version of those notions). She writes: "Never again did I wear slacks in Somaliland, not even in the desert evenings when the mosquitoes were thick as porridge, not even in the mornings when the hordes of glue-footed flies descended" (56). The two photographs of Laurence show her dressed as she describes. In one, probably taken about the time her sex was questioned, she sits on the steps of the Sheikh bungalow, wearing a dress (but as yet with no scarf over her head, as befitted a married Somali woman [fig. 3.1]). Her arm is around a dog, probably the "good-natured black dog of undeterminable breed" that was lent to her by a neighbouring schoolteacher to protect her while Jack was away (54). In the other image (fig. 3.8), she perches on a dozer blade between Jack and the Italian foreman, Gino, wearing an outfit similar to the one she describes as having horrified Somali governor Reece when he dropped in unexpectedly to their camp: "canvas tennis shoes which were caked with wet mud, a pair of Jack's socks, a wrinkled old cotton

3.8 "Jack, author, and Gino," *The Prophet's Camel Bell*. Courtesy of David and Jocelyn Laurence

skirt and blouse, and a kerchief wound around my head turban style" (97). Although she was ashamed of her dishevelment, the kerchief over her head and the skirt worn even in a desert camp contrast strikingly with Alys Reece's attire in the photograph in *To My Wife* (facing 80, fig. 3.2). In that image, Reece wears slacks and a floppy-brimmed hat and sits astride a camel. Laurence, meanwhile, notes that in Somaliland people never rode the camels but only led them (103). Thus while Reece participates in an activity of memsahibs and sahibs and dresses in a Westernized fashion, Laurence attempts to conform to Somali codes of behaviour and dress.

MATERNITY, CHILD PROSTITUTION, AND GENITAL EXCISION: QUESTIONING WESTERN INTERVENTION

Laurence's comments on gender roles are especially evident in her textual treatment of three specific issues: enforced maternity, child prostitution, and genital excision and infibulation.[29] She writes that she learned about attitudes toward mothering, as she learned about the silencing of women, through her own experiences. Because she was childless, Somali acquaintances repeatedly greeted her with the words, "I pray Allah grant you a son" (73; see also 56, 200). Thus her bodily functions, which in some autobiographical writing by women are only hinted at (Neuman 1–2), are more explicitly represented because they were of interest to the people who surrounded her. She writes that the "Somalis had been concerned for some time about my childless state, and they knew quite well that I was concerned about it, too" (145). In the desert, Jack's employees told her that an ostrich egg she and Jack had found would work as a fertility charm, and they recommended that she also eat lion fat if she wanted to become pregnant. When she became pregnant and moved from the desert to the city of Hargeisa to ensure the continuation of the pregnancy, a Somali woman suggested that Jack must be glad she was having a child: "You have been married five years – a long time," she told Laurence. "If you did not bear him a child soon, he would have had to divorce you" (255).

In Kenya, Reece faced similar concerns about her lack of offspring. During the first childless year of her marriage, she was given an ostrich egg festooned with seashells to hang over her bed (55). Her husband was repeatedly asked, "Has God sent her an embryo yet?" (67), and when Reece gave birth to a daughter, they were told that "God would do better for me next time" (84, 88; see also 91, 124). When she returned from Nairobi with her baby girl, she learned that people from the surrounding area would pay her a welcoming visit only if the child was a boy (91); when that boy was finally born in 1945, the family was inundated with gifts (169). Laurence and Reece thus learned first-hand that, in Micere Githae-Mugo's words, a "childless woman is nothing; she is as good as dead" (144). Indeed, after Laurence left Somaliland, she wrote in several works of fiction about the cultural imperative for women to have children.

In *This Side Jordan*, for example, the pain of childlessness is briefly explored through several characters. Nathaniel's wife, Aya, and her friend, Charity, both have difficulty conceiving and carrying a child to term, while a third character, the old servant Whiskey, takes a second, very young wife when his first fails to have children. In the story "A Fetish for Love," infertility is the main subject. Constance, the wife of a British colonial official in the Gold Coast, takes an interest in Love, the teenaged wife of their old servant, Sunday, when she discovers that he beats Love because she is unable to have children. Constance disapproves of the "ju-ju woman" Love consults and, instead, tries to substitute her own "fetish" – medicine from the European doctor to improve the woman's fertility. The medicine is of course useless because it is Sunday who is infertile; Constance eventually learns that he has already put aside two previous wives who have not borne children.[30]

Laurence's story reveals the conditions of some women's lives, including their forced early marriage, the cultural imperative for them to have children, the refusal of their husbands to admit to infertility, and the societal acceptance of spousal abuse. The story also serves as a criticism of Western meddling, something Laurence identified and condemned in herself. Eventually, Constance gives up on her attempts to get Sunday to stop beating Love, or Love to return to her mother; she even throws out Love's bottle of useless medicine. Constance takes the advice of her husband to "just do nothing" (171) and of her doctor, who questions whether Sunday could bear it "if he were forced to recognize and admit" that the infertility is "his burden" (180). In the haunting conclusion to the story, she watches as Love smears egg onto a carved wooden fertility figure, while "a hopeless and enduring hope burnished" her face (181). Laurence's story makes the point that for a Ghanaian woman, as for her husband, "[n]ot to have children is something of a disgrace. Not merely a heartbreak. A deep shame" (179). The story is also explicit in its portrayal of the helplessness of a Western woman to intervene when an African woman is being abused.

Laurence's own inability to intervene in the abuse of women and children is evident in her description of her experiences with child prostitution and genital excision and infibulation in Somaliland. She encountered prostitution when a family that ran a small "tea-shop-cum-brothel" attached itself to the construction camp in which she and Jack lived (PCB 156). Invoking her husband's opinion and equating it with her own, Laurence writes that she and Jack "did not mind" that the family was operating a brothel. Instead, they were more concerned that it was using up the camp's meagre water supply, since every time a construction employee visited the brothel, he took some water with him. Laurence describes her husband's reaction to the theft as "annoyance" and quotes him as saying that he decided to give the *jes*, or family group, a daily ration of water because the *jes* "provides amenities of one kind and another" (157).

The implications of the Laurences' hands-off approach are not evident until Laurence reveals that the prostitutes included not just an old woman and an "attractive girl of about sixteen" but also a girl of eight who "had a curiously vacant and withdrawn look" (156, 157). Laurence chillingly writes, "There was a special name for such children, which meant literally 'a small opening'" (157). As her comment indicates, the child was named by her vagina, just as in many patriarchal societies women are named in relation to the sexual services they provide.

In relating her dealings with this child, who was called Asha, Laurence foregrounds the problem of communicating in an unfamiliar language, a problem exacerbated by the fact that all her translators were men. She writes: "We did not talk much, Asha and I, for I did not know what to say to her. I never asked her about her life. My knowledge of Somali was too limited, and who would I get to translate?" (157). Translation was undoubtedly a difficulty, but Laurence's account only hints at a much larger concern that men who were part of her camp were abusing a little girl, and that both their colonial employer and their society appeared to condone such abuse. Laurence places most of the blame, and the source of her own passivity, on difficulties of communication and on another woman. As she writes, "If we forbade the *jes* to stay near the camp, the crone would only move her trade elsewhere, so the child would be no better off. Here at least Asha got enough water" (157).

Although Laurence recognized that she might find anti-child-prostitution allies within Somali society, she characterized any action she might take as "meddling": "I had the strong suspicion that I might easily make Asha's life worse by interfering. I could not take her away from the situation entirely, and what else would do any good? So, whether out of wisdom or cowardice, I did nothing" (157–8). Laurence might have felt unequal to the task of disrupting her husband's work camp, especially since, as she implies, he would not have supported such an action. She might also have considered the fact that the separation of the men from their families necessitated by colonial employment opportunities encouraged them to turn to prostitutes for sex. For whatever reason, Laurence (like her fictional character Constance) "did nothing" about Asha, but she was troubled enough by the experience that she later wrote a short story in which one of the characters is a child who is rescued from a life of prostitution and put into a Ghanaian boarding school run by two Englishwomen. In "The Rain Child," the girl is only six and has long been separated from her family, but she is significantly named Ayesha.

Ayesha is introduced in the story after she has been struck by an older girl, Ruth, who has been raised in England. Her teacher, Miss Neddon, explains why students and teachers at the school are protective of Ayesha: "She must have been stolen, you see, or sold when she was very young. She has not been able to tell us much. But the Nigerian police traced her back to several slave-dealers. When they discovered her she was being used as a child prostitute. She was very injured when she came to us here" (117). After Ruth expresses horror that "[t]hings like that really happen here?" Miss Neddon replies, "Not just here. Evil does not select one place for its province" (117). Miss Neddon, like Laurence in *The Prophet's Camel Bell*, attempts to avoid cultural stereotyping by recognizing that child prostitution is a problem not just in Africa but worldwide. Ayesha's place within the story, however, raises questions about Laurence's use of the issue of child prostitution. Ayesha is undoubtedly a kind of exorcism for Laurence: while she was unable to negotiate cultural differences that prevented her intervening on behalf of a real child, she was able to imagine such negotiation and such intervention in her fiction. At the same time, Ayesha is a minor character whose presence in the story serves mostly to forward a plot about the inability of a young woman raised in England to integrate into African society and the inability of her teacher to facilitate that integration.

Laurence's dealings with women who had experienced genital excision and infibulation, as reported in *The Prophet's Camel Bell*, show an increasing reluctance to meddle in an unfamiliar culture. When she first arrived in Somaliland, Laurence was willing to pose questions about the practice. She asked two young male teachers who spoke English a direct question: "Did the clitoridectomy make it impossible for Somali women to enjoy sex?" (47). Their answer to this question and to several other related questions (including "What did the Somali bride-price actually involve? Did men love their wives or merely regard them as possessions? Could a woman divorce her husband for infidelity?") was that they "did not know" (47). The two men instead taught her an independence song that advocated rising in arms against colonial oppressors (47–8).

Laurence embraced this anti-colonialist response, but interpreted the men's evasive reply to her questions about women as a reproof of her curiosity about gender issues. She writes that she was appalled by the brashness of her own questions and concluded, "People are not oyster shells, to be pried at" (51).

In *The Prophet's Camel Bell*, in her essay "The Very Best Intentions," and through the fictional character Miranda in *This Side Jordan*, Laurence represents herself as a well-meaning but overly inquisitive liberal.[31] In the essay, she writes that although she wanted to appear "sympathetic, humanitarian, enlightened" (28), a Ghanaian acquaintance perceived her as part of "yet another set of white liberals who went around collecting African acquaintances as though they were rare postage stamps" (25). In the novel, one of the Ghanaian characters says of Miranda: "These damn amateur anthropologists, they're all sincere. You couldn't insult them if you tried. Wait until one of them starts asking you about native customs, Nathaniel. You know, one of these ladies once asked me in what position Africans make love" (53). Despite her intense self-criticism, as evident in these subsequent writings, Laurence's questions to the two Somali schoolteachers were appropriate for someone interested in women's lives. The response of the men, however, led her to question her own sensitivity to cultural difference and thus transformed her curiosity into a reluctance to further interrogate gender difference. Laurence recognized that she had stepped back from making strong statements about women and colonialism in Somalia; she wrote to Adele Wiseman in August 1962 that *The Prophet's Camel Bell* was "too nice – I feel it will offend no one, although I didn't intend it to be that way" (*Selected Letters* 142).

Laurence's dilemma becomes evident in that book when she relates that several desert women, hearing of her skill in first aid, came to ask if she could give them any medication to relieve the menstrual pain caused by what is commonly called female circumcision (75). As it was and is practised in Somalia, the procedure consists not of circumcision or simple removal of the prepuce, or hood of the clitoris, but of excision or amputation of most of the external female genitalia, including the clitoris, labia minora, and inner part of the labia majora. Excision is almost always followed by infibulation, or tightly sewing together the resulting wound, leaving only a small opening for the exit of urine and menstrual fluid. The procedure may be done at age eight or younger (Hicks 58) and, as a reviewer of Somali filmmaker Soraya Mire's 1994 film *Fire Eyes* suggests, results in a "chastity belt" made of the girl's "own flesh" (Stoller 58).

The issue of language and translation is an unspoken one in Laurence's description of her interaction with the group of women. She does not indicate who is translating for her, although the fact that she had only male translators may have accounted in part for her apparent lack of curiosity and the abruptness of her reply. Her response emphasizes her desire not to be seen as rude or meddling, and it represents her as less informed than she was; she writes, "Somali girls underwent some operation at puberty, the exact nature of which I had been unable to determine, partly because in our early days here every Somali to whom I put this question gave me a different answer, and partly because I no longer questioned people in this glib fashion" (75). Although the word "operation" is perhaps inaccurate to describe a procedure done outside hospital and without anaesthetic, which often led to infection, Laurence goes on to give a fairly accurate description of the procedure: "The operation was either a removal of the clitoris, or a partial sewing together of the labia, or perhaps both. But whatever was done, apparently a great many women had considerable pain with menstruation and intercourse, and the birth of their children was frequently complicated by infection" (75). Laurence may only later have connected the women's menstrual difficulties with their experience of excision and infibulation; she does not make the connection in a letter to Wiseman on 9 November 1951 in which she describes meeting the women (*Selected Letters* 67). At some point between 1951 and the book's publication in 1963, she took the trouble to learn that ninety-eight per cent of Somali women underwent genital excision, and eighty to ninety per cent the most radical form of excision and infibulation.[32] As Laurence notes, the subsequent back-up of menstrual blood often caused pain, and the thick scar tissue led to painful sexual experiences for Somali women, especially in the early days of their marriages.[33] The inelasticity of the scar also brought complications at childbirth, when the tearing of surrounding tissue might be followed by chronic infection. To all these ongoing health problems Laurence alludes, and considering the era in which her account was written and the lack of theoretical models available to her, the feminist statement she made in broaching this practice is a powerful one. Because she wanted to avoid the cultural imperialism implied by too detailed questioning, however, Laurence did not delve deeply into societal reasons for excision, except to repeat the commonly held belief that women were responsible for the continuation of the practice. She quotes "an educated Somali friend" who told her that "the old women would never agree to its being abandoned" (75).

Laurence's dilemma is emphasized by her abrupt reply to the women: "I have nothing to give you. Nothing." The only painkiller she had was Aspirin, and as she concludes, "the lunatic audacity of shoving a mild pill at their total situation was more than I could stomach" (76). As with the child Asha, another female turned into "a small opening," Laurence did not know what to do. In her book, she does not explore the cultural motivations for the practice, although she does acknowledge that it is just one part of the women's "total situation."

A possible reason for Laurence's reluctance is that she wanted her narrative to act as a counter to imperialism; thus her desire to be sensitive to cultural difference outweighed her urge to make a feminist intervention. In her book-length study of Laurence's African writings, Sparrow approves of Laurence's hesitancy, arguing that because "Somali women lived according to customs totally different from her own, ... [i]t was not, indeed, right that she should criticize the practise openly" (37). Laurence's reluctance is understandable and in some respects commendable, especially in light of essays by writers such as Kadiatu Kanneh, who contends, "'Female circumcision' has become almost a dangerous trope in Western feminisms for the muting and mutilation of women – physically, sexually and psychologically – and for these women's *need for* Western feminism. Circumcision, clitoridectomy, infibulation, become one visible marker of outrageous primitivism, sexism, and *the* Third World woman" (347). Kanneh dismisses North American and European assessments of genital excision as "arrogant and culturally 'superior' Western interference and insult" (348). After reading her essay, it is easy to imagine why Margaret Laurence, a self-described anti-imperialist, might want to avoid interfering with or insulting Somali cultural practices, and thus might avoid commenting on them in detail.

In a 1981 essay, Gayatri Spivak points to "the inbuilt colonialism of First World feminism toward the Third" ("French Feminism" 153). Using studies of clitoridectomy as a starting point, she argues that Western criticism often downplays the existence of such cultural practices as part of a functional system and, at the same time, sidesteps the need to work toward "a sense of our common yet history-specific lot" (153). In another essay, she concludes that because oppressed people often cannot speak for themselves, the female intellectual "has a circumscribed task which she must not disown with a flourish" ("Can the

Subaltern Speak?" 308). Thus although Spivak calls on North American and European feminists to speak out on behalf of women who cannot speak for themselves, she recognizes that feminists' interventions come from positions of power that might invalidate them. She is joined by writers such as Chandra Mohanty, who claims that "feminist scholarly practices" which represent "a composite, singular 'third world woman'" exemplify "relations of power" that can perpetuate the colonization of women (197). Thus interventions by Western feminists, even discursive ones, may be interpreted as furthering oppression. The desire not to engage in what Linda Alcoff identifies as "discursive imperialism" (17) is a powerful one. The problem is that "if I don't speak for those less privileged than myself, am I abandoning my political responsibility to speak out against oppression, a responsibility incurred by the very fact of my privilege?" (Alcoff 8). Alcoff concludes, and I agree, that the answer to her question is yes – that while unequal power relations indeed exist among women, it is at the same time essential to speak out.

Françoise Lionnet provides an example of how a writer can comment on excision and infibulation while taking note of the potential for cultural and religious imperialism in doing so. In *Postcolonial Representations*, she points out that words feminists have sometimes used to denounce excision, such as "barbaric" or "anachronistic," "often smack of racist, anti-Islamic rhetoric" (129). She recognizes the conflict between, on one hand, the "respect for the cultural autonomy of African societies that denounce any feminist intervention as 'acculturation' to Western standards" and, on the other, the "universal ethical imperative against the physical torture and psychological impairment of millions of women" (131).

Lionnet does what Laurence was perhaps understandably unable to do, given her historical situation, her lack of models, and her self-imposed ideological constraints. She canvasses the cultural reasons for the procedure, the most prominent of which is its role as a rite of passage, "one purpose of which is precisely to test the mettle of the individual" (133). As Lionnet points out, "the reasons for the continued performance of this practice are compelling psychosexual ones for those involved, since it is embedded in a cultural context that encodes it as a beautifying and enriching phenomenon without which girls do not become women and will therefore never be able to marry, have some degree of economic security, and lead 'full' female lives" (157). Excision and infibulation, she concludes, "are not just irrational and aberrant abuses" but instead are "part of a coherent, rational, and workable system" (165). Indeed, justifications for the practice include its perceived role in protecting virginity, assuring paternity, focusing women on their tasks as mothers, and making polygynous marriages workable.

Understanding the practice does not mean that it cannot be criticized, and Lionnet's critique is evident in her analysis of literary works by writers such as Nawal El Saadawi who have experienced excision and who describe the practice as part of an overall patriarchal social system (xiv). Sylvie Fainzang puts it well when she writes, "The sexual marking provided by excision is the necessary condition of access to a specific social status, that of *woman subjected to the authority of man*" (178; translation by F. Lionnet). Like forced prostitution, excision and infibulation are cultural markers of men's ownership of women, since if women are property, they can either be sold into prostitution or sexually mutilated to raise their value in the marriage exchange. Documentary filmmaker Soraya Mire calls infibulation "a means of controlling women's sexuality," while a Somali man she interviewed, who wants the custom discontinued, calls it "a form of social control" (*Fire Eyes*). Excision thus is identified as one aspect of women's place within their society – what Laurence calls their "total situation."

In writing about excision and infibulation and about child prostitution, Margaret Laurence made a tentative link between these practices and women's status in Somali society. It is remarkable that in 1963 she wrote openly about issues that African women writers such as Efua Dorkenoo, Olayinka Koso-Thomas, El Saadawi, Aamina Warsame, and Sadiya Ahmed have only more recently discussed in detail, and that Mire filmed only in 1994. In her book, also written in 1994, Dorkenoo emphasizes that "some years ago it would have been impossible in most countries even to mention the subject [of female genital mutilation] in public" (62). Indeed, in her study of Somali oral literature, Kapteijns notes that traditional Somali stories "are remarkably silent about girls' circumcision (*gudniin*)" (23). When Laurence writes about the practice, she writes in advance of much public discussion of it and in advance of theoretical analysis that would have allowed her to place it within its patriarchal social context.

FICTION AS CRITICAL COMMENT

Laurence's own critique of female genital mutilation, like that of child prostitution, is more explicit in her fiction than in her travel narrative.

Both practices feature in a pivotal scene in *This Side Jordan*, published three years before *The Prophet's Camel Bell*. At first glance, Laurence's novel appears to resist a feminist analysis; it is, after all, told through two masculine viewpoints, rather than through the viewpoints of the women characters, who include Johnnie Kestoe's wife, Miranda, and Nathaniel Amegbe's wife, Aya. Miranda, with her brash questions and her naive enthusiasm for African culture, may be too much like Laurence to be placed comfortably at the centre of the narrative. Or, as Sparrow suggests, Laurence may have chosen male protagonists because "she felt her own foreignness most when she watched the women" (*Into Africa* 131). A more complex explanation is that in writing about the dismantling of a patriarchal colonial structure such as the one that existed in the Gold Coast, one is almost compelled to write about it from the perspective of those with power, the men.[34] Irish Londoner Johnnie Kestoe seeks to gain the power of the economic imperialist in Ghana, and Laurence's characterization of this man as someone whose family originates from an arguably colonized part of Europe is not accidental. Nathaniel Amegbe, meanwhile, seeks to retain the power of the patriarch. Laurence's choice of the masculine point of view, reflecting as it does the patriarchal nature of colonial power, is both disturbing and effective. So too is her decision to represent the struggle toward decolonization in Ghana alongside a parallel gender struggle between the male protagonists and their female partners.

Like Laurence in Somaliland (and again in the Gold Coast), the two female characters are pregnant, and pregnancy adds to the gender conflict both couples experience. Throughout the novel, Aya unsuccessfully resists Nathaniel's efforts to force her to have her baby in a hospital. He believes that his son's life must begin in the "new" way, while she is afraid to have a child without the support of her mother and other women of her family group. Miranda's pregnancy, meanwhile, brings to a head her husband's conflicting feelings of possessiveness toward and repulsion by the female body. Although the novel is written in the third person, the narrative is often limited to the perspectives of one or other of the male characters. Thus Miranda's pregnant body is described through Johnnie's eyes as "the mound that had once been a body belonging to her, and to him. Now it belonged to neither of them, but only to the half-formed sluglike thing inside her, straining food from her blood" (8–9).

In a scene of the novel that was politely ignored by early reviewers such as Mary Renault but has since been the focus of much feminist comment, Johnnie Kestoe rapes a young, excised woman who has just been sold into prostitution. While it is not surprising that this scene has received so much scrutiny, it is just one part of the exploration in *This Side Jordan* of attitudes toward women in general and African women in particular. Throughout the novel, Johnnie's simultaneous sexual attraction to and revulsion by African women is explicitly stated. This attraction-revulsion is part of a long-standing trope that links land to be conquered with woman to be raped in the imperialist literary tradition of texts such as Joseph Conrad's *Heart of Darkness*. As Abena Busia writes, in Western literature about Africa, white men are "seen with peculiar frequency lusting after the black female flesh of a people they continue to hold in contempt" ("Miscegenation as Metonymy" 367). Indeed, in the first pages of Laurence's novel, Johnnie, a man "who didn't like Africans," is dancing with a young African woman and feeling an "itch of desire" (1, 4). Johnnie's unwilling attraction to African women is pointed out several times in the novel (87, 134). His assault on the young prostitute is preceded by a scene in which he makes sexual advances toward an even younger girl and then, when he feels himself rebuffed, strikes her (135). The girl is his old servant's fourteen-year-old "small wife." The link between gender oppression and colonialism becomes evident when the man, learning of his employer's assault, beats the girl. He cannot take out his anger about the assault on his colonial employer, but he can take it out on what he considers his own property – his wife.

Patriarchy merges with imperialist brutality when, with the connivance of several Ghanaian men, including Nathaniel, Johnnie sexually brutalizes an inexperienced prostitute. Busia rightly notes that the "unacknowledged association" between the European and African men in this passage exemplifies the "complicit power of patriarchal institutions, native and colonial" ("Silencing Sycorax" 93, 92n). The girl, who is from the north of the country where female genital excision is practised, is "very young, not more than sixteen ... perhaps younger" (*TSJ* 229), and both Nathaniel and Johnnie speculate that she has been sold into prostitution by the male members of her family. She is also a kind of "human sacrifice," given to Johnnie so that he will not persecute Nathaniel (226–7). Even the language used to describe her is that of sacrifice: "She lay spreadeagled, sheeplike, waiting for the knife" (231).

Although Johnnie realizes that the girl he has been offered as a bribe is very young and may not be sexually experienced, he decides, as he has done about the beating of his servant's wife, that "[n]one of that was his concern. She was an African whore. That was all he needed to know about her" (229). Even when he discovers that she is a virgin, he ignores her cry of pain and indeed revels in hurting her. Restating the opinion of colonizers everywhere who justify oppression by representing colonized peoples as less than human, he views her as "an animal, a creature hardly sentient, a thing" (230).

The linkage of gender with imperialism is spelled out in a line that associates woman with geography: "She was a continent and he an invader, wanting both to possess and to destroy" (231). Feminist commentators have variously criticized or defended this restatement of the trope of Africa as woman to be conquered. Margaret Gail Osachoff commented as early as 1980 that the passage, in which "imperialism takes on sexual overtones," exemplifies "the rape of Africa by the white imperialist" (224). In the same year, Jane Leney criticized the "lack of subtlety" of "the trite symbol of the woman as African continent" (69). Leney fails to note, as do many critics, that the metaphor is not that of an omniscient narrator but one that Laurence has chosen to attribute to Johnnie Kestoe, since in this section of the text the narrative is presented through his point of view. The imagery is thus part of Johnnie's internal analysis of his actions and sets the scene for his own subsequent awareness of their consequences. In later examinations of the scene, Sparrow and Gabrielle Collu defend this passage; while Sparrow contends that "colonialism is condemned by means of a metaphor" (*Into Africa* 150), Collu argues that "Laurence's use of the imagery is not trite or unsubtle" but instead "reveals the brutal and exploitative use of the African woman and by extension the violent colonization of Africa by white men" (27–8). Indeed, she contends, Laurence's fiction shows a "revisionist use of the colonial/imperial trope of land-as-woman" (20).[35]

Busia astutely points out that in *This Side Jordan*, the narrative of the rape is expressed through a series of reflections in Johnnie's mind, "which serve as a deliberate ironic commentary on the use of the black woman as the symbol of the virgin land to be tamed by the European" ("Silencing Sycorax" 91). She argues that Laurence uses the trope in *This Side Jordan* to show that "the despised body-as-land/land-as-body of the native woman ... must be possessed, not as object of desire but as assaulted object, in order to signal dominion and establish 'civilized' order" (91). Extending this argument, I would suggest that Johnnie Kestoe, who is angry with both his wife and Nathaniel, brutally assaults a young woman in order to establish his dominance over women and Africans in general.

The woman he assaults, meanwhile, remains almost completely silenced. Although Laurence rewrites the trope, pointing out the patriarchal power of the encounter, she cannot go further and allow the woman the power of comprehensible speech (although she does say a few words and makes a "low rhythmical keening sound," which neither Johnnie nor the reader understands [232]). As Busia suggests, the collaborative powers of patriarchy and colonialism unite to repress any speech she might attempt. They even repress her name; she is known only as Emerald, a name chosen by her African procurers.

The silenced and unnamed Ghanaian woman in Laurence's novel is also an excised woman, a fact that reinforces her oppression by the joint patriarchal structures. Laurence's narrative provides some detail about genital excision, from Johnnie's perspective: "Among certain peoples, the clitoridectomy was performed at puberty. By a bush surgeon – some fetish priestess, perhaps. Some of them were said to use the long wicked acacia thorns as needles. The wounds often became infected and did not heal for a long time" (233). This brief passage both outlines the procedure and its results and reveals Johnnie's ignorance of the cultural bases for the practice. The narrative then emphasizes the fact that genital scarring is torn open during sexual intercourse. The subsequent description of the blood that pours from the young woman's genitals because the "scars had opened when he savaged her" (233) reverses the characters' roles by turning the colonizer-rapist into the savage.

While this reversal of roles is remarkable, the suffering young woman not only is silent but also, like the child prostitute Ayesha, is a very minor character whose role in the novel is primarily to effect a transformation in a protagonist. The woman suffers pain so that Johnnie can have a moment of redemption. He can look at a Ghanaian and see that she "was someone, a woman who belonged somewhere and who for some reason of her own had been forced to seek him here in this evil-smelling cell, and through him, indignity and pain" (233). Through her, he can recognize that the Ghanaians, whose colonial domination he has been perpetuating, are people, more like him than unlike him.[36] By having Johnnie recognize the error of his racist ways, Laurence attempts to bring about a closure that provides a critique of colonialism. Before he can experience his moment of redemption, however, he must first brutalize the woman; she must first be sacrificed. In Laurence's text, his conversion is consolidated through her silent forgiveness of his brutality and his subsequent tears. Osachoff concludes that "the forgiveness of the woman, and by implication of the dark continent, is somewhat sentimental and unbelievable" (224). The acts of forgiveness and repentance are, on the contrary, not sentimental but extremely disturbing, since brutality is in effect washed away by tears.[37]

The girl's rape and its outcome are just part of Laurence's commentary in *This Side Jordan* on gender conflicts, illustrated in part through Johnnie's involvement with European as well as African women. His interactions with white women have disturbing parallels to his sacrifice of the Ghanaian virgin. Three times in the novel, blood pours from the genitals of a woman who has been sacrificed to provide some form of self-knowledge for Johnnie, and that woman's pain or fear is both inarticulate and represented through his eyes as evidence of her animal nature. In the first passage, designed to show some motivation for the brutality of his sexuality (and of his nature in general), the reader learns that he has watched his mother die from a botched abortion; her cries sound to him like "animal paingrunting" (60). The second incident with the young excised woman is the climax of his imperialistic behaviour and the beginning of his conversion; the link between these two scenes is evident in the repetition of the phrase "a clot of blood on a dirty quilt" (59, 232). In the third scene, at the end of the novel, Johnnie watches the birth of his and Miranda's daughter. For a father to be present at a birth scene set in 1957 is highly unusual, but Laurence invents this scene so that her protagonist can witness blood coming from the genitals of a woman in the act of creation of life, rather than in death or rape. Still, as the narrator notes of Miranda, again through Johnnie's perspective, "She was no longer human. The voice that came from her throat was an animal's coarse voice" (266). The birth of his child provides his final release, and thus three inarticulate and animalistic women in pain serve as stages in the rehabilitation of this one male character.

The scene also provides a symmetry to the novel's closure, since Aya gives birth to a child in the same hospital after yielding to Nathaniel's insistent demands. Laurence's desire for symmetry, for a paralleling of events in the lives of Nathaniel and Johnnie, leads her to represent the two births through the men's eyes, a choice for which she later berated herself. As she wrote in *Dance on the Earth*, "How could I have been so stupid, so self-doubting? ... I, who had experienced such joy with sex, such anguish and joy in the birth of my children, not only didn't have the courage to describe these crucial experiences; it didn't even occur to me to do so" (5–6). In her fiction, including *This Side Jordan*, "The

Rain Child," and "A Fetish for Love," Laurence's desire for symmetry, for a critique of Western meddling, and for closure that provides a colonialist critique sometimes compromises her feminist commentary, just as in *The Prophet's Camel Bell* her reluctance to engage in cultural imperialism prevents her from making a detailed investigation of crucial issues of gender difference.

The tentativeness of the feminist commentary in some of Laurence's African writings is a reminder of what can happen when Western feminist writers are too wary of being labelled imperialist to interfere, even discursively. At the same time, given the fact that Laurence does write openly about female genital excision, child prostitution, and other often hidden aspects of women's lives, and does recognize some of the intersections between patriarchy and colonialism, her books take important steps toward breaking the silence about cultural practices that oppress women. She is not only an anti-imperialist writer but also a groundbreaking feminist whose ideas and theories, as expressed in her early travel writing, are limited in part by her historical position and her avowed anti-imperialism, but nevertheless provide a valuable initial map on which to base later feminist considerations of cross-cultural female life experiences.

GENDER, IMPERIALISM, AND HISTORY

On the last page of *The Prophet's Camel Bell*, Laurence elaborates on the metaphorical meaning of the title she has chosen for her book. During the time she and Jack spent in Somalia, she writes, they had heard "the Prophet's camel bell" because they "had come to know something of these desert people, their pain and their faith, their anger, their ability to endure" (260).[38] "The most prophetic note of that bell," and one they "scarcely heard at all, although the sound was there, if we had had ears for it," was the upcoming independence and merger of the two Somalilands that had been under British and Italian administration.

Laurence could not imagine Somali independence to be as near as it later proved, perhaps because the British colonial government (for which she briefly worked) was slow to prepare for it (Lewis 148). Yet her novel and her short stories do look forward to Ghana's independence, although not unrealistically. "A Gourdful of Glory" focuses on the disillusionment of market women whose day-to-day lives do not change after independence, while in *This Side Jordan* a friend of Nathaniel's is cynical about self-government: "You'll see such oppression as you never believed possible. Only of course it'll be all right then – it'll be black men oppressing black men, and who could object to that?" (117). As several critics have pointed out, these were concerns also expressed by Laurence's Ghanaian friend Ofosu, whom she called Mensah in the essay "The Very Best Intentions" (24). Laurence suggests in "Ten Years' Sentences" that while her African books do not "ignore some of the inevitable casualties of social change, both African and European, ... they do reflect the predominantly optimistic outlook of many Africans and many western liberals in the late 1950's and early 1960's" (11). She points out that in *This Side Jordan*, "victory of the side of the angels is all but assured ... This was the prevailing spirit, not only of myself but of Africa at that time" (12).

In *The Prophet's Camel Bell*, Laurence speculates about the future of Somalia. She comments that because the clan system is essential for the survival of desert camel-herders, its elimination is unlikely, and she wonders whether Somali people will be able to overcome inter-clan conflict to create a unified country. She points out that one advantage Somalia has over other African countries looking forward to inde-pendence is a common language and religion and, with "certain local variations," a common culture (100–1). A disadvantage, of course, is that Somalia was carved up by the colonizers into three distinct enti-ties, each with almost a hundred years of colonial history to contend with (including the imposition of three different colonial languages, laws, and customs). J.B. Harley calls the "scramble for Africa, in which the European powers fragmented the identity of indigenous territorial organisation" a "textbook example" of the divisive power of colonial mapping (283). Just as Laurence was unable to predict a Somali future that would include the formation of the Somali Republic as early as 1960, so she also could not predict that continuing divisions would result in the 1969 takeover by southern leader Muhammad Siyaad Barre, and that the ensuing internal conflict would lead to the northern uprising in 1988 and the collapse of the Somali state in 1990–91.

Although the history of colonization is not the complete account of a country, as Laurence's Somali narrative makes abundantly clear, its history is irreversibly inflected by colonial rule. Laurence hints at the exacerbation of internal cultural divisions by colonial rule when she discusses gender issues such as bride price, prostitution, and genital excision. She also alludes to the curtailment of women's social free-dom when she writes about the inaccessibility of women's oral poetry. Kapteijns argues more explicitly that in British Somaliland, the colonial

3.9 "Working on a Balleh," photograph by C.J. Martin. Courtesy of C.J. Martin

government's application of "authentic Somali tradition and customary law" created what she calls "state-sanctioned tradition, both suitably nativized to reflect the assumed 'tribal' nature of local society and appropriately cleaned up to suit European universalizing notions of orderliness and fairness" (152). This codification of tradition prevented women from gaining rights during the colonial period. Indeed, colonization had a profoundly negative impact on Somali gender relations during and after the country's independence from colonial rule, as evidenced in the subject matter of modern poetry in Somalia. In the period around independence, Kapteijns suggests, anti-colonialist intellectuals turned away from colonial interference by embracing tradition in their songs. Such an embrace "symbolized an authentically Somali national identity contrasting starkly with colonial (or neocolonial), 'modern,' European values" (155). Songs from the 1950s to the 1980s thus warned women against "the immorality of exercising certain 'modern' rights," including what Kapteijns summarizes as the rights "to wear western clothes, go out of the house, date men, and have opinions and make decisions of their own" (140). Thus, she writes, the return to tradition served "to bolster men's claims of authority over women and limit women's social freedom [and] autonomous decision-making" (140). The orature that Laurence translated and discussed in *A Tree for Poverty* and *The Prophet's Camel Bell* came to be used for explicitly political purposes and was revealed to have even more of an impact on gender relations than she had thought possible.

The Laurences were minor players in the colonial situation in Somalia, yet they both had a lasting impact on the country. Although Margaret Laurence makes it clear that Jack's work was initially viewed with suspicion by Somalis, the last chapter of her book includes a description of the herdsmen's quick adoption of one of the reservoirs after it filled with water during the rains. As she writes on the last page of *The Prophet's Camel Bell*, speaking for herself and her husband, "Whenever we think of Somaliland, we think of the line of watering places that stretches out across the Haud, and we think of the songs and tales that have been for generations a shelter to nomads on the dry red plateau and on the burnt plains of the coast, for these were the things through which we briefly touched the country and it, too, touched our lives, altering them in some way forever" (260). Laurence's legacy in Somalia thus is not her short-term administrative support work for the British colonial government as it prepared for independence but, rather, her translations and transcriptions of Somali orature and the thoughtful, often complicated, and conflicted mapping of issues of imperialism and gender evident in her travel narrative.

When Agnes Deans Cameron describes her 1908 travels with her niece on Great Slave Lake, she writes that she and Jessie Brown were "the first white women who have penetrated to Fort Rae" (309). The use of masculine, sexualized terminology such as that evidenced by the word "penetrated" to describe entering geographical space is typical of many turn-of-the-century travel narratives. The accompanying claim to be "first" to enter that space, however, carries even more ideological baggage for Cameron as a female traveller than it would for a male traveller. For Western explorers and travellers of either sex, the claim to primacy is almost always based on race, ethnicity, culture, and class – encompassed in Cameron's case by her adjective "white" – since usually other non-white people live in and thus have travelled to these so-called blank spots on the map, and since most explorers are led or accompanied on their travels by "Native" guides and servants. For women, as Cameron's statement makes clear, the claim to be first is often based on gender as well as on race, and thus she qualifies her first by adding the word "women" after "white."

The narratives examined in this study demonstrate that the bases of primacy can shift from one claim to another. Thus while Anna Jameson represents herself as the first person of any kind to transcribe certain examples of oral Anishinaabe literature, she is "the first European female" to shoot the rapids at Sault Ste Marie (*WWSR* 3: 199). And while Mina Hubbard writes that she will be the "first in the field" to explore the Naskaupi and George Rivers (*WW* 107), she later qualifies her claims with adjectives pertaining to race and culture, noting that she is "the first of the white race to trace the Nascaupee River to its source" (174) and that "I alone, save the Indians, have witnessed the great [caribou] migration" (167). Margaret Laurence is clearly isolated by gender and race on her travels, both because of her situation – there were no other women in the work camps where she lived with her husband – and because of language barriers. Despite this isolation, she self-consciously undercuts the conventional claim of the traveller to primacy by pointing out that while her footsteps were not the first in Somalia, neither were those of male British writer Richard Burton a hundred years earlier.

When one examines such claims from the opposite direction, representations of primacy and solitude can be identified as methods through which writers situate themselves and their travelling companions as members of certain cultural and gender groups. In public presentations of my research, I have been asked to speak in general about the differences between travel narratives by men and those by women. Such generalizations are difficult and perhaps even impossible to make, since all Western travel writers write from their own cultural and historical moments but are influenced by similar discursive traditions. One generalization that I can make, though, relates to women writers' discussions of their solitude in terms of sexuality. Because of their gendered "aloneness" on their journeys, women travellers historically often write about sexuality in different ways than do men. Their writings show an awareness of two types of sexual danger: both a physical danger to their persons and a potential danger to their reputations. These dangers lead Jameson to write about attractive men in aesthetic or artistic terms, and Hubbard to provide herself with the metaphoric companionship of her husband and to include a statement in her diary from her companions attesting to the moral propriety of the trip. For Laurence, who travels with her husband, questions of morality do not arise, but her sexuality does becomes the subject of much more interest among members of the visited culture than would a male writer's because of the intense focus directed by members of the visited society toward her reproductive capabilities as a young married woman.

Narratives of travel by Canadian women writers show that the related claims to be alone and to be first are often made through various and changing technologies of representation. Jameson's sketch of the canoe journey from Manitoulin to Penetanguishene in 1837 emphasizes markers of gender, including parasol and bonnet, that characterize her figurative solitude. Hubbard's last photograph of setting her foot on the ground at George River Post in the late summer of 1905 was staged to illustrate her claim to be the first white person to complete this journey, and thus a relatively new technology, the portable camera, was used to provide visual proof. Cameron, who travelled three years

C.1 "The First Type-writer on Great Slave Lake," *The New North*

after Hubbard, directly links a photographic first to a technology of textual representation – the typewriter. As several of her photographs demonstrate (119, 282, 309, 347; fig. C.1), Cameron took a typewriter with her on the journey and used it and the typewriting skills of her niece to record various stages of her travel. As one tongue-in-cheek caption, "The First Type-writer on Great Slave Lake," shows, she later made a claim to primacy based on that typewriter.

The technology of map-making also helps travellers and writers, including those analyzed in this book, to make explicit and implicit claims to be first. Just as Hubbard's photograph ostensibly proves that she is the first to have completed this particular journey, so her map is presented as proof that she is the first to have detailed geographical knowledge of that area of Labrador. Her naming of the geographical features of the landscape, meanwhile, implies that the landscape was unnamed before her journey. Laurence's map, in contrast, is typical of a frontispiece travel map of previously charted areas that emphasizes blank spaces by showing only locations of interest to the traveller. Figurative and literal mapping come together, however, when she demonstrates that the blank space on the Victorian atlas that represented Africa was, and has always been, a blank only in the colonialist imagination, and when she points out the destructive results of the carving up of the landscape that accompanied or preceded colonialism. Laurence also uses her fiction to rewrite a geographical trope in order to represent the oppression of a woman by colonial and patriarchal forces.

The use of metaphors of travel, place, and mapping in literature and criticism is a fraught and contested practice, particularly when such metaphors are used by feminist writers. Caren Kaplan argues that "terms such as 'borders,' 'maps,' 'location,' 'space,' and 'place' do not necessarily liberate critical practices from the very conundrum of aestheticization and universalization that spurred a search for alternative metaphors and methods in the first place" (144). Janet Wolff contends, meanwhile, that because of the masculinist historical bases for exploration and cartography, employing such vocabulary "necessarily produces androcentric tendencies in theory" (224). Despite this criticism, she concludes by calling, not for the avoidance of such metaphors, but instead for their "reappropriation" (235). The writers whose works I analyze engage in such metaphorical reappropriation in various complex ways. Marlene Goldman concludes that the use of mapping imagery in Canadian women's fiction calls into question "the privileged position of a wide variety of literary and non-literary discourses that have informed constructions of female identity" (209). In this study, metaphors of mapping, as well as the literal mapping of geographic space, point to the construction in writings by Canadian women travellers not just of a female identity but also of a colonial or postcolonial identity.

I want to conclude by considering the map that serves as frontispiece to the first chapter of Cameron's *The New North*. The map of her journey is peculiarly compressed (fig. C.2). Its east-west axis is shortened and its north-south axis elongated, so that Chicago appears to be very far south but only a little to the east of the community of Arctic Red River. The introductory words in Cameron's book point out her shift in geographical emphasis:

Most writers who traverse The Dominion enter it at the Eastern portal and travel west by the C.P.R., following the line of least resistance till they reach the Pacific. Then they go back to dear old England and tell the world all about

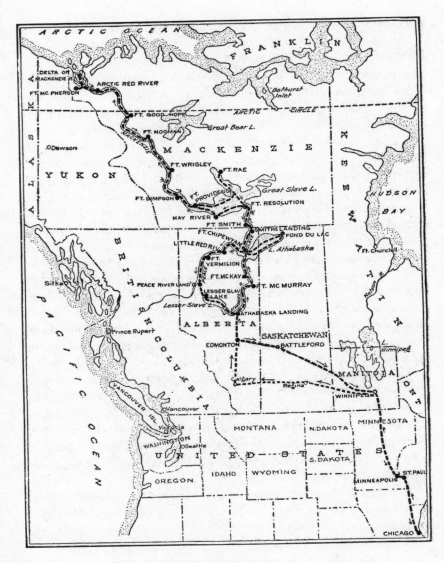

C.2   "Map of the Author's Route," *The New North*

Canada, their idea of the half-continent being Euclid's conception of a straight line, "length without breadth."

But Canada has a third dimension, a diameter that cuts through the Belt of Wheat and Belt of Fur, beginning south at the international boundary and ending where in his winter-igloo the Arctic Eskimo lives and loves after his kind and works out his own destiny. This diameter we are to follow. (2–3)

Cameron makes a claim in this passage to be unusual among turn-of-the-twentieth-century travellers. Using the relational pronoun "we," she posits that she and her travelling companion will use the map of Canada in a new way, as they journey south to north rather than east to west. The map printed in the book so that readers can trace this journey reflects that north-south orientation, focusing on "breadth" rather than "length" as it helps Cameron to make her geographical claim. A corresponding metaphorical claim to be alone on her journey is evident in the fact that she only once names her niece and travelling companion, three-quarters of the way through the book. For the remainder of the narrative, Jessie Brown is only "the Kid," a nickname that emphasizes both her youth and her lack of influence on the direction of the journey. Similarly, despite Cameron's use of the first-person plural pronoun "we," the full title of her book, *The New North: Being Some Account of a Woman's Journey through Canada to the Arctic*, implies that only one woman has made this journey, eliding the presence of both Brown and the other women whom Cameron met on various parts of her travels (including nuns in several northern residential schools and numerous First Nations women).

The complexity of the ways in which maps and narratives such as Cameron's complement and contradict one another as they exemplify the activities of travelling, perceiving people and places visited, and representing those perceptions through claims to primacy indicates a need for much more detailed study into the interconnections between mapping and travel writing. As both Hubbard's and Cameron's maps, photographs, and narratives demonstrate, more research is also necessary into the effects of technologies such as portable cameras and typewriters on travelling and writing at the turn of the twentieth century. In our current historical moment just after the turn of the twenty-first century, meanwhile, technologies that help voyagers both to travel and to represent those travels have proliferated. Global positioning systems, laptop computers, digital cameras, satellite telephones, and instant Internet access have radically changed the way that the visited world can be represented by the traveller and the speed with which those representations can be relayed home. These new technologies undoubtedly contribute both to new firsts and to new ways of critiquing claims to primacy. They also demonstrate new ways of mapping gender and cultural difference onto the landscape of Western narratives of travel.

notes

introduction

1 Cultural geographer Derek Gregory argues that cartography's objectivity has been challenged only in the past twenty-five years. In *Geographical Imaginations*, he points out the contradictory nature of cartography, calling it "a thoroughly practical and deeply politicized discourse" (7, 8).

2 Patrick Holland and Huggan point out, similarly, that travel writing as a mode of discourse is also ideological, because of the long-standing "connection between travel writing and imperial conquest" (15).

3 Such studies include *The Mind of the Traveler* (1991), in which Eric J. Leed characterizes the journey as "spermatic" and women as "sessile" or immobile. His most extensive commentary on women's relationship to travel is about their position as objects of exchange, "gifts" of hospitality provided to male travellers (117–26).

4 Holland and Huggan (1998) analyze travel writing as both an imperialist and a gendered discourse, while Steve Clark (1999) writes about travel writing in relation to empire. Authors such as Dorothy Middleton (1965), Catherine Barnes Stevenson (1982), Mary Russell (1986), Dea Birkett (1989), Shirley Foster (1990), Maria Frawley (1994), Susan Morgan (1996), and Mary Suzanne Schriber (1997) have rediscovered women travel writers, especially of the Victorian era. They approach the works of these writers mostly from the perspective of gender difference, as does Lawrence in her broader examination of women writers from the seventeenth to the twentieth centuries (1994) and Smith in her discussion of twentieth-century writers (2001). Gender and imperialism are more effectively combined in several other studies of travel writing, including those by Blunt (1994) and Inderpal Grewal (1996).

Responding to the plethora of books on Victorian women writers in Britain and, more recently, the United States, two 1997 theses, by Lisa LaFramboise and M. Susan Birkwood, examine Canadian women travel writers of the nineteenth and early twentieth centuries. A third dissertation, by Denise Adele Heaps, examines twentieth-century travel writing and, as the title indicates, makes gender the primary focus ("Gendered Discourse and Subjectivity in Travel Writing by Canadian Women," 2000). I found no general published studies of women's travel writing in Canada and few Canadian studies that make a concerted analysis of gender in relation to imperialism, although many essays have been published on specific Canadian women travel writers, and books and anthologies have included a number of these writers. Examples of such works are Germaine Warkentin's *Canadian Exploration Literature: An Anthology;* Eva-Marie Kröller's *Canadian Travellers in Europe, 1851–1900;* Elizabeth Waterston's entries on "Travel Books 1860–1920" and "Travel Books on Canada 1920–1960" in *Literary History of Canada;* Helen Buss's *Mapping Our Selves;* Karen Mulhallen's *Views from the North: An Anthology of Travel Writing;* Katherine Govier's *Without a Guide: Contemporary Women's Travel Adventures;* and Constance Rooke's *Writing Away: The* PEN *Canada Travel Anthology.*

5 See Sharpe for a discussion of Western women's alternating dominant and subordinate positions in colonial encounters (12) and Mills for an analysis of the possibilities for critique inherent in these women's marginal positions (23).

6 My study necessarily deals with shifting notions of gender. It is based on my own anti-racist, materialist approach, but examines Jameson in the context of early nineteenth-century feminism, with its focus on education; Hubbard in terms of Victorian conceptions of the domestic "Angel of the House"; and Laurence in relation to feminism of the 1960s.

7 Other writers make similar observations: Fussell points out that "reading about someone else's travel while traveling oneself was an action widely practiced" (*Abroad* 59); Holland and Huggan note, "It is an axiom of recent travel writing that writers offer tribute to their predecessors, homage often paid in adulatory terms" (7); Clark writes that travel books assert a "continuous re-enactment of earlier journeys" (11); and Porter points to the "sense of belatedness in a traveler, especially in a traveler who decides to give a written account of his travels," which includes pressure "to add something new and recognizably his own to the accumulated testimony of his predecessors" (12).

8 Toponymic researcher Bill Barry speculates that Canadian Northern officials were inspired by Canadian Pacific officials, who named the town on the junction between the two rail lines after Scottish essayist Thomas Carlyle (57). Another nearby literary place name is Kipling, on a CNR rail line.

chapter one

1 Jameson's letters to friends and family will be cited throughout as *Anna Jameson*. On the use of the name Anishinaabe, see note 20 below.

2 Jameson set out from England at the beginning of October 1836 and did not return until February 1838. Her decision to avoid discussion in her book of her lengthy trips to and from Toronto and of her return through the United States is conventional, since it avoids descriptions that might be repetitive of other travel narratives. At the same time, it allows her to avoid reference to the personal concerns about her reunion with her husband and their eventual financial settlement which motivated her journey and which she mentions in her letters to friends and family.

   Clara Thomas's 1967 biography *Love and Work Enough* contains a detailed and informative account of Jameson's life history. Anna Brownell Murphy was born in 1794, the oldest daughter of an Irish artist who moved his family to England when Anna was a small child. Until her marriage to lawyer Robert Jameson in 1825, she supported herself and contributed to the support of other family members by working as a governess. Her marriage was not a success, and she did not accompany her husband when he went to Dominica in 1829 and to Upper Canada in 1833. After she returned from her unsatisfactory visit in 1837 to her husband in Toronto, Jameson continued to support herself, her sisters, her parents, and a niece with her writing until her death in 1860. Her nominal status as a married woman allowed her the freedom to travel not just to Canada but throughout Europe and to establish unconventional friendships with people such as Ottilie von Goethe, daughter-in-law of the famous German writer.

3 Jameson's letters to Goethe will be cited throughout as *Letters*.

4 Jameson wrote to Goethe, "My journal, or at least the spirit of it, will be published, and I hope soon" (20 Oct. 1837, *Letters* 94). The numerous footnotes in Jameson's book indicate the extent of the rewriting she engaged in for the published work.

5 I quote from the 1838 three-volume edition of Jameson's work, available through Early Canadiana Online or in a facsimile edition, and retain, without comment, her idiosyncrasies of spelling, punctuation, and italicization. The title of the book is abbreviated to *WSSR* in parenthetical references.

6 See also Jameson's letter to her father, Denis Murphy, in which she writes, "Now take your Map and lay it before you, and trace my intended journey" (*Anna Jameson* 153). Bina Freiwald, Helen Buss ("Anna Jameson's *WSSR*"), Lisa LaFramboise (*Travellers in Skirts*), and Susan Birkwood all discuss Jameson's "specific, and intimate, addressee" (Freiwald 65).

7 Jameson spells the islands "Mackinaw" and "Manitoolin."

8 Gisela Sigrist contends, "As the title indicates, the structure is built on contrasts: the contrast of winter and summer, and of a contemplative and an active mode of life" (109). LaFramboise rightly notes, however, that Jameson's *Studies*, as well as her *Rambles*, must be considered a travel narrative (*Travellers in Skirts* 33). She points out that all three volumes begin by proposing an arduous journey that is farther and farther from the settled areas of Canada (34), and that the first volume, *Winter Studies*, is not just "a prolonged epistemological and aesthetic introduction to *Summer Rambles*," but also contains "conventional travel material: social analysis, travel description, the narrator's personal activities, reproductions of successful emigrant 'types'" (31).

9 Jameson consistently misspells the McMurrays' surname, calling them Mr and Mrs MacMurray. Except in direct quotations, I employ the spelling preferred by the McMurrays' brother-in-law Henry Schoolcraft (*Personal Memoirs* 561) and the *Dictionary of Canadian Biography* ("McMurray, William").

10 See Fraser 9–12 for discussion of Jameson's references to that political situation.

11 *Winter Studies and Summer Rambles* has been studied primarily from a feminist perspective in Thomas's biography and Marian Fowler's chapter in *The Embroidered Tent* (1982) and in works that focus on Jameson's writings, such as Judith Johnston's *Anna Jameson: Victorian, Feminist, Woman of Letters* (1997). Other recent studies of Jameson's works have analyzed *Winter Studies and Summer Rambles* either as feminist journal or epistolary writing (Freiwald, 1986; Buss, 1992) or as feminist travel writing (Sigrist, 1991; Birkwood, 1997; LaFramboise, 1997), while Adele Ernstrom (1997) has demonstrated links to Mary Wollstonecraft, and Jennifer Henderson (2003) has focused primarily on the transitional figure of the actress in Jameson's discussion of gender relations in her first volume, *Winter Studies*. Studies that examine the book from a post-colonial perspective are less common, although many essays comment on Jameson's writings about First Nations peoples. Lisa Vargo suggests in a 1998 article that Jameson demonstrates through her narrative that "domesticity subsumed by a masculinist ideology of nation subjugates both English women and Canadian native peoples" (61). Leslie Monkman argues in a 1984 essay, meanwhile, that Jameson "illuminates the tensions between aboriginal and European cultures in Upper Canada more clearly and more comprehensively than any of her contemporaries," and calls her book "one of pre-Confederation Canada's most important works of literary anthropology" (85, 86). Indeed, Jameson's book provides such detailed ethnographic descriptions and discussions of government policy toward indigenous peoples that it has been used as a source by contemporary historians (Rogers 122–3).

12 A few of the etchings were reproduced in Thomas's biography and Fowler's book and in journal articles by Lorraine York (1986) and Thomas Gerry (1990–91), while my 2003 essay "Here is the picture" examines and reproduces ten of the sketches.

13 Katharine Bassett Patterson kindly provided me with an initial transcription of this letter; see http://edocs.lib.sfu.ca/projects/VWWLP/ for her database on the letters of Anna Jameson, Harriet Martineau, and their friends.

14 Jameson refers to sexual contact between indigenous women and male European traders and settlers only obliquely when she notes that Henry avoids writing about "his adventures among the squaws" (3: 19) and when she writes critically about miscegenation (2: 244, 272; 3: 62).

15 Jameson's response to the dandy can be compared to Mina Hubbard's reaction to the Innu man who showed her his red leggings (WW 208; see also page 135 of this study).

16 Compare this passage to Hubbard's description of mosquitoes on her trip as "larger by far than any Jersey mosquitoes ever dreamed of being" with a bite "like the touch of a live coal" (WW 217–18).

17 Karen Dubinsky argues in *The Second Greatest Disappointment* that as more people visited Niagara Falls, "disappointment became an almost mandatory response" (10). Patricia Jasen suggests in *Wild Things* that by the early nineteenth century, "tourist angst" was already evident at the falls and that it increased "as commercial tourism began to transform Niagara" (34). As Elizabeth McKinsey points out in *Niagara Falls*, however, disillusionment over the commercialization of the falls and the impossibility of the high expectations generated by previous Romantic commentators being fulfilled was just beginning to be a common response at the time of Jameson's visit (154); Martineau wrote in 1838, for example, that she "expected to be disappointed" (*Retrospect* 1: 151).

18 Jameson was familiar with Martineau's work; she read excerpts from the newly published *Society in America* while she was in Canada and wrote that it "fulfilled the highest expectations I had previously formed" (2: 141). As a footnote reference indicates, she read the remainder of the book while she was preparing her own manuscript (1: 118–19n). Marryat's book was published after Jameson's, but she indicates in a letter home that she met Marryat in New York, where he gave her advice on publishing (*Anna Jameson* 159).

19 The cave was full of bones, and Jameson repeats Henry's speculation that they were those "of prisoners, sacrificed and devoured at war-feasts" (3: 67; see also Henry 110, from whom she quotes exactly).

20 I retain Jameson's spellings, such as Chippewa, Ottawa, and Pottowottomie, in direct quotations, but in my own text I use the spellings Ojibwa, Odawa, and Potawatomi current in books such as Steckley and Cummins's *Full Circle: Canada's First Nations*. I also employ that book's distinction

between the name of the cultural group (Ojibwa or, as they call themselves, Anishinabe or Anishinaabe) and its language (Ojibwe).

21 Jameson later describes herself as Johnston's "daughter Wa,sàh,ge,wo,-nò,quá" (3: 244), using a slightly different spelling. Two of her three new names contain the Ojibwe feminine suffix qua or quay.

22 As Jameson notes, George Johnston was indeed on Mackinac during her visit and sometimes acted as interpreter (3: 47).

23 *The Backwoods of Canada* focuses on settlement more than on travel, although it does begin with a description of the voyage to Canada. As Thomas and Johnston speculate (Thomas 239ch11n4; Johnston 111), Jameson may have been referring to Traill's newly published book when she wrote to Goethe just before she boarded the ship to North America on 1 October 1836: "I certainly did not send you the book about Canada to shew you in dark colours the hardships of a settler's life – quite the contrary. The book interested me, and pleased me very much, and it is thought to give so favourable a view of things, that they say it has made many persons emigrate" (*Letters* 59–60).

24 Similarly, Traill's sister Susanna Moodie commented in *Roughing It in the Bush* that "a mysterious destiny involves and hangs over them [Indian people], pressing them back into the wilderness, and slowly and surely sweeping them from the earth" (299). The notion of a "mysterious destiny" of course obfuscates the role played by trade, settlement, and government.

25 "Squaw" is the phonetic pronunciation of the word for "woman" in another Algonquian language, Massachusett. By the time of Jameson's travels, the word was widely used to refer to First Nations women in general and was beginning to take on pejorative connotations. In *The Last of the Mohicans* (1826), for example, James Fenimore Cooper describes a woman as a "crafty squaw" and a "squalid and withered ... hag" (258).

26 The *Dictionary of Canadian Biography* gives the Ojibwe names of Jameson's three friends as Oge-Buno-Quay, Obah-dahm-wawn-gezzhago-quay, and Oshaguscodawaqua ("McMurray, William" 680; "Johnston, John" 357). Jameson calls a more casual acquaintance, Johnston's sister-in-law, simply "Mrs. Wayish,ky" because, she writes, "I forget her proper name" (3: 188).

27 Ted Motohashi traces Columbus's use of the word "cannibal," the name given a group of people encountered in America, to tropes about man-eaters that were already of long standing (85; see also Hulme, *Colonial Encounters* 15, and Warner 163–4).

28 Schoolcraft's several publications, including his history of the Moravian missions and *Travels in the Central Portions of the Mississippi Valley*, are other important sources for Jameson's ethnographic information (*WSSR* 2: 109n; 3: 121n, 125n, 132n).

29 Henry writes of his life with Wa,wa,tam's family, "To fish and to hunt, to collect a few skins, and exchange them for necessaries, was all that I seemed destined to do, and to acquire, for the future" (113). He also notes that his companions were unable to converse about "the records of history, the pursuits of science, the disquisitions of philosophy, the systems of politics, the business and the amusements of the day, and the transactions of the four corners of the world" (148).

30 Jameson identifies the source for "[m]ost of the above particulars" as "oral communication" and Henry Schoolcraft's published papers (3: 132n).

31 The six stories appear in the 1956 edition of *Algic Researches*, renamed *Schoolcraft's Indian Legends*, under these titles: "Peboan and Seegwun, an Allegory of the Seasons" (39–40), "Sheem, or the Forsaken Boy" (92–6), "Iadilla, or the Origin of the Robin" (106–8), "Mishosha, or the Magician of the Lakes" (163–8), "Git-Chee-Gau-Zinee, or the Trance" (180–2; also published in *Travels* 410–12 as "Gitshee Gauzinee"), and "The Grave Light, or Adventures of a Warrior's Soul" (232–5; published in *Travels* 404–10 as "The Funeral Fire").

32 While Jameson adds a final paragraph outlining the remorse the brother and sister now feel about abandoning their younger brother, Schoolcraft includes a two-paragraph appendix noting, "The moral of this tale may be said to rebuke a species of cruelty." He then adds, to ensure that his readers do not confuse fiction with fact, that "we know of no recorded instance of abandonment of *children of either sex* by any North American tribes" (*Algic Researches* 95).

33 Paradoxically, Jameson wrote to Schoolcraft after the publication of her renditions of the stories, "The more exactly you can (in translation) adhere to the *style* of the language of the Indian nations, instead of emulating a fine or correct English style – the more characteristic in all respects – the more original – the more interesting your work will be" (qtd. in Schoolcraft, *Personal Memoirs* 634).

34 Head wrote that it was "very desirable indeed" to "discontinue the practice of giving presents to that portion of the visiting Indians who reside in the territory of the neighbouring states" (7). He argued both that such a policy would save money and that giving weapons to "Indians" living in another country and "engaged in civil war" with that country could be interpreted as "an act of hostility" (8). Jameson, meanwhile, quotes Jarvis as telling the First Nations chiefs assembled at Manitoulin that people in England had complained about "so large a sum of money" being spent on "Indian presents." Jarvis also told them that a rule of "civilised nations ... forbids your Great Father to give arms and ammunition to those Indians of the United States who are fighting against the government under which they live" (3: 280).

35 Historian Edward Rogers writes that the Delawares (Head's "Moravian Indians") were "induced" to give up fifteen square kilometres during Head's tenure as lieutenant-governor in exchange for an annuity (127).

36 Head had proposed that the Delawares be settled at Manitoulin (Rogers 127–8, Jameson 3: 266–7), but instead they moved to Kansas.

37 Jameson is not entirely sympathetic toward the people whose treaty was broken at Mackinac. In a footnote, she comments that as a result of the contravention of the treaty, several "whites" were killed: "The wretched individuals murdered were probably settlers, quite innocent in this business, probably women and children; but such is the *well-known* Indian law of retaliation" (3: 141n). Thus as well as criticizing government officials for their actions, she criticizes the "Indians" for what she perceives as their violent response and, in doing so, reveals her ingrained assumptions about probable targets for that violence and her inability to see the links between settlement and treaty issues.

38 The profits Jameson made from her books were legally the property of her husband (Thomas 101); the separation negotiations she conducted with him were designed not only to provide her with an allowance but also to ensure that she was left with a means of making her own living.

39 Jameson's classism is evident in the comment she makes about the faces of the men of Mackinac: "in none was there a trace of insolence or ferocity, or of that vile expression I have seen in a depraved European of the lowest class" (3: 139). In other passages, despite her own Irish heritage, she explicitly equates poor Irish immigrants with North American First Nations peoples. She writes that "little Red-skins" are "happy, healthy, active, dirty little urchins, resembling, except in colour, those you may see swarming in an Irish cabin. Poor Ireland! The worst Indian wigwam is not worse than some of her dwellings" (3: 253–4).

40 See Thomas 139–43 for a survey of those reviews.

41 Jameson's subsequent pamphlets and books on art include *Handbook to the Public Galleries of Art in or near London* (1842), *Companion to the Most Celebrated Private Galleries of Art in London* (1844), and *Memoirs of Early Italian Painters* (1845).

42 The album contains a notice indicating that it was sold at auction in London, England, on 20 December 1886. As well as containing the sixty-one sketches and watercolours of the Canadian and American journey, it includes thirty sketches showing Jameson's trip from England and travels in Europe. Thomas Gerry erroneously reports that none of the sketches has been published, but that Needler's booklet contains eight etchings based on the sketches (36). In fact, three of the eight illustrations in Needler's book appear to be reproductions of actual sketches from Jameson's album; four are etchings based on the sketches; and one is an etching that has no

counterpart in the album, although it is a summer version of a winter scene represented in an album sketch.

43 The differences between sketch and etching consist mostly in the stronger, darker lines of the etching and in variations in the trees, stumps, and one of the horses. In both sketch and etching, the female figure is almost covered by furs, but turns her face toward the viewer; her features are more subtly drawn in the sketch, giving her a pensive expression.

44 In several other sketches of modes of travel, including one of a bateau near St Joseph's island (album sketch 29), Jameson was probably also one of the small figures pictured.

45 Elizabeth Thompson argues that this picture "deviates from Traill's verbal representations of a similar site" because the stumps Traill describes "would preclude the picturesque by cluttering up the cleared space surrounding the cabin" (37).

46 In a letter to her friend Goethe, Jameson does not name her companion in the sleigh, but writes that by her side was "a *thing*, of which you can form no conception, a *Canada Dandy*" (*Letters* 77). Mr Campbell, she notes in her book, was driving the sleigh (1: 65).

47 In the etching of that scene in the Royal Ontario Museum's collection (fig. 1.2), white space has been cropped from the perimeter to give the canoes more emphasis. In addition, the parasol and bonnet of the female figure are more prominent in the etching than in the sketch, the faces of Jarvis and Head are turned toward the viewer, and some of the handkerchiefs around the heads of the paddlers are replaced by hats.

48 See Fowler (*Embroidered Tent*), Freiwald, and Buss ("Anna Jameson's *WSSR*") for discussions of Jameson's landscape descriptions in terms of their tendency toward sexualization or feminization.

49 The use of the word "sketch" to denote a picture in words was commonplace, as is evident from the titles of Jameson's *Visits and Sketches at Home and Abroad* (1834) and *Sketches in Canada, and Rambles among the Red Men* (1852, an abridged version of *Winter Studies and Summer Rambles in Canada*).

50 In contrast, the illustrators for Traill's book represent Montmorency Falls, near Quebec City, with a ship in the background, thus imbuing the landscape with the means for trade and settlement (23).

51 The imaginative portrait of "Peter, the Chief" used as the frontispiece for Traill's book also shows the upper body of a man, his head and eyes directed slightly to the side. In her text, she calls him simply "the old hunter, Peter" (163) and notes that he is "a sort of great man, though not a chief" (286). Her description of him is perfunctory: he is "dressed in a handsome blue surtout-coat, with a red worsted sash about his waist" (286). In the portrait, prepared by illustrators in London from this description, Peter is

depicted with European features, wearing a European-style frock coat and also a feathered conical hat. In *Roughing It in the Bush*, Moodie calls the same man the "old chief, Peter Nogan" (281) and writes that a "plainer human being than poor Peter could scarcely be imagined" (283). She also sketched Nogan wearing the hat pictured in Traill's portrait, "a blue cloth conical cap ... ornamented with a deer's tail dyed blue, and several cock's feathers" (290).

52 The page is erroneously labelled *The Widow Jones's – Stockbridge. Where Harriet Martineau lodged*. Several of the surrounding pages in the album are also mislabelled.

53 Jameson may have produced sketches of the Anishinaabe friends she made on the trip, including Johnston, McMurray, and Schoolcraft, but these drawings have not survived in her album or etchings.

54 The illustrators for Traill's *The Backwoods of Canada* also provide a wood-cut of two "Papouses" in bark cradles (166) to illustrate her comment that after carrying a child in a birchbark cradle on a strap around her neck, the mother would lean it up against a wall or chair, where the "passive prisoner" would stand, looking like "a mummy in its case" (167–8). The woodcut shows two peculiarly elongated cradles strung from a tree, with a dog barking at and worrying them. The children seem much larger than babies and have adult expressions and European features; the dog adds an element of humour to the illustration, taking it out of the realm of the ethnographic and into that of entertainment. Jameson's drawing of the woman and child (fig. 1.10) presents a more accurate portrayal of the activity of carrying a child in a cradle; the woman is pictured with the cradle on her back, held on by a tump-line over her forehead, rather than with the strap around her neck that Traill imagines.

chapter two

1 Unless otherwise stated, I cite the first edition of *A Woman's Way*, published by Murray in 1908. In quotations, I retain without comment Hubbard's spelling "Nascaupee" to refer to both river and cultural group, although in my own analysis I use the current accepted spellings "Naskaupi River" and "Naskapi" for the cultural group. *A Woman's Way* is abbreviated to WW in parenthetical references, while Dillon Wallace's *The Lure of the Labrador Wild* is shortened to LLW and *The Long Labrador Trail* to LLT. Diaries are identified using the initials of the writer.

2 See Anne Hart's biographical essay on Hubbard in *The Woman Who Mapped Labrador*, Sherrill Grace's introduction to the most recent edition of *A Woman's Way*, and James West Davidson and John Rugge's *Great Heart* for more biographical details about Hubbard and information about the three expeditions.

While Leonidas Hubbard took 120 pounds of flour for three people (Wallace, *LLW* 33), Mina Hubbard took 392 pounds for five people and had 105 pounds left over at the end of her trip, including some given to the Innu (*WW* 235). Despite his previous experience of starvation, Wallace took just 300 pounds of flour for five to six people. Less than a month into the trip he was already rationing flour (*LLT* 6, DW Diary 22 July), and eventually he sent most of his party back while he pushed on with one companion.

While Mina Hubbard was accompanied by four guides – three from the James Bay area of Ontario and one from Labrador – Wallace's single guide was an Ojibwa man from Minnesota (although a local trapper, Duncan McLean, did guide the group on the first part of the journey). Wallace boasted that the American guide, Peter Stevens, "was a Lake Superior Indian and had never run a rapid in his life" (16). He refused to take the advice of McLean, who suggested that the group keep to the Naskaupi River instead of trying to find the overgrown Innu trails (27). As a result, Wallace's expedition spent much more time searching for trails than did Mina Hubbard's, required more food, and at the same time had less success hunting.

Hubbard, in contrast, had on her crew expert whitewater canoeist Job Chapies and took the advice of local guide Gilbert Blake; she noted in her diary that her three James Bay guides told her that they would have missed the entrance to Seal Lake from the Naskaupi River had they not been travelling with someone familiar with the territory (17 July).

3 One anonymous and untitled review even compared Hubbard to Lady Jane Franklin, who "sent a ship to search for the relief of her lost husband" (*Literary Digest*).

4 See, for example, O'Flaherty (1979), Atwood (1996), and A.F. Williams (1996), all of whom either omit mention of Mina Hubbard's successful expedition or refer to it only as a footnote to her husband's unsuccessful trip.

5 The manuscript diaries of the Hubbards and George Elson were acquired by the Centre for Newfoundland Studies from Mina Hubbard Ellis's family in England during the 1990s; microfilm copies had earlier been deposited with the National Archives of Canada. Mina Hubbard's travel diary is an exact replica of the small, maroon, leather-covered diary her husband took on his expedition. With only a half page set aside for each day, the diaries did not provide enough space for daily entries and forced the Hubbards instead to hopscotch from middle to front to back as they wrote. Mina Hubbard also squeezed in two and sometimes three lines of writing to each ruled line of the diary.

See Niemi (1987) and Hoyle (1988) for discussions of the gender implications of the expedition. More recently, Roberta Buchanan has studied

Hubbard's descriptions of landscape (1997, 2001), Lisa LaFramboise has focused on *A Woman's Way* as a travel narrative that exhibits a balance of textual femininity and authority (1997, 2001), and Sherrill Grace has analyzed the book and the diary as autobiographical writings that negotiate a gendered identity (2000, 2001). *A Woman's Way* was long out of print until Newfoundland's Breakwater Books produced a facsimile of the first American edition in 1981. A new scholarly annotated edition of the book has been edited by Grace (2004) and, for the first time, Hubbard's diary will soon be published under the editorship of Buchanan and Bryan Greene. The Grace edition has a detailed introduction to Hubbard's expedition, and the diaries (forthcoming) will be accompanied by a biographical essay by Anne Hart, former director of the Centre for Newfoundland Studies, who was instrumental in establishing the Hubbard archival collection at the centre.

6 Parts of the Labrador Peninsula were claimed by both Quebec and the British colony of Newfoundland. The boundaries were settled by a ruling of the British Privy Council in 1927, which was confirmed when Newfoundland joined Canada in 1949. A Canadian government map published in 1952, however, indicates that the Quebec-Labrador boundary "had not been established at date of publication" (Labrador, Map 13E); the province of Quebec still disputes the boundary.

7 Duncan's book was based on a series of articles that she wrote for the Montreal *Daily Star* in 1888–89 under the masculine byline Garth Grafton. As Marian Fowler notes in her biography of Duncan, the last ten articles are signed either "Sara Jeannette [or, in one case, Jane] Duncan (Garth Grafton)" or simply "Sara Jeannette Duncan" (150). Duncan was by then an established writer whose works would be published even without the safeguard of a masculine pseudonym.

In the Canadian section of Duncan's fictionalized narrative, the narrator witnesses the condescension and discomfort of the newly arrived British emigrants to Winnipeg, who "all wear corduroys at first – to dances and the opera indiscriminately, by way of helping the 'natives' to feel on an equality with them," until they notice that everyone else is dressed according to "the usages of civilisation" (*Social Departure* 15). The narrator refers to Louis Riel and the Northwest Rebellion (37–8) and quotes a small boy at a glacier in British Columbia who tells her, "Ladies ain't meant fer explorin'" (49).

8 Binnie-Clark's next book, *Wheat and Woman* (1914), describes her efforts to run her own prairie farm.

9 Wallace's romantic tale of death in the wilderness was immediately popular with readers and remained a mainstay of North American wilderness narratives. In her autobiographical essay *The Labrador Fiasco*, Margaret

Atwood used the story as a metaphor for her father's "loss in the woods" after a stroke.

10 In her diary, Hubbard often refers to Wallace simply as "W": "Always there is much talk of the other party and their probable doings esp. the probability of their getting lost. All are familiar with the story of W's prowess in wilderness travel" (6 Aug.). Toward the end of her trip, she writes that she hopes to be able to "get my story and some of my pictures in print before W. is even heard from ... How grateful I should be and how complete would be my victory and how completely it would make of no account W's reflections" (26 Aug.).

   Once Wallace and his remaining companion, Clifford Easton, arrived at the post, Hubbard could barely tolerate Wallace's presence. She writes: "Felt a little nervous about their coming and now it is an end to peace of mind for me" (16 Oct.), and "This eve seemed as if I should go distracted with Wallace's clap trap in the kitchen" (17 Oct.). The anniversary of her husband's death was especially unpleasant: "Wallace & Easton not gone to their tents yet. I shall go to mine to-morrow unless they do. The view threatens to take away my appetite and the continual dropping of a not too melodious voice threatens to break up my nervous system ... Two years ago to-night 'the veil was drawn away and he stood before the Great Father'" (18 Oct.). Fortunately for Hubbard's peace of mind, the ship arrived on 19 October, and Wallace chose not to take it but instead to return overland by dogsled.

11 Feminist geographer Linda McDowell demonstrates that in late-nineteenth-century Europe and North America, the "ideology that 'women's place was in the home'" was held by all social classes and "exercised a vital hold on the lives and minds of all women" (79).

12 Twenty-one women were elected fellows of the Royal Geographical Society in 1892–93, but the society then voted to stop admitting women. Female members were not admitted again until 1913 (Blunt and Wills 117). Hubbard was elected to the society in 1927 on the basis of her Labrador expedition (Grace, Introduction 238n36).

13 A Labrador traveller quoted in the *New York Daily Tribune*, meanwhile, stated that Hubbard could not have "got into the interior ... in such short time" ("Thinks Wallace Safe").

14 After her marriage, Duncan was identified on the title pages of most of her works as "Mrs. Everard Cotes (Sara Jeannette Duncan)."

15 Hubbard notes in her preface that she is "indebted for the title of [her] book" to her pastor, James Sawyer (xi). The title ensured interest in her journey simply because a woman had made it, and implied that her travels were solitary, although in fact she was seldom alone.

16 Wallace also insisted that his expedition was a continuation of Leonidas Hubbard's and that Hubbard accompanied him in spirit: "Well, this, too,

is Hubbard's trip. His spirit is with me. It was he, not I, who planned this Labrador work, and if I succeed it will be because of him and his influence" (*LLT* 7–8). Because of his unstated rivalry with Mina Hubbard, he invoked his friend's spirit to argue that he, not she, was the valid completer of this journey.

17 Although the author is identified as "Mrs Leonidas Hubbard, Junior" on the title page of her book and in her articles (except the article in *Harper's Monthly Magazine*, which carries the byline "Mina B. Hubbard"), I list her as Mina Benson Hubbard in my bibliography. In identifying her in this way (as I similarly list Anna Brownell Jameson), I follow feminist literary convention that has, for example, permitted scholars to name Elizabeth Gaskell the author of her books, although she published either anonymously or as Mrs Gaskell.

18 In an article Leonidas Hubbard wrote about a canoe trip they took together, he calls his wife only "Madam" ("Off Days" 716, 721).

19 Wallace was blunt in stating that the "Indian" he hired was to be "woodsman, hunter and general camp servant" (*LLT* 4).

20 Hubbard's book exemplifies early twentieth-century terminology; for example, when she writes that others considered her husband "white" (43), she refers to his generosity and honour rather than his race. She uses the term in a similar way in her diary: "I tell you they have treated me white here [at George River Post]. I almost hate to go back again" (26 Sept.). See Cameron's *The New North* for a similar usage of the word (55).

21 Hubbard specifies Elson's cultural background in her magazine articles, but I question the editorial accuracy of a newspaper article about her journey in which she is quoted as calling him "[o]ne of my half-breeds" ("Mrs. Leonidas Hubbard's Own Story"). Several researchers have argued that Blake was Innu, of the cultural group known as Montagnais (see, for example, Cooke 43). Anne Hart's investigations have demonstrated, however, that he was indeed of Inuit descent.

22 Hart has determined Blake's age to be nineteen, although his daughter, Jean Crane, lists his age as seventeen in a review of the Breakwater edition of *A Woman's Way*.

23 Duncan's *A Social Departure*, Binnie-Clark's *A Summer on the Canadian Prairie*, and Cameron's *The New North* are exceptions in that they describe some travels "to" and, in Cameron's case, "from." One reason for these exceptions is that rail travel in Canada was still considered remarkable in the late nineteenth and early twentieth centuries.

24 Wallace also begins and ends the book about his 1905 expedition with brief mention of Leonidas Hubbard. The book opens with several quotations from Hubbard, including his admonishment "The work must be done, Wallace, and if one of us falls before it is completed the other must finish it" (*LLT* 2), and it ends with the words "The work of exploration

begun by Hubbard was finished" (288). Since Wallace is a man, he does not need to frame his narrative in the same way as Mina Hubbard does; a much briefer reference to Leonidas Hubbard can serve to authorize him as Hubbard's successor.

25 Leonidas Hubbard's expedition was criticized by contemporaries such as Robert T. Morris, who contended in a letter to *Forest and Stream* that there was always plenty of game in Labrador and that Hubbard's party must have been "not quite sufficiently skilled in woodcraft." In support of Hubbard, Labrador expert William Cabot argued that the delay caused by taking the wrong river meant that Hubbard's party had to attempt to survive by hunting during the fall, when there was little game. Cabot writes: "Lest it be thought that a good degree of practical woodsmanship would have kept them from arriving in such straits let it be realised that the little-known history of the dwellers in the country abounds with instances of distress in just such situations" (Introduction 23; see also Cabot's earlier defence of Hubbard in *Forest and Stream*).

26 The 1908 American edition, published by McClure, omits this introduction. Although the effect of this change should be to give Mina Hubbard's narrative more individual authority, in fact the title of the first chapter, "Leonidas Hubbard, Junior," and the first line, "There was an unusual excitement and interest in Mr Hubbard's face when he came home one evening in January of 1903," serve to position Hubbard's narrative firmly within the context of her husband's earlier expedition. Cabot was a friend of Leonidas Hubbard, and Mina may have asked him to write the introduction to her book after she saw his defence of Leonidas's expedition in *Forest and Stream*.

27 See Grace's introduction for a discussion of the "polyvocal" nature of *A Woman's Way* (l).

28 Hubbard is quoted in an interview with the *World* on 2 July 1905 as saying that she asked Elson to visit her in December 1904 to help her to write a book about her husband's expedition. The article notes that "Mr. Elson has written the true account of her husband's expedition, which account will be incorporated into the book now in preparation. This is the first attempt at literary work ever made by Mr. Elson, but this, Mrs. Hubbard says, is done in a wonderfully beautiful way" ("Why I Go to Labrador"). I was unable to locate the original of Elson's narrative, if indeed it still exists. Thus I can make no analysis of the kinds of alterations Hubbard may have made to this narrative.

29 In the process of writing her book, Hubbard also altered the original observations recorded in her own diary to make them less personal, more detailed, more literary, and, for contemporary readers such as me, less compelling. This editing is most obvious when she claims to quote directly from her diary entry of 24 August on pages 222–5, while in fact altering every line. Grace points out that Hubbard's diary is a "narrative" rather

than just field notes, since she writes as though she is "telling a story" and includes substantial amounts of dialogue ("Hidden Country" 278).

30 Buchanan comments on this obsession with food in Hart's CBC radio documentary on the Hubbard and Wallace expeditions (Hart, *Into Unknown Labrador*). Much of Leonidas Hubbard's diary is indeed filled with descriptions not only of food he and his companions ate on the trail but also of the food they plan to eat when they leave Labrador (30 Aug., 6, 8 Sept., 2, 11 Oct.); restaurants they hope to visit (5, 12, 14 Sept., with a list written on the final page of the diary), Indian dishes Hubbard wants to try (18, 20 Sept.), food he plans to leave at his office (26 Sept.), food he hopes to take on future camping trips (14 Sept.), meals Mina Hubbard previously served to him and his companions (23 Sept.), and meals he wants her to cook when he returns (19 Sept.). A typical entry is the following one, about future camp cooking plans, written on a day when he was in reality "[h]ungry all day": "with the outfit will go flour in plenty, sweet biscuit, bacon, chocolate, milk, heap sugar, marmalade, lime tablets, canned roast beef, onions, potatoes, rice, oatmeal, raisins, figs, dried fruit, tomatoes, with chickens when we can get them along the way. Then good stews, soups, French toast, syrup, pancakes, omlettes [*sic*], sweet biscuit and jam, with a broiled steak and a chicken roast when available, canned pork & beans, & canned plum pudding must also go in the menu. Mina & I must study delightful camp dinners now and carry out the nice little woods dinners we started. I must study camp cookery, too. And what fine little dinners we can have" (14 Sept.).

31 In the entry for 20 July, *A Woman's Way* includes Hubbard's sentence, omitted from *Outing*, "George worked like a hero" (246). While both *A Woman's Way* and *Outing* include the lines "All restless at inactivity but George. He calm, philosophical, cheerful, and hopeful always," *A Woman's Way* includes his subsequent words, "– a wonderful man" (Outing 667; WW 259). The wording of both is identical to that in Leonidas's diary for 24 August, with the exception of some abbreviations.

32 See also 15, 22 July, 14, 24, 25 September, and 8 October for examples of references to Mina and home. Hubbard's feelings about his wife and about food are often conflated in passages in his diary in which he longs for home.

33 The entry for 15 August in the diary held at the Centre for Newfoundland Studies reads: "I'd like to be home tonight to see the girl & the people & eat some bread & real sweet coffee or tea or chocolate." The original entry for 15 October similarly uses the abbreviations "N.Y." and "&."

34 Both *A Woman's Way* and *Outing* include almost word for word Hubbard's last remarkable diary entry before his death, in which he states his preparation for death while maintaining his continued resistance against its inevitability (18 Oct.). Mina Hubbard wrote in her own diary, "Oh <u>how</u>

noble must have been the spirit which in utter weakness and weariness and disappointment could keep so wonderfully sweet" (11 Aug.).

35 Grace's introduction to *WW* contains a detailed analysis of the articles written by Hubbard (xxxiv–xli).

36 In an interview with the *World* on 2 July 1905, Hubbard is quoted as saying that she made her decision to mount an expedition "as the work of writing the book progressed" – in other words, while she was editing her husband's travel diary and Elson's account of the last days of Leonidas's life ("Why I Go to Labrador").

37 Hubbard notes a few pages later that on one occasion she would not let Elson carry her rifle because "I was not pleased with him just then" (91). As her diary makes clear, she was "not pleased" because her movements had been restricted during the portage. At times she makes light of the restrictions – "George's tone of authority was sometimes amusing. Sometimes I did as I was told, and then again I did not" (88) – while at other times, especially in her diary, she describes them with bitterness: "When I suggested it [travelling to Fort Chimo] to George he opposed it as has been the rule with most of my suggestions" (28 Aug.). While she awaited the ship that would take her home from George River Post, she wrote: "Wish I were a man would try for a place in H.B.C. service for while in some of these out of the world places. Dread going back to face the crowd" (4 Oct.).

38 Cameron's niece dressed in an even more womanly manner; photographs (such as fig. 2.7) show her hatless, with her hair pinned up, wearing a skirt and jacket and with a flowing scarf knotted at her neck.

39 The portrait of Mina Hubbard appears as the frontispiece of all three first editions. A portrait of Leonidas Hubbard by the same artist appears opposite the first page of his diary excerpts in the Murray and Briggs editions and within the first chapter of the McClure edition. Based on a photograph of him published in *Outing*, it shows a similarly refined subject who rests his left hand against his face. Unlike his wife's body in her portrait, however, his directly faces the viewer, although he gazes away at an angle.

40 J.G. Millais was one of the few contemporaneous reviewers to mention this incident. In his 1909 review of Hubbard's book, he diminishes its impact by calling it "one of the poorest jokes on record," played out only for "the *fun* of throwing her four excellent helpers into a state of fear" (402).

41 A photograph labelled "From an Indian Grave" illustrates her Romantic description of this gravesite: "Back of this solitary resting-place were the moss-covered hills with their sombre forests, and as we turned from them we looked out over the bay at our feet, the shining waters of the lake, and beyond it to the blue, round-topped hills reaching upward to blend with exquisite harmony into the blue and silver of the great dome that stooped to meet them" (159). Elsewhere, Hubbard acknowledges the literary source

for her notions of the poetic Indian: "Everywhere along the way we found the camping places chosen from among the most beautiful spots, and there seemed abundant evidence that in many another Indian breast dwelt the heart of Saltatha, Warburton Pike's famous guide" (209).

42 Elson describes reaching the landmark in this way: "Job went to see he came to the canoes and said Georges river as Georges River boys. All glad to know the waters run North" (GE Diary 10 Aug.). In her analysis of these passages, LaFramboise points out that while Chapies gives George Elson a claim on the river by jokingly linking him to its name (which in fact honours King George III), Hubbard translates his comment into a reference to the biblical Jordan River and thus "situates the importance of the journey into the context of *her* life and belief system" ("Just a little" 36n68).

43 In her diary, Hubbard quotes Elson as admitting, "Well we fellows haven't hurried ourselves any. We have taken it easy" (25 July). Only the next day does she note that they were travelling at a relaxed pace in order not to tire her. She remains suspicious, however, that the men were moving slowly in order to ensure that they would have to take the Grand River route back (1 Aug.).

44 Hubbard also writes in her diary, "Would have been awfully frightened had I not had such implicit confidence in my men. Realize more & more what strain this trip would be were they not so brave and skillful and good" (1 July).

45 In an interview for Hart's CBC radio special, Blake's daughter, Jean Crane, says that from hints her father dropped, she believes there was a "love affair" between Elson and Hubbard: "[M]y father, Gilbert, would often smile as he talked about an affection between Mina and George. He told us that sometimes they would walk alone and they would tell the guides not to worry about them, that they would be all right. As they went out of sight, and often arm in arm, sometimes they would hold each other" (qtd. in Hart, *Into Unknown Labrador*).

46 Elson notes in his diary that Mina Hubbard sometimes cried as parts of the trip reminded her of her husband's journey and his subsequent death (23 July).

47 Travel theorist Dennis Porter comments on "the anxiety of travel writing," arguing that the travel writer feels pressure "to add something new and recognizably his own to the accumulated testimony of his predecessors" (12). Hubbard certainly exhibits some anxiety about her writing ability. Occasionally, she attributes difficulties to her companions; for example, she calls Iserhoff and Blake "childish" when they object to her writing that they became sick from overeating caribou meat (MH Diary 11 Sept.), and she notes that her work is going slowly because she is worried about Elson (24 Sept.). She also worries that her book will not properly honour

her husband's memory: "[I want to] make the book what it ought to be, something which will live and speak for him. Feel so uncertain of my ability to do it. Get dreadfully discouraged about it. Am afraid I am making a dreadfully flat uninteresting story of it and one which will look strange beside Laddie's diary and George's story" (15 Oct.). She was reassured about the interest in her narrative as soon as she reached Chateau Bay; after she sent a telegram announcing her safe arrival, editors at the *World* telegraphed back that they wanted five hundred words by wire. The article was published as "'Successful,' Mrs. Hubbard Wires *The World*."

48 The men's statement was drafted twice in Elson's handwriting (once on a left-hand page and once on a right-hand page), but was signed only once by all the men. Both their statement and Hubbard's are quoted below in their entirety:

> We the undersigned do hereby declare, each for himself, that during the trip across Labrador with Mrs Leonidas Hubbard Jr. leaving North-west River Post June 27th 1905 reaching George River Post August 27th 1905 he at all times treated Mrs Hubbard with respect, and each also declares his belief that Mrs Hubbard was always treated with respect by the other men of this Party. [E]ach also here records his promise that he will never by look or word or sign lead any human being to believe that during the trip there was anything in the conduct of Mrs Hubbard and her party towards each other which was unbecoming honorable Christian men and woman and also that he signs this statemen [*sic*] entirely of his own free will and accord.
>
> signed   George Elson
> September 16th 1905   J. C. Iserhoff
>   Gilbert Blake
>   *9 ι̇ ι ^°* [Job Chapies]

> George River Post
> Sept. 16th 1905
> I, Mina B. Hubbard, do hereby declare and solemnly avow that during the trip across Labrador, leaving Northwest River Post June 27th 1905, reaching George River Post Aug. 17th 1905, on which George Elson accompanied me, he at all times treated me with respect and as an honorable Christian man. I also record my promise that I will never by word or look or sign lead any human being to believe that he ever otherwise treated me and if that I should ever in any way intimate that he otherwise treated me I hereby declare it to be a lie.
>
> Mina B. Hubbard.

If Gilbert Blake's daughter is correct, he later contradicted his sworn statement, which thus might have been obtained under duress.

49 I am indebted to Anne Hart for pointing out the sexual implications of this passage.

50 See Barnley, Hind, McLean, Long, and Francis and Morantz for accounts of the killing of the staff of the Hudson's Bay Company post at Hannah Bay by a group of Cree.

51 Hubbard's declaration is a surprising echo of Samuel Hearne's comment to his First Nations companions of more than one hundred years earlier that "though I was no enemy of the Esquimaux, and did not see the necessity of attacking them without cause, yet if I should find it necessary to do it, for the protection of any one of my company, my own safety out of the question, so far from being afraid of a poor defenceless Esquimaux, whom I despised more than feared, nothing should be wanting on my part to protect all who were with me" (116). Hubbard thus appears to adopt the traditional masculine voice of the explorer and head of an expedition.

Fear was a common anticipatory response to such an encounter, as is evident in a newspaper clipping about Leonidas Hubbard's 1903 journey titled "Daring New Yorkers Lost in Labrador: Fears That Indians Have Slain Them." The anonymous author claims (erroneously on both counts) that expedition members "could scarcely die of hunger, for the country which they started to pierce is filled with game and fish" and that "only accident or the vengeance of the primitive tribe into whose haunts the fearless men undertook to penetrate could account for their failure to return in time."

52 The main differences between the American edition and the earlier British and Canadian editions (the latter produced from the British plates and printed by the same printers) are that the American edition omits Cabot's introduction; omits running heads provided at the top of alternate pages to summarize the action; reduces and occasionally crops photographs to allow printing two to a page; moves photographs and the portrait of Leonidas Hubbard to different locations in the text; changes two photograph captions; alters punctuation and some words ("journey" in the Murray edition [Preface ix] becomes "trip" in the McClure [Preface np]); uses a different typeface and pagination; binds the map into the book rather than folding it into a pocket inside the back cover; and omits the final index.

Some of these changes have a substantial impact on the reader and thus deserve more detailed study. For example, running heads in the British and Canadian editions provide summaries and glosses missing in the American edition, such as these headings for the "Scaring the Guides" chapter: "Scouting" (121), "Freed from My Guard" (123), "I Run Away" (125), "The Search" (127), "Recaptured" (129), and "I Am Admonished" (131). Photographs that appear in significantly different places include those moved from Cabot's introduction into the body of Hubbard's narrative; representations of the Naskapi and Montagnais, scattered throughout the earlier editions but consolidated in the American edition in the section in which Hubbard discusses her party's visits with the two groups; and the photograph illustrating Mina Hubbard's arrival with her companions at Ungava, which is moved from just before the final section of her narrative to the beginning of her husband's diary. That move in particular serves to link the completion of her journey more directly to the fulfillment of her husband's goal. All three editions, however, close with an evocative full-page landscape photograph labelled "Night-Gloom Gathers," in the section in which George Elson describes, in his appended narrative, the recovery and return of Leonidas Hubbard's body.

Of the photograph captions that are altered, one appears to be an editorial change: a photograph of Job Chapies poling up rapids, labelled "Up the Fierce Nascaupee" in the British edition, becomes "Job Was in His Element" (a line from Hubbard's book) in the American. The other alteration transposes the original caption from the rapids photograph onto a second, unrelated photograph: thus a photograph of the men looking at and walking beside a set of rapids, originally labelled "A Study in Rapids," becomes "The Fierce Nascaupee."

All editions of the book perpetuate a typographical error which indicates that the expedition started out on 27 July 1905, when in fact it embarked one month earlier, on 27 June (Murray and Briggs editions 54; McClure and Breakwater editions 24; McGill-Queen's edition 4–5).

53 Of his guide Peter Stevens, Wallace wrote that he had the "Indian instinct to kill" (*LLT* 53); of the Innu, that they "live according to their lights, and their lights are those of the untutored savage who has never heard the gospel of Christianity and knows nothing of the civilization of the great world outside" (215). Mills argues that "women travel writers were unable to adopt the imperialist voice with the ease with which male writers did" (3), but as Duncan's work indicates, women writers were nevertheless subject to the same imperialist discursive inheritance as their male counterparts.

54 As Marie Wadden notes, the people that Hubbard identified as "Nascaupee" and that others have since called Naskapi "call themselves Mushuau-Innu, which means 'the barren ground people,' because they traditionally hunted above the tree line" (22). Hubbard also sometimes calls them "the Barren Ground People" and even provides an Innu or Cree version: "Mush-a-wau e-u-its" (200, 192; see also diary memorandum 98).

55 Hubbard wrote the Innu words for "go away" (which she transcribed as "Ă wă' sik," a spelling probably provided by Elson) in the back of her diary. In contrast, although Wallace could not understand what was being said by the Innu group he met, he assumed they were saying that "we are glad to have you with us" (*LLT* 133): "we were jabbering, each in his own tongue, neither we nor they understanding much that the other said. I did

make out from them that we were the first white men that had ever visited them in their hunting grounds and that they were glad to see us" (134). Because of this communication difficulty, his claim to originality in this case is suspect.

56 The 1969 translation, which incorrectly gives Rich's first name as Edward, contains a few inaccuracies and inconsistencies regarding Hubbard's route and her reasons for taking the journey. Rich says that Hubbard was looking for her missing husband, who was supposed to be travelling to Davis Inlet, and that she was travelling with a white man (probably Elson) and two Indians who did not understand their language. (If they did not in fact understand one another's language, his mother would have been unable to quote their conversation.) A new translation, made by Marguerite Mackenzie of Memorial University of Newfoundland from the Innu version of the interview in *Sheshatshui-atanukana mak tipatshimuna* (29–30), reads in part:

> Then they saw the Innu, they [Innu] did not do anything to them [Hubbard and companions]. Then when they most likely reached them, the Innu, the men were not there. Kamushuasht is the name of the place there, it is very far, indeed. That's where they reached my late mother, [as] only the women were there; all the men had gone to Davis Inlet.
>
> "Then they called out to us," my late mother said. "We were afraid."
>
> "Don't be afraid of us, we are people/human," they were saying to us ...
>
> Then they [Hubbard party] followed the current there on that side, right there again at George River they reached other Innu. Then they stayed there for a long time, taking pictures of the Innu. Still they [Innu] didn't do anything to them [Hubbard party], they did not bother them.

This version includes a passage in which "Âkaneshâss," or Little White Guy – presumably Elson – describes the party's encounter with the migrating caribou, a conversation Hubbard also describes (205). While the original translation ends with the words "They went back on the ship. I don't know the rest – what they used to tell about that. I was very young. I didn't have much sense. That's all I know" (78), Mackenzie's new translation omits mention of the ship and ends with the words "I do not know where she told this story about, because I did not think about it much, I was still a child."

57 See, for example, the photograph credited to George Richards (*LLT* facing 120). Cameron's publisher also chooses not to give photograph credits to her travelling companions; instead, all photographs, even those showing Cameron, are credited on the title page to "the author."

58 Innu men had certainly travelled the complete route, as was clear when the "chief" of the more northerly group told Elson that he had taken the route south to North West River and had also canoed north to Ungava (204).

59 Nevertheless, Hubbard's narrative is written as though she can understand what the Innu are saying. She bases her account on subsequent conversations with Elson and the other men of her party and, in places where she quotes the Innu directly, on the account of the trip found in Elson's diary. Half a decade later Margaret Laurence also had difficulty communicating with Somali women because she did not speak the language and had to rely on male translators.

60 LaFramboise interprets Hubbard's description of the man in red leggings as an eruption of "the idea of the woman explorer as both an object and an agent of desire, in an interracial context" (*Travellers in Skirts* 206). She argues that the man serves as a "displacement of the attraction" that historians speculate was developing between Hubbard and Elson, and that "the spectre of forbidden sexual attraction to the racial 'other' is raised and disposed of" in this safe context (206).

61 "Geography at the British Association," *Geographical Journal*, October 1907, describes a talk Hubbard gave on 6 August 1907 titled "Traverse of Two Unexplored Rivers of Labrador" (425), and "Meetings of the Royal Geographical Society, Session 1907–1908," *Geographical Journal*, February 1908, lists her speech of 6 January 1908 titled "Journeys through Lonely Labrador."

62 On Wallace's map of his 1903 journey, he also named Mountaineer Lake, Elson Lake (in Labrador, not the Lake Elson in Quebec that Mina Hubbard named), Ptarmigan Lake (where he shot three ptarmigans, *LLW* 86), Hope Lake, and Mary Lake ("Let us call it Mary Lake" [*LLW* 103]). On his 1905 journey, he named lakes Portage (*LLT* 77), Namaycush (where he caught his first Namaycush fish, 80), Desolation (98), and Bibiquasin (95, now spelled Bibikwasin [Labrador, Map 13L, 1990]). He also adopted guide Peter Stevens's names for lakes Washkagama (Crooked Lake [67]) and Kasheshebogamog ("which in his language means 'Lake of Many Channels'" [108]). All of Wallace's toponyms can be found on current topographical maps, except lakes Windbound and Kasheshebogamog (which were subsumed in the Smallwood Reservoir) and Mount Hubbard.

63 Marc Richard's Web posting identifies almost all of the topographic features in Quebec named by Hubbard and still in existence today. Labrador toponyms have been identified through a comparison of Hubbard's textual references and the toponyms on her map to current topographical maps of the area. I am also indebted to biographical research on names of Hubbard's family members conducted by Anne Hart.

64 Hubbard acknowledged James Sawyer in her preface and wrote near the end of her trip that she would be very glad to see "the Sawyers" (25 Aug.).

Mrs Sawyer's first name is spelled "Lucy" in the *National Cyclopedia of American Biography*.

65 Hart has identified those nieces as Dorothy McCall, Marie Underhill, Orma Benson, Agnes Underhill, Gertrude Cruikshank, and Marion McCall. See Martin et al. for names of other female relatives (225).

Grace suggests that photographs such as those labelled "Wild Maid Marion" and "Bridgman Mountains" serve to "illustrate specific locations in her narrative" and "consolidate and confirm her attempt to name and claim aspects of the country" (Introduction lviii). There is also, of course, a Romantic tradition of naming places for people (including women), as William Wordsworth's "Poems on the Naming of Places" demonstrate. A difference between his naming technique and Hubbard's is that while Wordsworth writes of naming geographical features for people who visited locations with him or whose presence is evoked by those locations, Hubbard often arbitrarily inscribes names on certain features of the landscape simply because she wants to honour or recognize the holders of those names. (The geographical features she named after her husband are of course exceptions, since the landscape of Labrador certainly evoked feelings about him.)

66 Again, these toponyms are examples of Hubbard's practice of naming adjacent geographical features for a husband and wife. For her middle name, see the copy of the birth certificate for "Benson, Nina [*sic*] Adelaide" in the Centre for Newfoundland Studies Archives. Hubbard also named Resolution Lake to commemorate her party's decision to push on to Ungava rather than turning back (*WW* 189).

67 Indeed, in his diary George Elson uses the first-person plural pronoun to describe naming several geographical features; he writes: "crossed a little brook (Ka-co-shepish) we called" (8 July) and "had Lunch at point Lucy [Lucie in superscript above line] – we called" (29 June). The brook name did not make its way onto Mina Hubbard's map. Similarly, on 22 July Elson wrote vertically in the margin of his diary, "Mount Elson"; although Hubbard's map includes Lake Elson, the name Mount Elson does not appear.

68 See "Innu lakes damaged," "Innu, Natives of Quebec," and "Selected Innu Placenames."

69 See Pratt's *Lost Lands* and "Paddling the Wild East." A group of women canoeists in 1982 avoided the difficulties posed by the reservoir by arranging to be flown to a point north of it, on the George River (Ford; Niemi). In 1996 Susan Musgrave used only established means of travel, including airplanes and boats, in her travels through Labrador. She evoked Mina Hubbard's canoe journey, however, through the title of her essay about changes to Labrador ("Another Woman's Way through Unknown Labrador").

chapter three

1 Laurence notes that many Somalis doubted whether the water reservoirs Jack was building would really help them (*PCB* 44). One group of Somali herdsmen suggested that a better option would be for the government to send out truckloads of water to each Somali camp during the dry season (70). For more biographical details about Laurence, see James King's *The Life of Margaret Laurence* and Lyall Powers's *Alien Heart: The Life and Work of Margaret Laurence*. *The Prophet's Camel Bell* is abbreviated to *PCB* in parenthetical references, and *A Tree for Poverty* as *TFP*.

2 Laurence's African prose has been fully incorporated into the canon of her work only within the past decade and a half. The most comprehensive examination of her African works is Fiona Sparrow's *Into Africa with Margaret Laurence* (1992), which includes a chapter on *The Prophet's Camel Bell*. Shorter works on that travel memoir include essays by George Woodcock (1978) and Konrad Groß (1986) and a chapter in David Lucking's book (2002).

   Laurence's African fiction has been the subject of more detailed analysis. Recently, several commentators have looked at gender-specific metaphors (Coger, 1996–97) and at the intersections of imperialism and gender in her fiction (Busia, 1989–90; Collu, 1997; Pell, 1997), while others have also noted such intersections in her travel memoir (Buss, "Reading" 2001; Roy, "Anti-imperialism" 2001). The critical interest in Laurence's African texts has led to McClelland and Stewart New Canadian Library editions of *This Side Jordan, The Tomorrow-Tamer,* and *The Prophet's Camel Bell* and more recently to Donez Xiques's edition of *A Tree for Poverty* (1993) and Nora Foster Stovel's edition of *Long Drums and Cannons* (2001). Those two non-fiction texts have also been the subject of several recent critical essays (Sparrow, "Margaret Laurence" 1996; Na'Allah, 2001).

3 See Quinby for a discussion of the relational nature of memoir (299).

4 Reece also published articles about her time in Somaliland, including "Carpets to Somaliland" (1956) and "Somaliland Safari" (1957). Her position as the wife of the governor of the British Somaliland Protectorate, a man who had been knighted in 1950, would have prevented any intimacy between the two women.

5 Laurence dedicates much of her text to debunking that romantic view of travel, but her representation of Somali culture retains a romantic perspective. After Jack and several employees have recovered some stolen instruments, she imagines that in years to come the story will be told by the Somalis as one of bravery against all odds, "although by that time it will have been forgotten what was stolen and from whom" and the box of instruments will have been transformed "into some rare carved chest laden with golden coins and necklaces like the sun" (110).

6 Laurence writes later in *PCB*, "Whether Mohamed Abdullah Hassan [*sic*] was a madman and a religious fanatic, as the British claimed, or an early nationalist and divinely inspired leader, as the Somalis claimed, was not a matter that could ever be settled" (240). In 1964 she drafted an essay on the man, whose name she then spelled Mahammed 'Abdille Hasan (a spelling similar to that using Somali orthography, Maxammed Cabdille Xasan [Kapteijns 4]). In "The Poem and the Spear," published in *Heart of a Stranger* in 1976, she claimed that the "deeply ingrained imperialism" of the British prevented them from seeing him "as a nationalist leader with a legitimate aim" (65). David Richards has criticized the "distortions" inherent in parallels Laurence makes between Mahammed 'Abdille Hasan and Louis Riel (Richards 24).

7 Unless otherwise indicated, the short stories quoted are from Laurence's collection *The Tomorrow-Tamer* and the essays from *Heart of a Stranger*.

8 Just as she includes only first names of friends and employees in Somalia, so Laurence does not name the Reeces or Philip Shirley; he is identified in Sparrow's *Into Africa with Margaret Laurence* (46), King's *The Life of Margaret Laurence* (94), and Powers's *Alien Heart* (112-13).

9 For a contrasting portrayal of African speech, see Joyce Cary's *Mister Johnson*, in which African characters consistently speak only pidgin English. African writer Micere Githae-Mugo defends Laurence against charges of appropriation and, indeed, against her own self-criticism. Githae-Mugo writes that, unlike many Western writers on Africa, Laurence never claimed to "understand the *native* mind," and yet she has "a reasonable grasp of what Africa is all about." She concludes that Laurence – "perhaps above any other Western writer on Africa – richly contributed to the field of African literature" (13).

10 Jack Laurence is sometimes Margaret Laurence's excuse for inaction when she might otherwise be actively anti-imperialist or feminist. Thus I disagree with Sparrow's assessment that "Jack Laurence is the hero of the book [*The Prophet's Camel Bell*]" (*Into Africa* 40). Although Laurence is enthusiastic about her husband's work and presents him in a generally positive light, her narrative also emphasizes Jack's more conservative approach and her sometimes enforced deferral to him in matters related to their relations with Somalis.

11 That retrospective self-criticism is evident again and again in Laurence's narrative. For example, she describes her involvement in Mohamed's marital squabbles and then disparages her assumption "that Mohamed's mother-in-law trouble was identical with the situations I had read about in the lovelorn columns of North American newspapers, and that his request for advice meant precisely the same as it would to a person at home" (188).

12 My thanks to David Brooks of the *Journal of the Anglo-Somali Society* for providing me with Mrs Shirley's first name.

13　Laurence provides more information about the two poets in the essays "The Poem and the Spear" and "The Epic Love of Elmii Bonderii."

14　Lyall Powers suggests in his biography of Laurence that the word *belwo* or *balwo* in fact means "mischief" or "trouble" (125). As Kapteijns points out, the *balwo* was a very new and ephemeral genre. It was introduced in the 1940s and was quickly replaced by the similar but longer *heello* or *hees*. She also notes that stories were not as highly regarded as poetry. In both *A Tree for Poverty* and *The Prophet's Camel Bell*, Laurence includes almost as many *balwo* as *gabay* and many more pages of stories than of poems, probably because *balwo* were popular at the time and because she had access to storytellers in her husband's work camp.

15　Andrzejewski later worked at the London School of Oriental and African Studies, while Musa Galaal was employed in the Somali Ministry of Education developing the orthography for the Somali language. (According to Kapteijns, the Somali man's name is spelled Muuse Haaji Ismaa'iil Galaal in Somali orthography [220].) Laurence also credits the two men with giving her advice about spelling and pronunciation.

16　For details on Omar's project, see her Web site at <http://www.nationofpoets.com/>.

17　In "Books that Mattered to Me," Laurence records that she read *Prospero and Caliban* after *This Side Jordan* was published in 1960, while she was reworking her short stories and contemplating writing her Somali travel narrative. She used Mannoni, she says, as a way of "trying to *understand* our African experience" (244). If Laurence's dating of her reading is accurate, writers such as Richards and Leney who argue for the influence of Mannoni on *This Side Jordan* are mistaken.

18　Laurence also refers to Mannoni in her essay on Mahammed 'Abdille Hasan when she discusses his followers' belief in the supernatural powers of their leader ("The Poem and the Spear" 72–3). She notes that Mannoni "describes precisely the same thing in the uprising of Malagasy people in Madagascar in 1947" and writes that "recourse to magic in one form or another is common in battles in which an essentially tribal people are faced with an enemy which has not a superior culture but only more efficient weapons, more efficient means of killing" (73).

19　Other markers of gender common to narratives by Jameson, Hubbard, and Laurence include descriptions of insects and concern about appearance. Laurence's reference to the "dozen detached ant-wings and several frantic beetles ... floating like croutons on the surface of the venison soup" (90) parallels Jameson's and Hubbard's descriptions of insects and food (*WSSR* 3: 166–7; *WW* 93). Similarly, just as Elson is quoted as telling Hubbard that it was probably a good thing that she could not see herself in a mirror (88), so Laurence describes her dismay when she looked into the Land Rover's mirror: "I was covered with clay and grime, my clothes filthy and dishevelled" (85). Later she relates her embarrassment at being caught in a similar state of dishevelment when Governor Reece arrived for a visit (97–8).

20 Laurence thus echoes Jameson's comment that hunting repays the beauty of nature "with pain and with destruction" (*WSSR* 3: 331).

21 Compare this passage to Hubbard's approving comment that her travelling companions did not fire a shot at the massive caribou herd they encountered, even though "Gilbert was wild for he had in him the hunter's instinct in fullest measure" and the "trigger of Job's rifle clicked longingly" (*WW* 164). Jameson also comments on what she calls "the destructive propensities" of her travelling companions, "all keen and eager sportsmen" (*WSSR* 3: 322).

22 Laurence's disapproval did not prevent her and Jack from keeping the cheetah skin and eventually smuggling it out of the country when they left (147, 259).

23 Jameson's even earlier narrative downplays personal danger, but as I pointed out in chapter 1, she reportedly did carry a concealed knife for protection.

24 Reece writes of similarly helpful behaviour she and her husband encountered when they made a cross-country trip during the Somali rainy season in about 1950 ("Somaliland Safari" 62–3).

25 Kapteijns identifies these women as Khadiija Cabdullaahi Dalays and Shamis Abokor, who sang under the pseudonym Guduudo Carwo (104–5).

26 Laurence's comments about women's work echo Jameson's reasoning about the gendered division of First Nations work in Canada: "This division of labour was not as unfair as it sounded. The men protected the tribe with their spears, and led the herds to new grazing grounds, often going ahead to find the way. Men had to reserve their strength for their own demanding work" (75).

27 The photographs were scattered throughout the 1963 British edition published by Macmillan, collected after page 110 of the 1964 American edition issued by Knopf, omitted from the 1963 McClelland and Stewart version in Canada, and then restored in McClelland and Stewart's 1988 New Canadian Library edition.

28 C.J. Martin noted in an e-mail dated 4 October 2003 that he took the photograph in the family compound of a young Somali staff member. I am grateful to Mr Martin for supplying copies of his Somali photographs and for granting permission to reproduce them.

29 These life experiences for women are not, of course, restricted to Somalia. Genital excision has in the past been practised by the medical profession in North America to control what was diagnosed as women's excessive

sexuality; today it is practised not only in several northern and central African countries but also in countries such as Canada by immigrants from those areas. The North American obsession with reproductive technologies demonstrates the importance of parenthood for Western societies. Child prostitution is a problem throughout North America and Europe as well as in countries where "tourist" prostitution is common.

30 Reece writes of one woman in Kenya who was so upset by her childless state that she had a false pregnancy, "by no means uncommon among African women where fertility means so much" (*To My Wife* 103). Reece took the woman to a female Western doctor, who prescribed exercises that might or might not help and a medicine that would act as a placebo (104).

31 Commentators have interpreted Miranda as a thinly disguised version of Laurence (Morley 84; Martens 13; Pell 41).

32 See Warsame and Ahmed (4), Dorkenoo (63, 88, 118), and World Health Organization (11, 17).

33 Warsame and Ahmed (10) and Dorkenoo (13) report that a husband might use a knife to open up his wife's genital scars enough to allow for intercourse, but Kapteijns suggests that if intercourse proved difficult, it would be more common for a female midwife or relative to open the infibulation surgically (31). Somali researchers Warsame and Ahmed contend that because deinfibulating a bride was a test of the groom's "virility and courage," deinfibulation by others was usually done in secret (10).

Laurence's early predecessor in Somalia, Richard Burton, tried to include an appendix on infibulation in his 1856 book. The appendix was in Latin and thus would presumably have been accessible only to those interested in scientific study. His account, which refers to texts that described a practice called "fibulation" as early as 1806 and 1845, was suppressed by the publisher sometime during the publication process, with the result that the appendix title appeared in some tables of contents, but the appendix itself was omitted. A 1966 edition of Burton's book includes a translation of part of his account of infibulation, from a first edition in which the first two pages of the censored appendix were mistakenly included (1966: 285–6). His description is surprisingly detailed; he writes that removal of the clitoris and cutting away and sewing together of the labia was performed by a Midgan woman, and he indicates that if a new husband was unable to break through the scar tissue with his penis, he used a finger or a knife. An inaccuracy in Burton's account is his notion that lacings used to sew up the labia could be undone years later.

34 In Laurence's first draft of the novel, the two protagonists were Miranda and Nathaniel. Laurence wrote Johnnie into the role of main character in the European side of the story after criticism from the Atlantic Monthly Novel Contest led her conclude that his story paralleled Nathaniel's in a

more "natural & inevitable way" (Laurence and Wiseman, *Selected Letters* 97, 103).

35 As Collu points out, the trope is also reworked in Laurence's story "The Drummer of All the World," first published in 1956. In that story, the European protagonist refers to Africa as a queen that the Europeans had "sought to force our will upon" (18) and represents an African woman with whom he makes love as someone who "belonged to earth": "Possessing her, I possessed all earth" (12).

36 Leney calls Johnnie's experience an "epiphany" in which he "comes to see the girl as a person, one of the Others who has to be respected" (69), while Pell comments that Johnnie's "recognition of the humanity of the black virgin (who symbolizes Africa) and his kindness to her are the first evidences of his humanity and respect for the Other" (40).

37 When Eustace argues that "the decolonising potential of the gesture is severely limited by the rape's association with an indigenous discourse on human sacrifice" (372), he fails to acknowledge that the "discourse on human sacrifice" is part of Laurence's recognition of the multiple and joint effects of colonialism and patriarchy.

38 The epigraph and original title of *The Prophet's Camel Bell* are taken from a passage in James Elroy Flecker's "The Gates of Damascus" which refers to the gate that leads to Mecca: "God be thy guide from camp to camp, / God be thy shade from well to well. / God grant beneath the desert stars / Thou hearest the Prophet's camel bell." In Laurence's book, the title refers to at least three aspects of life in Somaliland: the Somalis' Islamic faith, which allowed them to live in such a harsh country; a bell the Laurences received as gift from a Somali man, which indicated support for Jack's work; and Margaret's belief that she and Jack had heard the bell figuratively when they became acquainted with Somali culture.

bibliography

Achebe, Chinua. *Morning Yet on Creation Day*. London: Heinemann Educational, 1975.

Alcoff, Linda. "The Problem of Speaking for Others." *Cultural Critique* 20 (1991–2): 5–32.

Andrew, Mary Adele (Mani-Aten). "Set My People Free." Byrne and Fouillard 231–3.

Andrzejewski, B.W., and I.M. Lewis. *Somali Poetry: An Introduction*. Oxford: Clarendon Press, 1964.

Ashcroft, Bill, Gareth Griffiths, and Helen Tiffin. *The Empire Writes Back: Theory and Practice in Post-Colonial Literatures*. New York: Routledge, 1989.

Atwood, Margaret. *The Labrador Fiasco*. London: Bloomsbury Publishing, 1996.

Barnley, George. *Kenooshao: A Red Indian Tragedy*. London: C.H. Kelly, 1899.

Barratt, Alexandra, ed. *Women's Writing in Middle English*. London: Longman, 1992.

Barry, Bill. *People Places: Saskatchewan and Its Names*. Regina: Canadian Plains Research Centre, 1997.

"Benson, Nina [*sic*] Adelaide." Birth certificate, 15 April 1870; issued 26 May 1946. Ms. Coll. 241.1.01. Centre for Newfoundland Studies Archives, Memorial University, St John's.

Berton, Pierre. Foreword. *A Woman's Way through Unknown Labrador*. By Mina Hubbard. 1908. St John's: Breakwater Books, 1981.

– *The Wild Frontier: More Tales from the Remarkable Past*. Toronto: McClelland and Stewart, 1978.

Binnie-Clark, Georgina. *A Summer on the Canadian Prairie*. London: E. Arnold, 1910.

– *Wheat and Woman*. Toronto: Bell and Cockburn, 1914.

Birkett, Dea. *Spinsters Abroad: Victorian Lady Explorers*. Oxford: B. Blackwell, 1989.

Birkwood, M. Susan *"[D]ifferent sides of the picture": Four Women's Views of Canada (1816–1838)*. Diss. University of Western Ontario, 1997. Ann Arbor: UMI, 1998.

Blanton, Casey. *Travel Writing: The Self and the World*. New York: Twayne Publishers, 1997.

Blunt, Alison. *Travel, Gender, and Imperialism: Mary Kingsley and West Africa*. New York: Guilford Press, 1994.

Blunt, Alison, and Gillian Rose, eds. *Writing Women and Space: Colonial and Postcolonial Geographies*. New York: Guilford Press, 1994.

Blunt, Alison, and Jane Wills. *Dissident Geographies: An Introduction to Radical Ideas and Practice*. Harlow, Eng.: Prentice Hall, 2000.

Bohls, Elizabeth A. *Women Travel Writers and the Language of Aesthetics, 1716–1818*. Cambridge: Cambridge University Press, 1995.

Brennan, Matthew. *Wordsworth, Turner, and Romantic Landscape: A Study of the Traditions of the Picturesque and the Sublime*. Columbia, SC: Camden, 1987.

Bridgman, Helen Bartlett. *Within My Horizon*. Boston: Small, Maynard, 1920.

Buchanan, Roberta. Interview and e-mails, 2000–4.

– "Is Landscape Gendered? Mina Hubbard's Diary of Her Expedition to Labrador in 1905 in the Context of Exploration Culture." Unpublished paper, Centre for Newfoundland Studies, Memorial University, St John's, 25 May 2001.

– "The Langscape before Her: Mina Hubbard's Description of Labrador, 1905." Unpublished paper, Canadian Women's Studies Association Conference, Memorial University, St John's, 9 May 1997.

Buchanan, Roberta, and Bryan Greene. Introduction. *The Woman Who Mapped Labrador: The Life and Expedition Diary of Mina Hubbard*. McGill-Queen's University Press, forthcoming.

Burke, Edmund. *A Philosophical Enquiry into the Origin of Our Ideas of the Sublime and Beautiful*. 1757. Notre Dame: University of Notre Dame Press, 1968.

Burton, Sir Richard Francis. *First Footsteps in East Africa; or, An Exploration of Harar*. 1856. 2 vols. London: Tylston and Edwards, 1894. Rpt. in 1 vol. New York: Praeger, 1966.

Busia, Abena P.A. "Miscegenation as Metonymy: Sexuality and Power in the Colonial Novel." *Ethnic and Racial Studies* 9.3 (1986): 360–72.

– "Silencing Sycorax: On African Colonial Discourse and the Unvoiced Female." *Cultural Critique* 14 (1989–90): 81–104.

Buss, Helen. "Anna Jameson's *Winter Studies and Summer Rambles in Canada* as Epistolary Dijournal." *Essays on Life Writing: From Genre to Critical Practice*. Ed. Marlene Kadar. Toronto: University of Toronto Press, 1992. 42–60.

– *Mapping Our Selves: Canadian Women's Autobiography in English*. Montreal: McGill-Queen's University Press, 1993.

– "Reading Margaret Laurence's Life Writing: Toward a Postcolonial Feminist Subjectivity for a White Female Critic." *Margaret Laurence: Critical Reflections*. Ed. David Staines. Ottawa: University of Ottawa Press, 2001. 39–58.

Byrne, Nympha, and Camille Fouillard, eds. *It's like the Legend: Innu Women's Voices*. Charlottetown: Gynergy Books, 2000.

Cabot, William B. *In Northern Labrador*. London: J. Murray, 1912.

– Introduction. *A Woman's Way through Unknown Labrador: An Account of the Exploration of the Nascaupee and George Rivers*. By Mina Hubbard (Mrs Leonidas Hubbard Jr). London: J. Murray, 1908. 1–29.

– "The Labrador Expedition." Letter to the editor. *Forest and Stream* 62 (11 June 1904): 478.

Cameron, Agnes Deans. *The New North: Being Some Account of a Woman's Journey through Canada to the Arctic*. New York: D. Appleton, 1909.

Campbell, Mary B. *The Witness and the Other World: Exotic European Travel Writing, 400–1600*. Ithaca: Cornell University Press, 1988.

Carter, Paul. *The Road to Botany Bay: An Essay in Spatial History*. London: Faber and Faber, 1987.

Cary, Joyce. *Mister Johnson*. 1939. London: M. Joseph, 1952.

Césaire, Aimé. *Discourse on Colonialism*. 1955. Trans. Joan Pinkham. New York: Monthly Review Press, 1972.

Clark, Steve, ed. *Travel Writing and Empire: Postcolonial Theory in Transit*. London: Zed Books, 1999.

Clifford, James. "Traveling Cultures." *Cultural Studies*. Eds. Lawrence Grossberg, Cary Nelson, and Paula Treichler. New York: Routledge, 1992. 96–112.

Coger, Greta M.K. McCormick. "The Development of Girls into Women and Women as Women: Metaphors of Love, Marriage, and Motherhood in *A Tree for Poverty* and *This Side Jordan* with a Post-colonial Perspective." *Margaret Laurence Review* 6–7 (1996–7): 13–28.

Collu, Gabrielle. "Writing about Others: The African Stories." Riegel 19–32.

Cooke, Alan. "A Woman's Way." *Beaver* 291 (1960): 40–5.

Cooper, James Fenimore. *The Last of the Mohicans*. 1826. London: G.G. Harrap, 1925.

"Country Life: Literary Notes." Rev. of *A Woman's Way through Unknown Labrador*, by Mina Hubbard. Clipping from unidentified journal 22 May 1908: np. Mina Hubbard clipping file. Centre for Newfoundland Studies, Memorial University, St John's.

Crane, Jean. Rev. of *A Woman's Way through Unknown Labrador*, by Mina Hubbard. *Newfoundland Quarterly* 79.4 (1984): 37.

"Daring New Yorkers Lost in Labrador: Fears that Indians Have Slain Them." Clipping from unidentified journal 13 Nov. 1903: np. Ms. Coll.

244.6.02.001, Centre for Newfoundland Studies Archives, Memorial University, St John's.

Davidson, James West, and John Rugge. *Great Heart: The History of a Labrador Adventure*. 1988. Montreal: McGill-Queen's University Press, 1997.

Davidson, Lillias Campbell. *Hints to Lady Travellers at Home and Abroad*. London: Iliffe, 1889.

de Beauvoir, Simone. *The Second Sex*. 1949. Trans. H.M. Parshley. New York: A.A. Knopf, 1953.

Dickason, Olive. *Canada's First Nations: A History of Founding Peoples from Earliest Times*. Toronto: Oxford University Press, 1992.

Dinesen, Isak (Karen Blixen). *Out of Africa*. 1937. New York: Random House, 1952.

Dorkenoo, Efua. *Cutting the Rose: Female Genital Mutilation*. London: Minority Rights Group, 1994.

Driver, Felix. *Geography Militant: Cultures of Exploration and Empire*. Oxford: Blackwell, 2001.

– "Geography's Empire: Histories of Geographical Knowledge." *Environment and Planning D: Society and Space* 10 (1992): 23–40.

Dubinsky, Karen. *The Second Greatest Disappointment: Honeymooning and Tourism at Niagara Falls*. Toronto: Between the Lines, 1999.

Duncan, James, and Derek Gregory, eds. Introduction. *Writes of Passage: Reading Travel Writing*. London: Routledge, 1999. 1–13.

Duncan, Sara Jeannette (Garth Grafton). "Cow-Catcher Comments." *Montreal Daily Star*. 3 Nov. 1888: 2.

– "The Men of Moosomin." *Montreal Daily Star*. 20 Oct. 1888: 2.

– "Regina and Its People." *Montreal Daily Star*. 27 Oct. 1888: 2.

– "The Sad City by the Sea." *Montreal Daily Star*. 10 Nov. 1888: 2.

– *A Social Departure: How Orthodocia and I Went Round the World by Ourselves*. New York: D. Appleton, 1890.

– "Winnipeg Whisperings." *Montreal Daily Star*. 6 Oct. 1888: 2.

DuPlessis, Rachel Blau. *Writing beyond the Ending: Narrative Strategies of Twentieth-Century Women Writers*. Bloomington: Indiana University Press, 1985.

Elson, George. Diary, 1905. Ms. Coll. 241.3.03. Centre for Newfoundland Studies Archives, Memorial University, St John's.

Ernstrom, Adele. "The Afterlife of Mary Wollstonecraft and Anna Jameson's *Winter Studies and Summer Rambles in Canada*." *Women's Writing* 4.2 (1997): 277–96.

Eustace, John C. "Containing Nationalism: Neo-colonial Gestures in Margaret Laurence's *This Side Jordan*." *Literature of Region and Nation: Proceedings of the 6th International Literature of Region and Nation Conference*. Ed. Winnifred M. Bogaards. Saint John: University of New Brunswick, 1998. 362–75.

Fainzang, Sylvie. "Excision et ordre social." *Droit et cultures* 20 (1990): 177–82.

Fanon, Frantz. *Black Skin, White Masks*. 1952. Trans. Charles Lam Markmann. New York: Grove Press, 1967.

- *A Dying Colonialism*. 1959. Trans. Haakon Chevalier. New York: Grove Press, 1967.

- *The Wretched of the Earth*. 1961. Trans. Constance Farrington. New York: Grove Press, 1968.

Finnegan, Ruth, ed. *The Penguin Book of Oral Poetry*. London: A. Lane, 1978.

Ford, Jesse. "What did flies matter when you were free?" *Rivers Running Free: Stories of Adventurous Women*. Ed. Judith Niemi and Barbara Wieser. Minneapolis: Bergamot Books, 1987. 7–18.

Foster, Shirley. *Across New Worlds: Nineteenth-Century Women Travellers and Their Writings*. New York: Harvester Wheatsheaf, 1990.

Fowler, Marian. *The Embroidered Tent: Five Gentlewomen in Early Canada*. Toronto: House of Anansi Press, 1982.

- *Redney: A Life of Sara Jeannette Duncan*. Toronto: House of Anansi Press, 1983.

Francis, Daniel, and Toby Morantz. *Partners in Furs: A History of the Fur Trade in Eastern James Bay, 1600–1870*. Kingston: McGill-Queen's University Press, 1983.

Fraser, Wayne. *The Dominion of Women: The Personal and the Political in Canadian Women's Literature*. New York: Greenwood Press, 1991.

Frawley, Maria. *A Wider Range: Travel Writing by Women in Victorian England*. Rutherford: Fairleigh Dickinson University Press, 1994.

Freiwald, Bina. "'Femininely Speaking': Anna Jameson's *Winter Studies and Summer Rambles in Canada*." *A Mazing Space: Writing Canadian Women Writing*. Ed. Shirley Neuman and Smaro Kamboureli. Edmonton: Longspoon Press; NeWest Press, 1986. 61–73.

Friedan, Betty. *The Feminine Mystique*. 1963. New York: Dell Publishing Co., 1983.

Fussell, Paul. *Abroad: British Literary Traveling Between the Wars*. New York: Oxford University Press, 1980.

- Introductions. *The Norton Book of Travel*. Ed. Paul Fussell. New York: Norton, 1987. 13–17, 21–5.

"Geography at the British Association." *Geographical Journal* 30 (Oct. 1907): 421–5.

Gerry, Thomas M.F. "'I Am Translated': Anna Jameson's Sketches and *Winter Studies and Summer Rambles in Canada*." *Journal of Canadian Studies* 25.4 (1990–1): 34–49.

Gikandi, Simon. *Maps of Englishness: Writing Identity in the Culture of Colonialism*. New York: Columbia University Press, 1996.

Gilbert, Sandra, and Susan Gubar. *No Man's Land: The Place of the Woman Writer in the Twentieth Century*. Vol. 1, *The War of the Worlds*. New Haven: Yale University Press, 1988.

Gilman, Chandler R. *Life on the Lakes: Being Tales and Sketches Collected during a Trip to the Pictured Rocks of Lake Superior*. 2 vols. New York: George Dearborn, 1836.

Gilpin, William. *An Essay on Prints*. 1768. 3rd ed., London: Printed by G. Scott for R. Blamire, 1781.

Githae-Mugo, Micere. *Visions of Africa: The Fiction of Chinua Achebe, Margaret Laurence, Elspeth Huxley and Ngugi wa Thiong'o*. Nairobi: Kenya Literature Bureau, 1978.

"Givins, James." *Dictionary of Canadian Biography*. Vol. 7. Toronto: University of Toronto Press, 1988. 347–48.

Glickman, Susan. *The Picturesque and the Sublime: A Poetics of the Canadian Landscape*. Montreal: McGill-Queen's University Press, 1998.

Goldie, Terry. *Fear and Temptation: The Image of the Indigene in Canadian, Australian, and New Zealand Literatures*. Kingston: McGill-Queen's University Press, 1989.

Goldman, Marlene. *Paths of Desire: Images of Exploration and Mapping in Canadian Women's Writing*. Toronto: University of Toronto Press, 1997.

Govier, Katherine, ed. *Without a Guide: Contemporary Women's Travel Adventures*. Toronto: Macfarlane, Walter & Ross, 1994.

Grace, Sherrill. *Canada and the Idea of North*. Montreal: McGill-Queen's University Press, 2001.

– "'Hidden Country': Discovering Mina Benson Hubbard." *biography* 24 (2001): 273–87.

– "'A Woman's Way': Canadian Narratives of Northern Discovery." *New Worlds: Discovering and Constructing the Unknown in Anglophone Literature*. Ed. Martin Kuester, Gabriele Christ, and Rudolf Beck. München: E. Vögel, 2000. 177–202.

– "A Woman's Way: From Expedition to Autobiography." Introduction to *A Woman's Way through Unknown Labrador*, by Mina Hubbard. Montreal: McGill-Queen's University Press, 2004. xvii–lxxvi, notes 233–8.

Graham, Jean. "The Woman Explorer." Rev. of *A Woman's Way through Unknown Labrador*, by Mina Hubbard. *Canadian Magazine* 31 (Sept. 1908): 468–71.

Greene, Graham. *In Search of a Character: Two African Journals*. London: Bodley Head, 1961.

Greer, Germaine. *The Female Eunuch*. 1970. London: Paladin, 1971.

Gregory, Derek. *Geographical Imaginations*. Cambridge, MA: Blackwell, 1994.

Grewal, Inderpal. *Home and Harem: Nation, Gender, Empire, and the Cultures of Travel*. Durham: Duke University Press, 1996.

Groß, Konrad. "Margaret Laurence's African Experience." *Encounters and Explorations: Canadian Writers and European Critics*. Ed. Franz K. Stanzel and Waldemar Zacharasiewicz. Würzburg: Königshausen & Neumann, 1986. 73–81.

Harley, J.B. "Maps, Knowledge, and Power." *The Iconography of Landscape: Essays on the Symbolic Representation, Design and Use of Past Environments*. Ed. Denis Cosgrove and Stephen Daniels. Cambridge: Cambridge University Press, 1988. 277–312.

Hart, Anne. "Finding Her Way." Biographical essay in *The Woman Who Mapped Labrador: The Life and Expedition Diary of Mina Hubbard*. Montreal: McGill-Queen's University Press, forthcoming.

– Interviews with and e-mails to the author, 2000–1.

– "Into Unknown Labrador." *Rediscovering Canada – Image, Place and Text*. Ed. Gudrun Björk Gudsteins. Reykjavik: University of Iceland, 2001. 53–62.

– researcher and narrator. *Into Unknown Labrador*. Ideas series. CBC Radio. 28 May 1999.

Havens, Munson Aldrich. "A Woman in Unknown Labrador." Rev. of *A Woman's Way through Unknown Labrador*, by Mina Hubbard. *Dial* 45 (1 Nov. 1908): 286–9.

Head, Sir Francis Bond. "Memorandum on the Aborigines of North America." Appendix A of *A Narrative*. 3rd ed. London: J. Murray, 1839.

Heaps, Denise Adele. "Gendered Discourse and Subjectivity in Travel Writing by Canadian Women." Diss. University of Toronto, 2000.

Hearne, Samuel. *A Journey from Prince of Wales's Fort in Hudson's Bay, to the Northern Ocean*. London: A. Strahan and T. Cadell, 1795.

Henderson, Jennifer. *Settler Feminism and Race Making in Canada*. Toronto: University of Toronto Press, 2003.

Henry, Alexander. *Travels and Adventures in Canada and the Indian Territories between the Years 1760 and 1776*. 1809. Edmonton: M.G. Hurtig, 1969.

Herriot, Trevor. *River in a Dry Land: A Prairie Passage*. Toronto: Stoddart, 2000.

Hicks, Esther. *Infibulation: Female Mutilation in Islamic Northeastern Africa*. 2nd ed. New Brunswick, NJ: Transaction Publishers, 1996.

Hind, Henry Youle. *Explorations in the Interior of the Labrador Peninsula, the Country of the Montagnais and Nasquapee Indians*. Vol. 2. London: Longman, Green, Longman, Roberts, & Green, 1863.

"Historic Innu Photos." Innu Nation Web site. 23 May 2001 <http://www.innu.ca/historic.html>.

Holland, Patrick, and Graham Huggan. *Tourists with Typewriters: Critical Reflections on Contemporary Travel Writing*. Ann Arbor: University of Michigan Press, 1998.

Hoyle, Gwyneth. "Hubbard and Wallace: The Rivals." *Canexus: The Canoe in Canadian Culture*. Ed. James Raffan and Bert Horwood. Toronto: Betelgeuse Books, 1988. 135–49.

Hubbard, Leonidas, Jr. "The Children of the Bush." *Outing* 41 (Feb. 1903): 529–40.

– Diary, 1903. Ms. Coll. 241.3.01. Centre for Newfoundland Studies Archives, Memorial University, St John's.

– "The Leonidas Hubbard, Jun., Expedition into Labrador: The Diary of Leonidas Hubbard, Jun." Ed. Caspar Whitney. *Outing* 45 (March 1905): 643–89.

– "Off Days on Superior's North Shore." *Outing* 42 (Sept. 1903): 716–24.

Hubbard, Mina Benson (Mrs Leonidas Hubbard Jr). Diary, 1905. Ms. Coll. 241.3.02. Centre for Newfoundland Studies Archives, Memorial University, St John's.

– "Exploring Inner Labrador." *Windsor Magazine* 27 (Dec. 1907–May 1908): 554–61.

– *The Woman Who Mapped Labrador: The Life and Expedition Diary of Mina Hubbard*. Ed. Roberta Buchanan and Bryan Greene. Montreal: McGill-Queen's University Press, forthcoming.

– "Labrador, from Lake Melville to Ungava Bay." *Bulletin of the American Geographical Society* 38 (Sept. 1906): 529–39. Rpt. as "A Woman's Way through Unknown Labrador." *Journal of the Manchester Geographical Society* 23.4 (1907): 169–82.

– "My Explorations in Unknown Labrador." *Harper's Monthly Magazine* 112 (May 1906): 813–23.

– "'Successful,' Mrs. Hubbard Wires *The World*." *World* 11 Nov. 1905: 4.

– "Through Lonely Labrador." *Englishwoman's Review* 15 Apr. 1908: 82–8.

– *A Woman's Way through Unknown Labrador: An Account of the Exploration of the Nascaupee and George Rivers*. London: J. Murray; Toronto: W. Briggs, 1908.

– *A Woman's Way through Unknown Labrador: An Account of the Exploration of the Nascaupee and George Rivers*. New York: McClure, 1908. Facsimile rpt., St John's: Breakwater Books, 1981.

– *A Woman's Way through Unknown Labrador: An Account of the Exploration of the Nascaupee and George Rivers*. 1908. Ed. Sherrill Grace. Montreal: McGill-Queen's University Press, 2004.

Hubbard, Mina, and Dillon Wallace. Agreement, 1 Oct. 1904. Ms. Coll. 244.1.01.001. Centre for Newfoundland Studies Archives, Memorial University, St John's.

Huffman, Nikolas H. "Charting the Other Maps: Cartography and Visual Methods in Feminist Research." *Thresholds in Feminist Geography: Differ-*

ence, Methodology, Representation. Ed. John Paul Jones III, Heidi J. Nast, and Susan M. Roberts. New York: Rowman & Littlefield, 1997. 255–83.

Huggan, Graham. *Territorial Disputes: Maps and Mapping Strategies in Contemporary Canadian and Australian Fiction.* Toronto: University of Toronto Press, 1994.

Hulme, Peter. *Colonial Encounters: Europe and the Native Caribbean, 1492–1797.* London: Methuen, 1986.

– "Introduction: The Cannibal Scene." *Cannibalism and the Colonial World.* Ed. Francis Barker, Peter Hulme, and Margaret Iversen. Cambridge: Cambridge University Press, 1998. 1–38.

Hunter, J.A., and Daniel P. Mannix. *Tales of the African Frontier.* New York: Harper, 1954.

"Innu lakes damaged or lost due to flooding associated with the Churchill Falls hydro electric development." Innu Nation Web site. 8 March 2003 <http://www.innu.ca/lostlake.html>.

"Innu, Natives of Québec: Cree, Atikamekw, Montagnais." GeoNative Web site. 18 Feb. 2004 <http://www.geocities.com/Athens/9479/innu.html>.

Jameson, Anna Brownell. Album of Sketches. Ms. Coll. 966-6L. Toronto Public Library (Toronto Reference Library), Toronto.

– *Anna Jameson: Letters and Friendships (1812–1860).* Ed. Mrs Steuart Erskine. London: T.F. Unwin, 1915.

– *Characteristics of Women: Moral, Poetical and Historical.* 1832. 2 vols., London: Saunders & Otley, 1853.

– *A Commonplace Book of Thoughts, Memories, and Fancies, Original and Selected.* London: Longman, Brown, Green and Longmans, 1854.

– *Diary of an Ennuyée.* London: H. Colburn, 1826.

– *Early Canadian Sketches.* Ed. G.H. Needler. Toronto: Burns & MacEachern, 1958.

– Etchings. 1837. Ms. Coll. 961.220. Royal Ontario Museum, Toronto.

– Letter from Anna Jameson to Charlotte McMurray. Toronto, 26 Aug. 1837. Ms. Coll. 47.1.93, Harry Sproat Collection. Thomas Fisher Rare Book Library, University of Toronto.

– *Letters of Anna Jameson to Ottilie von Goethe.* Ed. G.H. Needler. London: Oxford University Press, 1939.

– *Sketches in Canada, and Rambles among the Red Men.* London: Longman, Brown, Green, and Longmans, 1852.

– *Visits and Sketches at Home and Abroad.* 1834. 3 vols. London: Saunders and Otley, 1835.

– *Winter Studies and Summer Rambles in Canada.* 3 vols. London: Saunders and Otley, 1838. Facsimile ed. Toronto: Coles, 1972.

"Jarvis, Samuel Peters." *Dictionary of Canadian Biography.* Vol. 8. Toronto: University of Toronto Press, 1985. 430–3.

Jasen, Patricia. *Wild Things: Nature, Culture, and Tourism in Ontario, 1790–1914*. Toronto: University of Toronto Press, 1995.

"Johnston, John." *Dictionary of Canadian Biography*. Vol. 6. Toronto: University of Toronto Press, 1987. 356–9.

Johnston, Judith. *Anna Jameson: Victorian, Feminist, Woman of Letters*. Aldershot, Eng.: Scolar Press, 1997.

Jones, James A. *Tales of an Indian Camp*. 1829. London: H. Colburn and R. Bentley, 1830.

Kanneh, Kadiatu. "Feminism and the Colonial Body." *The Post-Colonial Studies Reader*. Ed. Bill Ashcroft, Gareth Griffiths, and Helen Tiffin. New York: Routledge, 1995. 346–8.

Kaplan, Caren. *Questions of Travel: Postmodern Discourses of Displacement*. Durham: Duke University Press, 1996.

Kaplan, E. Ann. *Looking for the Other: Feminism, Film and the Imperial Gaze*. London: Routledge, 1997.

Kapteijns, Lidwien, with Maryan Omar Ali. *Women's Voices in a Man's World: Women and the Pastoral Tradition in Northern Somali Orature, c. 1899–1980*. Portsmouth, NH: Heinemann, 1999.

King, James. *The Life of Margaret Laurence*. Toronto: A.A. Knopf Canada, 1997.

Kingsley, Mary. *Travels in West Africa, Congo Français, Corisco and Cameroons*. 1897. 2nd ed. London: Macmillan, 1898.

Klein, Clayton. *Challenge the Wilderness: The Legend of George Elson*. Fowlerville, MI: Wilderness Adventure Books, 1988.

Koso-Thomas, Olayinka. *The Circumcision of Women: A Strategy for Eradication*. London: Zed Books, 1987.

Kröller, Eva-Marie. *Canadian Travellers in Europe, 1851–1900*. Vancouver: University of British Columbia Press, 1987.

– "First Impressions: Rhetorical Strategies in Travel Writing by Victorian Women." *Ariel* 21.4 (1990): 87–99.

"Labrador." Rev. of *A Woman's Way through Unknown Labrador*, by Mina Hubbard. *Geographical Journal* 32 (Dec. 1908): 614.

Labrador. Maps 13E ("Winokapau Lake" 1952 and 1989), 13F ("Goose Bay" 1965 and 1990), 13K ("Snegamook Lake" 1968 and 1990), 13L ("Kasheshibaw Lake" 1968, "Red Wine Lake" 1990), 23H ("Ossokmanuan Lake" 1964, "Ossokmanuan Reservoir" 1990). Ottawa: Government of Canada.

Labrador-Quebec. Map 23I ("Michikamau Lake" 1953, "Woods Lake" 1983). Ottawa: Government of Canada.

LaFramboise, Lisa. "'Just a little like an explorer': Mina Hubbard and the Making of *A Woman's Way*." *Papers of the Bibliographical Society of Canada* 39.1 (2001): 7–44.

- *Travellers in Skirts: Women and English-Language Travel Writing in Canada, 1820–1926.* Diss. University of Alberta, 1997. Ann Arbor: UMI, 1998.
Laurence, Margaret. "Books that Mattered to Me." Verduyn 239–49.
- *Dance on the Earth: A Memoir.* Toronto: McClelland and Stewart, 1989.
- "Gadgetry or Growing: Form and Voice in the Novel." Woodcock, ed., 80–9.
- *Heart of a Stranger.* 1976. Toronto: McClelland and Stewart, 1981.
- "Ivory Tower or Grassroots?: The Novelist as Socio-Political Being." *A Political Art: Essays and Images in Honour of George Woodcock.* Ed. W.H. New. Vancouver: University of British Columbia Press, 1978. 15–25.
- *Long Drums and Cannons: Nigerian Dramatists and Novelists, 1952–1966.* London: Macmillan, 1968. Rpt. Edmonton: University of Alberta Press, 2001.
- "Mask of Beaten Gold." *Journal of Canadian Fiction* 27 (1980): 23–40.
- *The Prophet's Camel Bell.* London: Macmillan, 1963; and Toronto: McClelland and Stewart, 1963. Rpt. as *New Wind in a Dry Land,* New York: A.A. Knopf, 1964. Rpt. Toronto: McClelland and Stewart, 1988.
- "Ten Years' Sentences." *Canadian Literature* 41 (1969): 11–16.
- *This Side Jordan.* 1960. Toronto: McClelland and Stewart, 1989.
- *The Tomorrow-Tamer and Other Stories.* 1963. Toronto: McClelland and Stewart, 1970.
-, ed. *A Tree for Poverty: Somali Poetry and Prose.* 1954. Toronto: ECW Press, 1993.
- "Uncertain Flowering." *Story: The Magazine of the Short Story in Book Form* 4 (1953): 9–34.
Laurence, Margaret, and Adele Wiseman. *Selected Letters of Margaret Laurence and Adele Wiseman.* Ed. John Lennox and Ruth Panofsky. Toronto: University of Toronto Press, 1997.
Lawrence, Karen. *Penelope Voyages: Women and Travel in the British Literary Tradition.* Ithaca: Cornell University Press, 1994.
Leed, Eric J. *The Mind of the Traveler: From Gilgamesh to Global Tourism.* New York: Basic Books, 1991.
Leney, Jane. "Prospero and Caliban in Laurence's African Fiction." *Journal of Canadian Fiction* 27 (1980): 63–80.
Lewis, I.M. *A Modern History of Somalia: Nation and State in the Horn of Africa.* Rev. ed. London: Longman, 1980.
Lionnet, Françoise. *Postcolonial Representations: Women, Literature, Identity.* Ithaca: Cornell University Press, 1995.
Long, John S. "The Reverend George Barnley and the James Bay Cree." *Canadian Journal of Native Studies* 6 (1986): 313–31.
"Love's Labour." Rev. of *A Woman's Way through Unknown Labrador,* by Mina Hubbard. *Evening Standard and St. James's Gazette* 5 June 1908: 5.

Lucking, David. *Ancestors and Gods: Margaret Laurence and the Dialectics of Identity.* Bern: Peter Lang, 2002.

McClintock, Anne. *Imperial Leather: Race, Gender and Sexuality in the Colonial Contest.* New York: Routledge, 1995.

McDowell, Linda. *Gender, Identity, and Place: Understanding Feminist Geographies.* Minneapolis: University of Minnesota Press, 1999.

McKinsey, Elizabeth. *Niagara Falls: Icon of the American Sublime.* Cambridge: Cambridge University Press, 1985.

MacLaren, I.S. "Exploration/Travel Literature and the Evolution of the Author." *International Journal of Canadian Studies* 5 (1992): 39–68.

McLean, John. *John McLean's Notes of a Twenty-Five Year's Service in the Hudson's Bay Territory.* Ed. W.S. Wallace. Toronto: Champlain Society, 1932.

"McMurray, William." *Dictionary of Canadian Biography.* Vol. 12. Toronto: University of Toronto Press, 1990. 680–2.

Mannoni, O. *Prospero and Caliban: The Psychology of Colonization.* 1950. Trans. Pamela Powesland. New York: Praeger, 1964.

Marryat, Frederick. *A Diary in America, with Remarks on its Institutions.* 6 vols. London: Longman, Orme, Brown, Green & Longmans, 1839.

Martens, Debra. "Laurence of Africa." *Paragraph* 16.1 (1994): 9–13.

Martin, Norma, Donna S. McGillis, and Catherine Milne. *Gore's Landing and the Rice Lake Plains.* Cobourg: Heritage Gore's Landing, 1986.

Martineau, Harriet. *Retrospect of Western Travel.* 3 vols. London: Saunders and Otley, 1838.

– *Society in America.* 3 vols. London: Saunders and Otley, 1837.

Maxwell, Anne. *Colonial Photography and Exhibitions: Representations of the "Native" and the Making of European Identities.* London: Leicester University Press, 1999.

"Meetings of the Royal Geographical Society, Session 1907–1908." *Geographical Journal* 31 (Feb. 1908): 228.

Mellor, Anne K. *Romanticism and Gender.* New York: Routledge, 1993.

Merrick, Elliott. *The Long Crossing and Other Labrador Stories.* Orono: University of Maine Press, 1992.

Middleton, Dorothy. *Victorian Lady Travellers.* London: Routledge & Paul, 1965.

Millais, J.G. "Through the Heart of Labrador." Rev. of *A Woman's Way through Unknown Labrador,* by Mina Hubbard. *Nature* 79 (4 Feb. 1909): 401–3.

Millett, Kate. *Sexual Politics.* 1969. New York: Avon Books, 1971.

Mills, Sara. *Discourses of Difference: An Analysis of Women's Travel Writing and Colonialism.* London: Routledge, 1991.

Mire, Soraya, writer, dir., and prod. *Fire Eyes.* Persistent Productions, 1994.

Mohanty, Chandra Talpade. "Under Western Eyes: Feminist Scholarship and Colonial Discourses." *Feminist Review* 30 (1988): 65–88. Rpt. in *Colonial*

Discourse and Post-colonial Theory: A Reader. Ed. Patrick Williams and Laura Chrisman. New York: Columbia University Press, 1994. 196–220.

Monkman, Leslie. "Primitivism and a Parasol: Anna Jameson's Indians." *Essays on Canadian Writing* 29 (1984): 85–95.

Moodie, Susanna. *Roughing It in the Bush; or, Life in Canada.* 1852. Toronto: McClelland and Stewart, 1989.

Morgan, Susan. *Place Matters: Gendered Geography in Victorian Women's Travel Books about Southeast Asia.* New Brunswick, NJ: Rutgers University Press, 1996.

Morley, Patricia. "Canada, Africa, Canada: Laurence's Unbroken Journey." *Journal of Canadian Fiction* 27 (1980): 81–91.

Morris, Robert T. "Mr. Hubbard's Death in Labrador." Letter to the editor. *Forest and Stream* 62 (2 April 1904): 270.

Motohashi, Ted. "The Discourse of Cannibalism in Early Modern Travel Writing." Clark 83–99.

"Mrs. Leonidas Hubbard's Own Story of Her Trip through the Wilderness of Labrador." *World* 26 Nov. 1905: np. Ms. Coll. 244.6.02.004. Centre for Newfoundland Studies Archives, Memorial University, St John's.

"Mrs. Hubbard Safe." *North Adams Evening Transcript* 10 Nov. 1905: 8.

Mukherjee, Arun. *Oppositional Aesthetics: Readings from a Hyphenated Space.* Toronto: TSAR Publications, 1994.

Mulhallen, Karen, ed. *Views from the North: An Anthology of Travel Writing.* Erin, ON: Descant/Porcupine's Quill, 1984.

Musgrave, Susan. "Another Women's Way through Unknown Labrador." *Imperial Oil Review* 80 (1996): 14–19.

Na'Allah, Abdul-Rasheed. "Nigerian Literature Then and Now." *Long Drums and Cannons.* By Margaret Laurence. Edmonton: University of Alberta Press, 2001. lv–lxiii.

Neuman, Shirley. "'An appearance walking in a forest the sexes burn': Autobiography and the Construction of the Feminine Body." *Signature* 2 (1989): 1–26.

New, W. H., ed. *Margaret Laurence.* Toronto: McGraw-Hill Ryerson, 1977.

– "The Other and I: Laurence's African Stories." Woodcock, ed., 113–34.

Niemi, Judith. "Following Mrs. Hubbard through Labrador." *Rivers Running Free: Stories of Adventurous Women.* Ed. Judith Niemi and Barbara Wieser. Minneapolis: Bergamot Books, 1987. 219–29.

O'Flaherty, Patrick. *The Rock Observed: Studies in the Literature of Newfoundland.* Toronto: University of Toronto Press, 1979.

Olsen, Tillie. *Silences.* New York: Delacort Press/Seymour Lawrence, 1978.

Omar, Deeqa. "A Nation of Poets." Web site. 8 Jan. 2002 <http://www.nationofpoets. com/>.

Osachoff, Margaret Gail. "Colonialism in the Fiction of Margaret Laurence." *Southern Literary Review* 13.3 (1980): 222–38.

Page, P.K. *Brazilian Journal*. Toronto: Lester & Orpen Dennys, 1987.

Pasteen, Mary Jane (Miste Mani-Shan). "Women Speared the Caribou." Byrne and Fouillard 34–6.

Pell, Barbara. "The African and Canadian Heroines: From Bondage to Grace." Riegel 33–46.

Penashue, Elizabeth (Tshuaukuish). "Like the Gates of Heaven." Byrne and Fouillard 157–75.

Peterman, Michael. Introduction. *The Backwoods of Canada: Being Letters from the Wife of an Emigrant Officer, Illustrative of the Domestic Economy of British America*. By Catharine Parr Traill. 1836. Ottawa: Carleton University Press, 1997. xix–lxix.

Porter, Dennis. *Haunted Journeys: Desire and Transgression in European Travel Writing*. Princeton: Princeton University Press, 1991.

Powers, Lyall. *Alien Heart: The Life and Work of Margaret Laurence*. Winnipeg: University of Manitoba Press, 2003.

Pratt, Alexandra. *Lost Lands, Forgotten Stories: A Woman's Journey to the Heart of Labrador*. Toronto: HarperCollins, 2002.

– "Paddling the Wild East: Retracing the Route of Mina Hubbard." *Paddler* 22.4 (2002): 52–3.

Pratt, Mary Louise. *Imperial Eyes: Travel Writing and Transculturation*. London: Routledge, 1992.

Quebec. Maps 23P ("Whitegull Lake" 1967, "Lac Résolution" 1978), 24A ("Lac Brisson" 1968 and 1983), 24H ("Lac Henrietta" 1983), 24I ("George River" 1968 and 1978), 24J ("Lac Ralleau" 1968 and 1981). Ottawa: Government of Canada.

Quinby, Lee. "The Subject of Memoirs: *The Woman Warrior*'s Technology of Ideographic Selfhood." *De/Colonizing the Subject: The Politics of Gender in Women's Autobiography*. Ed. Sidonie Smith and Julia Watson. Minneapolis: University of Minnesota Press, 1992. 297–320.

"Recent Crossing of Labrador." Rev. of *A Woman's Way through Unknown Labrador*, by Mina Hubbard. Geographical Journal 29 (March 1907): 349.

Reece, Alys. "Carpets to Somaliland." *Corona* 8.9 (1956): 337–8.

– "Somaliland Safari." *Corona* 9.2 (1957): 61–4. Excerpted as "Journey Back from Zeila." *Journal of the Anglo-Somali Society* 30 (2001): 7–8.

– *To My Wife – 50 Camels*. London: Harvill Press, 1963.

Renault, Mary. "On Understanding Africa." Rev. of *This Side Jordan*, by Margaret Laurence. *Saturday Review* 10 Dec. 1960: 23–4. Rpt. in New, ed., 103–4.

The Revenge of Mina Hubbard. Videorecording. Narr. Pierre Berton. Oakville, ON: Magic Lantern Communications, 1985.

Rich, Adrienne. "Notes toward a Politics of Location." *Blood, Bread, and Poetry: Selected Prose, 1979–1985*. New York: W.W. Norton, 1986. 210–31.

Rich, Shushep (Joseph) [attributed to Edward Rich]. "Missus Hubbard." Trans. Matthew (Matiu) Rich. *What They Used to Tell About: Indian Legends from Labrador.* Ed. Peter Desbarats. Toronto: McClelland and Stewart, 1969. 78.

Rich, Shushep (Joseph). "Mrs. Hubbard." *Sheshatshui-atanukana mak tipatshimuna [Myths and Tales from Sheshatshit].* Ed. José Mailhot. Collected by Madeleine Lefebve and Robert Lanari, 1967. St John's: Labrador Innu Text Project, 1999. Narrative translated by Marguerite Mackenzie, Memorial University, St John's, 2003.

Richard, Marc. "L'expédition de Mina Benson Hubbard au Labrador et dans l'Ungava (1905)." Gouvernement du Québec, 1999. 9 Jan. 2001 <http://www.toponymie.gouv.qc.ca/femmes.htm>

Richards, David. "'Leave the dead some room to dance!': Margaret Laurence and Africa." *Critical Approaches to the Fiction of Margaret Laurence.* Ed. Colin Nicholson. London: Macmillan, 1990. 16–34.

Riegel, Christian, ed. *Challenging Territory: The Writing of Margaret Laurence.* Edmonton: University of Alberta Press, 1997.

Rimmer, Mary. "(Mis)Speaking: Laurence Writes Africa." Riegel 1–18.

Rogers, Edward S. "The Algonquian Farmers of Southern Ontario, 1830–1945." *Aboriginal Ontario: Historical Perspectives on the First Nations.* Ed. Edward S. Rogers and Donald B. Smith. Toronto: Dundurn Press, 1994. 122–66.

Rooke, Constance, ed. *Writing Away: The PEN Canada Travel Anthology.* Toronto: McClelland and Stewart, 1994.

Rose, Gillian. "On Being Ambivalent: Women and Feminisms in Geography." *New Words, New Worlds: Reconceptualising Social and Cultural Goegraphy.* Ed. Chris Philo. Lampeter, Wales: St. David's University College, 1991.

Roy, Wendy. "Anti-imperialism and Feminism in Margaret Laurence's African Writings." *Canadian Literature* 169 (2001): 33–57.

– "'Here is the picture as well as I can paint it': Anna Jameson's Illustrations for *Winter Studies and Summer Rambles in Canada.*" *Canadian Literature* 177 (2003): 97–119.

Russell, Mary. *The Blessings of a Good Thick Skirt: Women Travellers and Their World.* London: Collins, 1986.

Saadawi, Nawal El. *The Hidden Face of Eve: Women in the Arab World.* Trans. Sherif Hetata. London: Zed Press, 1980.

Said, Edward W. *Orientalism.* New York: Random House, 1978.

"Sawyer, Lucy Sargent." *National Cyclopedia of American Biography.* Vol. 5. 1894. 71–2.

Scadding, Henry. *Mrs. Jameson on Shakespeare and the Collier Emendations.* Toronto: The Week, 1892.

Schoolcraft, Henry Rowe. *Algic Researches, Comprising Inquiries Respecting the Mental Characteristics of the North American Indians: Indian Tales and*

Legends. 2 vols. New York: Harper & Brothers, 1839. Rpt. as *Schoolcraft's Indian Legends.* 1956. Ed. Mentor L. Williams. East Lansing: Michigan State University Press, 1991.

– *Personal Memoirs of a Residence of Thirty Years with the Indian Tribes on the American Frontiers.* Philadelphia: Lippincott, Grambo and Co., 1851.

– *Travels in the Central Portions of the Mississippi Valley.* New York: Collins and Hannay, 1825.

Schriber, Mary Suzanne. *Writing Home: American Women Abroad, 1830–1920.* Charlottesville: University Press of Virginia, 1997.

"Selected Innu Placenames in Nitassinan." Innu Nation Web site. 8 March 2003 <http://www.innu.ca/Topo1.htm>.

Shakespeare, William. *A Midsummer Night's Dream.* 1595–96. *The Riverside Shakespeare.* Ed. G. Blakemore Evans. Boston: Houghton Mifflin, 1974. 222–49.

– *The Winter's Tale.* 1611. *The Riverside Shakespeare.* Ed. G. Blakemore Evans. Boston: Houghton Mifflin, 1974. 1569–1605.

Sharpe, Jenny. *Allegories of Empire: The Figure of Woman in the Colonial Text.* Minneapolis: University of Minnesota Press, 1993.

Sigrist, Gisela. "'On my Way to that Ultimate Somewhere': Anna Jameson's *Winter Studies and Summer Rambles in Canada.*" *Probing Canadian Culture.* Ed. Peter Easingwood, Konrad Groß, and Wolfgang Kloos. Augsburg: AV-Verlag, 1991. 107–16.

Silvis, Randall. *Heart So Hungry: The Extraordinary Expedition of Mina Hubbard into the Labrador Wilderness.* Toronto: A.A. Knopf Canada, 2004.

Sluyter, Andrew. *Colonialism and Landscape: Postcolonial Theory and Applications.* Lanham: Rowman & Littlefield, 2002.

Smith, Sidonie. *Moving Lives: Twentieth-Century Women's Travel Writing.* Minneapolis: University of Minnesota Press, 2001.

Snively, Judith. "Female Bodies, Male Politics: Women and the Female Circumcision Controversy in Kenyan Colonial Discourse." Diss. McGill University, 1994.

Sparrow, Fiona. *Into Africa with Margaret Laurence.* Toronto: ECW Press, 1992.

– "Margaret Laurence of Hargeisa: A Discussion of *A Tree for Poverty.*" *New Perspectives on Margaret Laurence: Poetic Narrative, Multiculturalism, and Feminism.* Ed. Greta McCormick Coger. Westport, CT: Greenwood Press, 1996. 129–35.

Spivak, Gayatri Chakravorty. "Can the Subaltern Speak?" *Marxism and the Interpretation of Culture.* Ed. Cary Nelson and Lawrence Grossberg. London: Macmillan, 1988. 271–313.

– "French Feminism in an International Frame." *In Other Worlds: Essays in Cultural Politics.* New York: Routledge, 1988. 134–53.

Steckley, John, and Bryan D. Cummins. *Full Circle: Canada's First Nations*. Toronto: Prentice Hall, 2001.

Stevenson, Catherine Barnes. *Victorian Woman Travel Writers in Africa*. Boston: Twayne Publishers, 1982.

Stoller, Joyce. "*Fire Eyes* – Fire between the Legs." Rev. of *Fire Eyes*, film by Soraya Mire. *Monthly Review* 46.9 (1995): 58–60.

Stovel, Nora Foster. "Talking Drums and Dancing Masks." Introduction. *Long Drums and Cannons*. By Margaret Laurence. Edmonton: University of Alberta Press, 2001. xvii–liii.

Strong, William Duncan. *Labrador Winter: The Ethnographic Journals of William Duncan Strong, 1927–1928*. Ed. Eleanor Leacock and Nan Rothschild. Washington: Smithsonian Institution Press, 1994.

Tapping, Craig. "Margaret Laurence and Africa." *Crossing the River: Essays in Honour of Margaret Laurence*. Ed. Kristjana Gunnars. Winnipeg: Turnstone Press, 1988. 65–80.

"Thinks Wallace Safe." *New York Daily Tribune* 14 Nov. 1905: 5.

Thomas, Clara. *Love and Work Enough: The Life of Anna Jameson*. Toronto: University of Toronto Press, 1967.

Thompson, Elizabeth. "Illustrations for *The Backwoods of Canada*." *Studies in Canadian Literature* 19.2 (1994): 31–56.

"Through Unknown Labrador." Rev. of *A Woman's Way through Unknown Labrador*, by Mina Hubbard. *Times Literary Supplement* 21 May 1908: 165a.

"Through Unknown Labrador: Explorations of a Plucky Woman." Rev. of *A Woman's Way through Unknown Labrador*, by Mina Hubbard. *Western Mail* 13 June 1908: np. Mina Hubbard clipping file. Centre for Newfoundland Studies, Memorial University, St John's.

Tobin, Beth Fowkes. *Picturing Imperial Power: Colonial Subjects in Eighteenth-Century British Painting*. Durham: Duke University Press, 1999.

Todorov, Tzvetan. *The Conquest of America: The Question of the Other*. Trans. Richard Howard. New York: Harper & Row, 1984.

Traill, Catharine Parr. *The Backwoods of Canada: Being Letters from the Wife of an Emigrant Officer, Illustrative of the Domestic Economy of British America*. London: C. Knight, 1836.

"Travel and Topography." Rev. of *A Woman's Way through Unknown Labrador*, by Mina Hubbard. *Evening Standard and St. James's Gazette* 19 May 1908: np. Mina Hubbard clipping file. Centre for Newfoundland Studies. Memorial University, St John's.

Vargo, Lisa. "An 'Enlargement of *Home*': Anna Jameson and the Representation of Nationalism." *Victorian Review* 24.1 (1998): 53–68.

Verduyn, Christl, ed. *Margaret Laurence: An Appreciation*. Peterborough, ON: Broadview Press, 1988.

W., W.H. Rev. of *A Woman's Way through Unknown Labrador*, by Mina Hubbard. *Journal of the Manchester Geographical Society* 24 (1908): 133–4.

Wadden, Marie. *Nitassinan: The Innu Struggle to Reclaim Their Homeland.* Vancouver: Douglas & McIntyre, 1991.

Wallace, Annie. Letter to Dillon Wallace. 22 Nov. 1905. Ms. Coll. 244.5.01.004. Centre for Newfoundland Studies Archives, Memorial University, St John's.

Wallace, Dillon. Diaries, Labrador Expedition, 20 May 1905–27 April 1906. 5 vols. Ms. Coll. 244.3.02. Centre for Newfoundland Studies Archives, Memorial University, St John's.

– *The Long Labrador Trail.* Toronto: F.H. Revell, 1907.

– *The Lure of the Labrador Wild: The Story of the Exploring Expedition Conducted by Leonidas Hubbard, Jr.* New York: F.H. Revell, 1905. Rpt. St John's: Breakwater Books, 1983.

Ware, Vron. *Beyond the Pale: White Women, Racism and History.* London: Verso, 1992.

Warkentin, Germaine. *Canadian Exploration Literature: An Anthology.* Toronto: Oxford University Press, 1993.

Warner, Marina. "Fee fie fo fum: The Child in the Jaws of the Story." *Cannibalism and the Colonial World.* Ed. Francis Barker, Peter Hulme, and Margaret Iversen. Cambridge: Cambridge University Press, 1998. 158–82.

Warsame, Aamina, and Sadiya Ahmed. *Social and Cultural Aspects of Female Circumcision and Infibulation: A Preliminary Report.* Mogadishu and Stockholm: Somali Academy of Sciences and Arts and Swedish Agency for Research Co-operation with Developing Countries, 1985.

Waterston, Elizabeth. "Travel Books 1860–1920." *Literary History of Canada: Canadian Literature in English.* Carl F. Klinck, gen. ed. 2nd ed. Vol. 1. Toronto: University of Toronto Press, 1976. 361–79.

– "Travel Books on Canada 1920–1960." *Literary History of Canada: Canadian Literature in English.* Carl F. Klinck, gen. ed. 2nd ed. Vol. 2. Toronto: University of Toronto Press, 1976. 108–18.

Waterston, Elizabeth, Ian Eastbrook, Bernard Katz, and Kathleen Scott. *The Travellers: Canada to 1900.* Guelph: University of Guelph, 1989.

Whitney, Caspar. "The Leonidas Hubbard, Jun., Expedition into Labrador." *Outing* 45 (March 1905): 643–89.

"Why I Go to Labrador: Mrs. Hubbard's Own Story." *World* 2 July. 1905: 2.

Williams, Alan F. "Explorers Wild: The Hubbards in Labrador." *Kunapipi* 18.1 (1996): 72–84.

Williams, Mentor L. Introduction. *Schoolcraft's Indian Legends.* 1956. East Lansing: Michigan State University Press, 1991. xi–xxiv.

Rev. of *Winter Studies and Summer Rambles in Canada*, by Anna Brownell Jameson. *British and Foreign Review* 8 (1839): 134–53.

Wolf, Eric R. *Europe and the People without History*. Berkeley: University of California Press, 1982.

Wolff, Janet. "On the Road Again: Metaphors of Travel in Cultural Criticism." *Cultural Studies* 7.2 (1993): 224–39.

Wollstonecraft, Mary. *Letters Written during a Short Residence in Sweden, Norway, and Denmark*. London: J. Johnson, 1796. Rpt. in *A Short Residence in Sweden, Norway and Denmark and Memoirs of the Author of "The Rights of Woman."* Ed. Richard Holmes. London: Penguin, 1987.

– *A Vindication of the Rights of Woman; with Strictures on Political and Moral Subjects*. London: J. Johnson, 1792. Rpt. ed. Miriam Brody. London: Penguin, 1992.

"A Woman Explorer." Rev. of *A Woman's Way through Unknown Labrador*, by Mina Hubbard. *Spectator* 101 (3 Oct. 1908): 472–73.

Rev. of *A Woman's Way through Unknown Labrador*, by Mina Hubbard. *Englishwoman's Review* 15 July 1908: 212–16.

Rev. of *A Woman's Way through Unknown Labrador*, by Mina Hubbard. *Literary Digest* 37 (7 Nov. 1908): 673.

Rev. of *A Woman's Way through Unknown Labrador*, by Mina Hubbard. *Nation* 88.2275 (1908): 114.

Woodcock, George. "Many Solitudes: The Travel Writings of Margaret Laurence." *Journal of Canadian Studies* 13.3 (1978): 3–12. Rpt. in Verduyn 21–37.

–, ed. *A Place to Stand On: Essays by and about Margaret Laurence*. Edmonton: NeWest Press, 1983.

World Health Organization. *Female Genital Mutilation: An Overview*. Geneva: WHO, 1998.

Xiques, Donez. Introduction. *A Tree for Poverty: Somali Poetry and Prose*. By Margaret Laurence. Toronto: ECW Press, 1993. 7–15.

York, Lorraine. "'Sublime Desolation': European Art and Jameson's Perceptions of Canada." *Mosaic* 19.2 (1986): 43–56.

index

Abdi (the Laurences' Somali driver), 157, 173, 188; and guns and hunting, 176–9; photograph, 175, 188

Abokor, Shamis (Guduudo Carwo), 244n25

abolition, 56

abuse: child, 193–5; sexual, 193–5, 202–4; spousal, 60, 62, 152, 186

Achebe, Chinua, 153, 169; *Morning Yet on Creation Day*, 175; universalization, 175

Adelaide Lake, 146

adoption, trope of, 34–9, 82

adventurousness. *See under* Hubbard, M.B.; Jameson, A.B.

Agnes, Lake, 145–6, 240n65

Ahmed, Sadiya, 200, 245nn32–3

Aiktow River, 16

Alcoff, Linda, 199; "The Problem of Speaking for Others," 151–2

Algonquian language group, 123–4, 222n25

Ali, Maryan Omar, 167; *Women's Voices in a Man's World*, 182

Alma, John Lees, 66

Amadi, Elechi, 176; *The Concubine*, 181

Amegbe, Aya, 192–3, 201, 205

Amegbe, Nathaniel, 159, 192, 196, 201–3, 205–6, 245n34

American Geographical Society, 104, 141–3

American War of Independence, 54

Andrew, Mary Adele (Mani-Aten), 147–8

Andrzejewski, B.W. (Guś), 166–8, 243n15

Anishinaabe, 34, 219n1, 222n20; culture, 82–3; orature, 11, 13, 17, 46–52, 82–3, 210, 223nn31–3; represented by A. Jameson, 17, 42, 70; sketches of, 80; women, 10, 20, 42

anti-imperialism, 10, 14, 64. *See also under* Laurence, M.

appropriation of voice, 160, 242n9

Arabian Nights, 182

Arctic Red River, 213

Asha (Somali child), 194–5, 198

Ashcroft, Bill, 159, 164

Ashini, Jean Pierre (Napes), 148

Atlantic Monthly Novel Contest, 245–6n34

Atwood, Margaret, 227n4; *The Labrador Fiasco*, 228–9n9

authority: and travel writing, 12, 32–3, 169; over women, 209. *See also under* Hubbard, M.B.

Ayesha (character in *The Rain Child* [M. Laurence]), 195, 204

clitoridectomy, 180, 195, 198, 204. *See also* female genital mutilation

code-switching, 159

Coger, Greta M.K. McCormick, 241n2

Colborne, John, 52–3, 55

Coleridge, Samuel Taylor, 139

collaboration, 117, 128–9

Collu, Gabrielle, 203, 241n2, 246n35

colonialism, 16, 64, 213; and gender, 9–10, 199, 208; and imagination, 169. *See also* imperialism; *see also under* Hubbard, M.B.; Jameson, A.B.; Laurence, M.

Columbus, Christopher, 158, 222n27

Congers, NY, 97, 102, 119

Conrad, Joseph: *Heart of Darkness*, 202

contact zone, 10, 17, 82–3, 132

Cooke, Alan, 86, 230n21

Cooper, James Fenimore, 32; *The Last of the Mohicans*, 222n25

counter-narrative, 14, 168–72

Crane, Jean, 230n22, 234n45, 235n48

Cree, 15–16, 87, 121, 126, 236n50; language, 114, 123–4, 147, 237n54

cultural sensitivity, 152, 154, 167, 172, 193–200, 206

Cummins, Bryan D.: *Full Circle*, 221–2n20

Dalays, Khadiija Cabdullaahi, 244n25

danger: for women travellers, 11, 23, 26, 211. *See also* weapons: for protection on travels

Davidson, James West, 86, 90, 117–19; *Great Heart*, 226n2

Davidson, Lillias Campbell: *Hints to Lady Travellers at Home and Abroad*, 107

Davis Inlet, 126

Davis Inlet band, 124, 126–7, 238n56. *See also* Montagnais

de Beauvoir, Simone: *The Second Sex*, 180

Delaware, 52, 54–5, 224nn35–6

dependence complex, 172–4

Desolation Lake, 239n62

Detroit, 19, 27

Dial, 95

diaries. *See under* Elson, G.; Hubbard, L.; Hubbard, M.B.; Wallace, D.; *see also* journals

Dickason, Olive, 52

Dictionary of Canadian Biography, 34, 220n9, 222n26

Dinesen, Isak (Karen Blixen), 182

Disappointment Lake (Keshikash-kau), 144, 148

Djibouti, 154, 186

domesticization, 6–7; of wilderness (*see under* Hubbard, M.B.)

Dorkenoo, Efua, 200, 245nn32–3

Dorothy Lake, 145, 240n65

Dubinsky, Karen: *The Second Greatest Disappointment*, 221n17

Duncan, James, 150

Duncan, Sara Jeannette (Garth Grafton; Mrs Everard Cotes), 14, 93, 98, 229n14; articles in Montreal *Daily Star*, 228n7; use of racist or stereotypical language, 123, 237n53; *A Social Departure*, 87–8, 123, 228n7, 230n23

DuPlessis, Rachel Blau, 180

Early Canadiana Online, 219n5

Eastman, George, 128

135; orature, 11–14, 17, 46–52, 126–7, 210, 223nn31–2, 238n56; pejorative descriptions, 35, 37–46, 70, 123, 135–6, 222n25, 230n19, 237n53; receiving gifts as allies, 24, 53, 56, 61, 223n34; and religious conversion, 54, 56–8, 135; and reserve land, 52–6; and sexuality, 25–6, 116–17, 122, 126; as "specimens," 35, 37–9, 41, 65, 75; and trade, 33, 43, 53, 57; and treaties, 56, 83; as types, 65, 77, 82, 132–5; as warlike, 22, 57–8, 80, 116–17, 122–4, 127, 236n51; women, 10, 17–18, 20–2, 41–2, 44, 58–64, 131–2, 215. *See also* Anishinaabe; Cree; Delaware; Innu; Odawa; Ojibwa; Potawatomi; Six Nations

Flecker, James Elroy: "The Gates of Damascus," 246n38

Ford, Jesse, 240n69

Ford, John, 116, 130, 132, 144

Ford, Mrs John, 116, 145

Ford Island, 144

Ford River, 144

Forest and Stream, 231nn25–6

Fort Chimo, 233n37

Fort Michilimackinac, 33–5

Fort Rae, 210

Foster, Shirley, 7, 21, 217n4

Fouillard, Camille, 147

Fowler, Marian, 228n7; *The Embroidered Tent*, 7, 27, 59, 220n11, 221n12, 225n48

framing narratives, 13, 98–100, 150, 231n24

Francis, Daniel, 236n50

Franklin, Jane, 227n3

Fraser, Wayne, 220n10

Frawley, Maria, 217n4

Freiwald, Bina, 219n6, 220n11, 225n48

French Somaliland, 153–4, 160, 186; map, 170–1. *See also* Djibouti

Friedan, Betty: *The Feminine Mystique*, 180

Fussell, Paul: *Abroad*: 31, 218n7; *The Norton Book of Travel*, 8

gabay (*gabei*), 165–7, 182–3, 243n14

Galaal, Musa Haji Ismail, 166–7, 243n15

Gardiner Dam, 16

Gaskell, Elizabeth, 93, 230n17

gender, 3, 12, 16, 107–9, 129, 210, 216, 218n5; and geography, 6, 203; and imperialism, 5, 8–10, 12–13, 59, 86, 149–52, 203, 206, 208–9, 218n4; markers of, 243n19. *See also under* First Nations; Hubbard, M.B.; Jameson, A.B.; Laurence, M.

genital excision, 185, 192–3, 195–200, 202, 204–7, 244–5n29. *See also* female genital mutilation

Genoa, 158

Geographical Journal, 128, 142, 239n61

geography: and gender, 6, 149, 203; and imperialism, 6, 8–9, 142, 146–8; and naming, 14–16, 23, 87, 143–50, 212, 234n42, 239nn62–3, 240nn65–8; and primacy, 6, 143, 215

Geological Survey of Canada: maps, 90

George River (Mushuau-shipu), 90, 94, 98, 112, 126, 141, 210, 238n56, 240n69; headwaters, 104, 113–14; mapping, 86, 137, 143; naming, 114, 147, 234n42; navigation, 86, 121, 137

Hearne, Samuel, 236n51
heello, 243n14
hees, 243n14
Helen Falls, 143–5
Henderson, Jennifer, 220n11
Henry, Alexander, the Elder, 12–13, 20, 82, 84, 221n14, 221n19; *Travels and Adventures in Canada and the Indian Territories*, 13, 22, 32–5; and Wa,wa,tam, 33–5, 47–8, 223n29
heroism: and exploration and travel, 6, 8, 99, 101
Herriot, Trevor: *River in a Dry Land*, 16
Hicks, Esther, 196
Hind, Henry Youle, 236n50
Holland, Patrick, 217n2, 217n4, 218n7
Hope Lake, 239n62
Hoyle, Gwyneth, 227n5
Hubbard Lake, 94, 144, 146
Hubbard, Leonidas, Jr, 7, 13–14, 88, 129, 229–30n16, 230–1n24, 231n26; "The Children of the Bush," 111, 123; criticism of 1903 expedition, 231n25; death of, 90, 99–100, 229n10, 236n51, 237n52; diary, 90, 99–102, 227n5, 232nn30–4, 233n36, 235n47, 237n52; discussions of food, 101–2, 232nn30–3; and geographical naming, 144, 240nn65–6; and home, 101–2, 232nn32–3; and landscape, 137–8; 1903 expedition, 84–7, 90, 92, 94, 99–102, 140, 227n2, 227n4; "Off Days on Superior's North Shore," 88, 230n18; portrait, 233n39, 236n52; relationship with and perceived by M. Hubbard, 92–5, 97–102, 112, 117–18, 121, 140–1, 211,

232–3n34, 234n46, 234–5n47, 240n65; racist or stereotypical language, 123
Hubbard, Mina Benson (Mrs Leonidas Hubbard Jr), 3–5, 7–16, 84–150, 221n15, 226–40; adventurousness, 104, 109; and authority, 10, 87, 99, 102, 110–11, 115–16, 129, 150, 228n5, 233n37, 234n43; biography, 226n2, 228n5, 240n66; and canoeing, 88, 91, 98–9, 111–15, 120–1, 131, 136, 138; and caribou migration, 91, 109, 114, 128, 210, 238n56, 244n21; as childlike, 110–11; and civilization and savagery, 101, 107, 133–5, 141; and class, 86–7, 95, 112, 116–17, 119; and collaboration, 117, 128–9; and colonialism, 9, 86–7, 92, 149; and cultural and racial typing, 132–5; declaration of honourable behaviour, 121–2, 211, 235n48; diary, 13–14, 23, 86, 94–5, 97, 105, 109–24, 128, 131, 138–41, 149, 178, 226–35, 237n54; and domesticization of wilderness, 87, 93–8, 101, 107, 138, 140–1, 150, 218n6; equipment and provisions, 105–7, 110, 128, 141, 227n2; ethnographic project, 127–8, 132–6; as expedition leader, 10, 87, 94, 107, 114–16, 129, 236n51; as explorer, 86–8, 92, 102, 104–5, 109–14, 129, 140–3, 210, 236n51; and femininity, 23, 87, 93, 102–9, 129–30, 228n5; and figurative solitude, 112–14, 116, 141, 150, 229n15; and First Nations violence, 117, 122–4, 127, 150, 177–8; framing narratives, 13, 98–100, 150, 231n24; frontispiece

land as woman, trope of, 141, 202–4, 213, 246n35

landscape discourse: by male travellers, 137–8. *See also* picturesque; sublime; *see also under* Hubbard, M.B.; Jameson, A.B.

language: and imperialism, 237n53; racist and stereotypical, 39–40, 44–6, 123, 135–6, 160–1, 173, 222n25, 230n19, 237n53. *See also* Ojibwe language; Somali language; *see also under* Hubbard, M.B.; Innu; Jameson, A.B.; Laurence, M.

Laurence, Jack, 7, 152–3, 155, 173, 192, 206, 241n5, 242n10, 246n38; construction of *ballehs*, 153, 164, 170, 187–8, 209, 241n1; and hunting and guns, 176–8, 244n22; photograph, 174, 190–1; response to child prostitution, 193–4

Laurence, Margaret, 5, 7–14, 151–209, 241–6; and anti-imperialism, 14, 151–2, 154, 157, 159, 175, 196, 198–9, 206, 241–6, 242n10; and appropriation of voice, 160, 242n9; biography, 241n1; on child prostitution, 14, 152, 184–5, 192–5, 200–7; and colonialism, 9, 14, 151–4, 157–61, 168–9, 172, 174–5, 196, 201–4, 206–7, 213, 264n37; counter-narrative, 14, 168–72; cultural sensitivity, 152, 154, 167, 172, 193–200, 206; on female genital mutilation, 14, 152, 180, 192–3, 195–207; and feminism, 14, 152, 154, 179–80, 206, 218n6, 242n10; and figurative solitude, 178, 210–11; on gender, 14, 151–2, 154, 161, 176–87, 189–207, 209–10, 241n2,

243n19, 244n26; and hunting and guns, 176–9, 244nn20–2; and imperialism, 10, 14, 151–4, 158–61, 163–5, 171–2, 197, 203, 205–6, 241n2, 246n6; imperialist discursive inheritance, 14, 168, 172, 175–6, 211; journals, 156–7, 173; language and speech, 52, 159–61, 161, 163–7, 173, 207; Manawaka cycle, 154, 179–80 (*see also* individual titles); and mapping, 5, 151–2, 169–71, 206, 209, 212–13; on marriage, 152, 181, 184–7, 193, 195, 207, 242n11; on maternity, 14, 152, 180–1, 184, 192–3, 197, 201, 205, 245n29; and patriarchy, 10, 14, 154, 179, 186, 194, 200–3, 206, 213, 246n37; photographs, 156, 187–91, 244n27; and primacy, 169, 211; and purdah, 186–7; and race, 160–1, 187, 210; and relational motives for travel, 7–8, 155–6; and religion, 160, 162–3, 207, 246n38; and sexuality, 14, 152, 154, 180, 194–7, 202–5, 211; and Somali orature, 11, 14, 153, 155, 163–8, 181–3, 190, 207–9, 243nn14–15; on spousal, sexual, and child abuse, 152, 186, 193–5, 202–4; subject position, 158–9; and translation, 11, 14, 153, 155, 159, 164–8, 181–2, 194, 197, 209, 239n59; and universalization, 152, 168, 175–6

Laurence, Margaret, works of: "Books that Mattered to Me," 153, 173, 179, 243n17; *Dance on the Earth*, 179–80, 205; "Drummer of All the World," 246n35; "The Epic Love of Elmii Bonde-

Manitoulin Island, 69, 71, 77, 211; First Nations settlement, 52, 224n36; gift distribution, 24, 37, 53, 56, 61, 223n34; Indian farming village, 52; A. Jameson's travels to, 20, 45, 47, 73–4; spelling of, 219n7

Mannix, Daniel P., 169

Mannoni, O., 14; dependence complex, 172–4; *Prospero and Caliban*, 171–3, 243nn17–18

mapping, 3–6, 8, 171, 210; figurative, 3, 5, 10, 17, 82–4, 143, 150–2, 169–70, 206, 209, 212–13, 216; and imperialism, 6, 8, 142, 146, 149; politics of, 6; and primacy, 6, 212–15. *See also* cartography; *see also* under Hubbard, M.B.; Jameson, A.B.; Laurence, M.

maps: and gender and imperialism, 6, 13; as objective, 12–13. *See also under* British Somaliland Protectorate; Labrador; Quebec

Marie Lake, 145, 240n65

marriage, 27, 59, 60–1, 200. *See also under* Laurence, M.

Marryat, Frederick, 13, 20, 221n18; and First Nations, 46; and Mackinac Island, 31; and Niagara Falls, 31

Martens, Debra, 245n31

Martin (A. Jameson's steersman), 25, 69, 80

Martin, C.J.: photographs by, 188–90, 244n28

Martin, Norma, 240n65

Martineau, Harriet, 13, 20, 221n13, 226n52; and First Nations, 46; and Mackinac Island, 31; and Niagara Falls, 29–31, 221n17; *Retrospect of Western Travel*, 29,

221n17; *Society in America*, 22, 29-31, 46, 59, 221n17

Mary Lake, 239n62

maternity, 245n30. *See also under* Laurence, M.

Maxwell, Anne, 108, 132–3; *Colonial Photography and Exhibitions*, 75

Mealy Mountains (Akamiuapishkᵘ), 147

Mellor, Anne K., 139

memoir, 154–6, 160

Memorial University of Newfoundland, 238n56

Merrick, Elliott, 86

Michikamats, Lake, 90, 147

Michikamau, Lake, 90, 94, 137, 147–8

Middleton, Dorothy: *Victorian Lady Travellers*, 12, 217n4

Millais, J.G., 86, 132, 233n40

Millet, Kate: *Sexual Politics*, 180

Mills, Sara, 11, 127–8, 218n5, 237n53; *Discourses of Difference*, 8

Mire, Soraya: *Fire Eyes*, 196–7, 200

miscegeny, 57, 117

Mohamed (the Laurences' cook), 161–2, 164, 176, 178, 187, 190, 242n11; photograph, 188

Mohanty, Chandra, 199

Mokomaun,ish, 73–5, 77, 82

Monkman, Leslie, 39, 43, 220n11

Montagnais, 124; photographs, 132–3, 236–7n52. *See also* Davis Inlet band; Innu

Montmorency Falls, 225n50

Moodie, Susanna: *Roughing It in the Bush*, 222n24, 226n51

Morantz, Toby, 236n50

Moravian missionaries, 52, 54

Morgan, Susan, 217n4

Morley, Patricia, 245n31
Morris, Robert T., 231n25
Motohashi, Ted, 222n27
Mountaineer Lake, 239n62
Mukherjee, Arun, 158, 175
Mulhallen, Karen: *Views from the North*, 218n4
Munro, Alice, 179
Murphy, Denis, 219n2, 219n6
Musgrave, Susan, 240n69
multivocality, 99, 127, 231

Na'Allah, Abdul-Rasheed, 241n2
Namaycush Lake (Atshuku-nipiss), 148, 239n62
naming: people, 35–7, 44–5, 92–5, 97–8, 150; geographical features, 14–16, 23, 87, 143–50, 212, 234n42, 239nn62–3, 240nn65–8; and imperialism, 147–9
Nasir, Ahmed (Arabetto), 167, 186; photograph, 188
Naskapi, 123–4, 127, 141, 178, 226n1, 237n54; photographs, 131–2, 236–7n52. *See also* Barren Ground People; Innu
Naskaupi River, 88, 90–1, 112, 115, 210, 226n1, 227n2; headwaters, 104, 113–14; mapping, 86, 137, 142–3; navigation of, 137, 148–9; photograph, 138
Nation, 143
National Archives of Canada, 227n5
National Cyclopedia of American Biography, 240n64
Nature, 132
navigation, 90, 111, 137, 148–9
Needler, G.H., 20; *Early Canadian Sketches* (A. Jameson), 65, 224–5n42
neo-colonialism, 158, 175, 208
Neuman, Shirley, 192

New York, 18, 23, 102
New York Daily Tribune, 229n13
Newfoundland, 90, 228n6
Niagara Falls, 19, 22, 27–31, 53–4, 65–7; disappointment in, 28–9, 221n17; sketches by A. Jameson, 30, 65, 73, 138
Niemi, Judith, 86, 227n5, 240n69
Nigeria, 153–4; gender relations, 181; literature, 153, 168, 175, 181
Nogan, Peter, 225–6n51; wife of, 44
North, the, 88
North Adams Evening Transcript, 92
North West River Post, 91, 98, 105, 149, 235n48, 239n58
Northwest Rebellion, 228n7
Nwapa, Flora: *Efuru*, 181

Odawa, 34, 44, 45–6, 52, 57, 60, 221n20; sketches of, 72–4
Odyssey, 34, 45, 84
O'Flaherty, Patrick, 227n4
Ojibwa, 44, 52, 57, 60, 72, 221–2n20; women, 10. *See also* Anishinaabe; Chippewa
Ojibwe language, 43–4, 47, 52, 222nn20–1, 222n26
Olsen, Tillie: *Silences*, 179
Omar, Deeqa, 168, 243n176
Ontario, 90, 98. *See also* Upper Canada
Ontario, Lake, 66; illustration of, 67
orature: Anishinaabe or Ojibwa, 11, 13, 17, 46–52, 82, 210, 223nn31–3; Innu, 12, 14, 126–7, 238n56; Somali, 11, 14, 153, 163–8, 181–3, 186, 190, 207–9, 243nn14–15
Orma Lake (Nisukaka), 145, 148, 240n65

Tapping, Craig, 174
technologies of representation and
    travel, 105–7, 128, 141, 157,
    211–12, 215–16
Tecumseh, 42
Tema, 153
This Side Jordan. See under
    Laurence, Margaret, works of
Thomas, Clara, 21, 42, 59, 222n23,
    224n38, 224n40; *Love and Work
    Enough*, 219n2, 220n11, 221n12
Thompson, Elizabeth, 68, 225n45
Thomson, James, 169, 172
Tiffin, Helen, 159, 164
Times Literary Supplement, 104
Tobin, Beth Fowkes, 75, 77, 80;
    Picturing Imperial Power, 64
toponymy, 15, 143–8, 218n8,
    239n63, 240n66. *See also* naming:
    geographical features
Toronto, 18, 23, 43, 219n2;
    A. Jameson's views on, 20–1, 63;
    Public Library, 65
tourism, 28, 31, 35; scenic, 72
Traill, Catharine Parr, 11, 13, 20;
    The Backwoods of Canada,
    42–4, 68, 82, 222n23, 225n45,
    225nn50–1, 226n54; and civiliza-
    tion and conversion, 56–7; and
    First Nations, 42–4; illustrations
    for *Backwoods*, 68, 225n45,
    225nn50–1, 226n54; and Ojibwe
    language, 47; and the picturesque,
    68, 225n45; and settlement, 43–4
translation, 11, 14, 44, 52, 129,
    132, 237n55, 238n56. *See also
    under* Laurence, M.
travel writing, 17–19, 98, 210,
    220n8, 220n11; and authority,
    12, 32–3, 169; as discursively
    constructed, 32, 33–4, 168–9,
    210; as domesticating, 7, 150; as
    gendered, 6–9, 11, 21, 88, 211,

216, 217n3, 217–18n4; as heroic,
    6, 8, 99, 101; as imperialistic,
    6, 8–9, 82, 158, 168–9, 217n2,
    217–18n4; and mapping, 5–6,
    141–50, 215; and memoir, 154; as
    objective, 6, 11–12; and precur-
    sors, 12–13, 28, 31–4, 62, 82, 88,
    234n47, 218n7; relational, 7–8,
    19, 90, 100, 155–6
treaties, 56, 83, 224n37
Tree for Poverty, A. See under
    Laurence, Margaret, works of
typing, cultural and racial, 65, 77,
    82, 132–5

Ulysses (Odysseus), 34, 84
Ungava Bay, 91, 114, 239n58; M.
    Hubbard's arrival at, 91, 130–1,
    237n52
Ungava District, 86, 90–1, 98,
    113–16, 118–29; geographical
    mapping and naming, 143–7;
    photographs, 129–34, 137
Ungava Peninsula, 86
United States: government of, 53–4,
    56
universalization, 152, 168, 175–6,
    208, 213
Upper Canada, 7, 9, 13, 17–84,
    219n2; First Nations reserves
    and treaties, 52–6, 224nn35–6;
    government, 20, 43, 53–4, 59;
    settlement, 13, 20, 43–4, 53–5,
    57, 63, 68, 70, 222n23
Upper Canada Rebellion, 20

Vargo, Lisa, 57, 82, 220n11
Victoria (queen), 59

Wadden, Marie, 237n54
Wallace, Annie, 117
Wallace, Dillon, 14, 100–1, 116,
    128, 232n30; diary, 227n2; and

landscape, 137–8; and geographical naming, 144–5, 148–9, 239n62; *The Long Labrador Trail*, 91, 123, 135–6, 226n1, 227n2, 229–30n16, 230n19, 230–1n24, 237–8n55, 238n57, 239n62; *The Lure of the Labrador Wild*, 13, 90, 226n1, 227n2, 228n9, 239n62; 1903 expedition, 84, 90, 92; 1905 expedition, 84–6, 90–1, 98, 227n2; and personal naming, 95; and primacy, 91–2, 237–8n55; rivalry with M. Hubbard, 12–13, 84, 90–1, 229n10, 230n16; use of racist or stereotypical language, 123, 135–6, 230n19, 237n53

warfare, 10, 57–8

Warkentin, Germaine, 7; *Canadian Exploration Literature*, 218n4

Warner, Marina, 222n27

Warsame, Aamina, 200, 245nn32–3

Washkagama Lake, 239n62

Waterston, Elizabeth, 218n4

Waub-Ojeeg, 37, 48–9

Wa,wa,tam, 33–5, 48, 223n29

Wayish,ky, 37; description and illustration of lodge, 37–8, 65, 80–2

Wayish,ky, Mrs, 222n26

weapons, 77, 233n37; for protection on travels, 11, 26, 110, 177–8, 187, 244n23; of war, 58. *See also* hunting

Western Mail, 86, 95, 104, 128, 143

Whitney, Caspar, 101–2

Williams, Alan F., 227n4

Williams, Mentor L.: *Schoolcraft's Indian Legends* (*Algic Researches*), 49–51

Wills, Jane, 6, 141, 146, 229n11

Windbound Lake, 144, 239n62

Windsor Magazine, 104

Winter Studies and Summer Rambles in Canada. See under Jameson, Anna Brownell, works of

Wiseman, Adele: *Selected Letters of Margaret Laurence and Adele Wiseman*, 164–7, 179, 196–7, 246n34

Wolf, Eric R., 44

Wolff, Janet, 213

Wollstonecraft, Mary, 19, 220n11; *Letters Written during a Short Residence in Sweden, Norway, and Denmark*, 19; *A Vindication of the Rights of Woman*, 80

woman as land, trope of, 202–4, 213, 246n35

"Woman Question," 58–64

woman's place, 6–7, 21, 84, 87, 92, 97, 107, 140, 150, 229n11

Woman's Way through Unknown Labrador, A. See under Hubbard, Mina Benson, works of

Woodcock, George, 241n2

Woolf, Virginia, 179–80

Wordsworth, William, 139, 240n65

World, 231n28, 233n36, 235n47

World Health Organization, 245n32

Xiques, Donez: *A Tree for Poverty* (M. Laurence), 168, 241n2

York, Lorraine, 71, 221n12

Zeilah (Saylac), 169, 186